POSTAL
CLERK-CARRIER
EXAMINATIONS
AND
MAIL HANDLER
EXAMINATIONS

by

Harry Walter Koch, M.A., LL.B.

This is a Ken-Book

ISBN 0-913164-89-5

We are pleased to offer this fourth edition of our book designed to help

you to prepare for and pass examinations for employment with the United

States Postal Service.   As in previous editions, we include a great deal

of material that was prepared by the United States Civil Service Commis-

sion or the Postal Service.   We also include, however, explanatory

material and suggestions of our own, particularly on how to pass the

written and oral examinations.

This booklet, issued by the United States Postal
Service, contains the material shown on page 15.
It carries its own page numbers at the bottom,
pages 1-70 and references therein are to those
numbers unless they are preceded by a KB.

NOTE: In most of this book, we have used the "circle" answer sheets as shown here (directions as to their use are on page KB-20):

1 Ⓐ ● Ⓒ Ⓓ Ⓔ

2 Ⓐ Ⓑ Ⓒ ● Ⓔ

3 Ⓐ Ⓑ Ⓒ Ⓓ Ⓔ

However, for some of the tests taken from older material, we use the rectangular form. Their use is the same.

The only difference is that the circular form runs in number sequence down the page; rectangles run across the page in number sequence.

POST OFFICE JOBS OFFER

JOB SECURITY	LIBERAL RETIREMENT	CASH FOR SUGGESTIONS
PAID VACATIONS	SICK LEAVE WITH PAY	PROMOTION OPPORTUNITIES
ON THE JOB TRAINING	LOW COST LIFE INSURANCE	PAID HOLIDAYS
	LOW COST HEALTH INSURANCE	

Getting the Sack

Pounding the pavement with a heavy sack slung over the shoulder may not be heaven on earth, but there are still lots of folks who'd like to give it a try. Work applications for the U.S. Postal Service are running so high (for clerk-carrier jobs that start at *about $9 per hour) that a handful of New York City openings recently brought in more than 100,000 applications. In Baltimore, police had to be called in to handle a crowd of 7000 people that formed after word got out that some postal jobs were being filled.

Despite recent roadblocks to federal employment, applications for federal jobs are high and increasing daily. Between October 1979 and March 1980, 3,592,000 people made inquiries — telephone, walk-in or written — for federal employment.

Apparently, many would-be workers think government employment is more appealing than eight hours with a shovel in a coal mine, eight hours polishing bumpers on an auto assembly line or eight hours pushing papers at a corporate desk. □□

San Francisco Chronicle, May, 1981

*Salary, of course, is always subject to change -- could be more -- or less -- when you read this.   Editor

Although methods of examining for the United States Postal Service employment are always subject to change, apparently the examinations at the present time are limited to the following subjects:

FOR CLERK CARRIER

Address Checking

Memory for Addresses

FOR MAIL HANDLER

Address Checking

Meaning of Words

Following Oral Directions

FOR DISTRIBUTION CLERK, MACHINE

Number Series

Memory for Addresses

Address Checking

HERE ARE SOME POST OFFICE JOBS

- You could be a MAIL HANDLER.
  You would help move the mail (it's heavy) within the Post Office building.

- You could be a DISTRIBUTION CLERK.
  You would sort the mail (in some places by hand, in some places by machine) and do other things to keep the mail moving

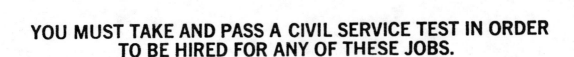

- You could be a MAIL CARRIER.
  You would deliver mail to homes, stores, and offices.

YOU MUST TAKE AND PASS A CIVIL SERVICE TEST IN ORDER TO BE HIRED FOR ANY OF THESE JOBS.

How Do You Apply for a Post Office Job?

FIRST: Go to your nearest Post Office or Federal Job Information Center. Tell them you want to apply for a Post Office job. You will get a form to fill out.

(If they are not accepting applications now, find out when they expect to accept them again. It might be a good idea to start getting ready for the examination anyway.)

You can find the address of your nearest Post Office or Federal Job Information Center in the telephone book.

Editor's Note: Post Offices are not now giving out applications except when a job is open. They may refer you to the regional Postal Service Personnel Office. In big cities, look for this in your telephone book: United States -- Postal Service -- and under that: Personnel.

When you get this form, be sure to find out WHEN you have to send it in, and WHERE you send it.

SECOND: Look over the form. If you don't know how to answer all the questions, ask someone in the office or someone you know for help. If there is no one to help you,

- Answer all the questions the best you can.
- Be sure to print your name and address.

This is what the Application Form looks like

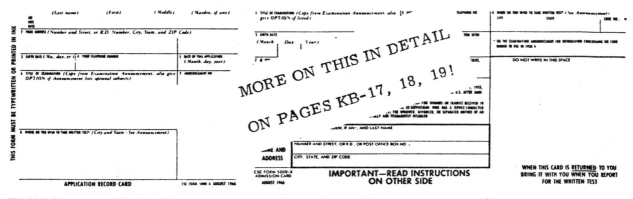

MORE ON THIS IN DETAIL ON PAGES KB-17, 18, 19!

THIRD: Mail the form as soon as you can. (Part of it will be returned to you, telling you when and where to report for the test.)

LETTERS

**DON'T GET JITTERY JUST BECAUSE
YOU HAVE TO TAKE A TEST.**

Go over the tests in this booklet as carefully as you can.
This will help you get ready to take the real test.

AND REMEMBER WHEN YOU SHOW UP

- **Be Sure You Have Had
  A Good Night's Sleep**

- **Be On Time**

- **Bring Your Admission Card**

**IF YOU FORGET TO BRING YOUR ADMISSION CARD, YOU WILL
HAVE TO COME BACK ANOTHER TIME, DON'T FORGET**

GOOD LUCK...

PLEASE NOTE!

THE NEXT 70 PAGES ARE FROM THE BOOKLET ISSUED BY THE

UNITED STATES POSTAL SERVICE FOR CLERK-CARRIER

EXAMINATIONS.

THERE IS A GREAT DEAL OF REFERENCE FROM ONE PAGE TO ANOTHER.

THEREFORE WITHIN THAT 70 PAGES, PLEASE USE THEIR OWN PAGE

NUMBERS AT THE BOTTOM OF THE PAGE FOR ANY PAGE REFERENCE.

THE NUMBERS AT THE TOP OF THE PAGE, PRECEDED BY KB ARE OUR

OWN KEN-BOOK PAGE NUMBERS AND ARE SEQUENTIAL THROUGHOUT

THE BOOK.

CONTENTS

Editor's Note: "This booklet" here refers to the Postal Service pamphlet included herein, pages KB-15-85, with its own page numbers as noted before, pages 2-70 -- rather than to this entire Ken-Book.

WHAT IS THIS BOOKLET ALL ABOUT?

This booklet will give you a good idea of what you have to do when you take the Postal Service tests for jobs in the Post Office.

- It shows how to apply for the test.

- It explains how to do the different kinds of questions.

- It describes how to mark your answers on the answer sheet.

- It gives some of each kind of question to try.

- Finally, it gives you a chance to test yourself with tests just like those used in the examination--same kinds of questions, same difficulty, same length.

The material is arranged so that you can study by yourself. Read the explanation, try the questions, check your answers. For the questions you get wrong, try to figure out why the correct answer is right and why you made a mistake. If you are working by yourself and you can't figure out why the correct answer is right, try to get some help. Ask a teacher; a librarian; perhaps a brother, a sister, or friend who has gone to high school.

- You must be at least a certain age. (See the examination announcement).

- You have to pass a physical examination.

- You have to be a United States citizen or have permanent resident alien status.

- YOU HAVE TO PASS A TEST.

In this booklet you will find tests that are very much like the tests you have to take to get a job in the Postal Service.

READ AND STUDY THIS BOOKLET CAREFULLY.

HOW DO YOU APPLY FOR A POSTAL SERVICE JOB?

First: Go to your nearest Post Office or Federal Job Information Center. Tell them you want to apply for a Post Office job. You will get an APPLICATION FORM to fill out.

> (If they are not accepting applications now, find out when they expect to accept them again. It might be a good idea to start getting ready for the examination anyway.)

You can find the address of your nearest Post Office or Federal Job Information Center in the telephone book.

When you get this form, be sure to find out WHEN you have to send it in, and WHERE you send it.

Second: Look over the form. If you don't know how to answer all the questions, ask someone in the office or someone you know for help. If there is no one to help you,

> * Answer all the questions the best you can.

> * Be sure to print your name and address.

This is what the instructions on the Application Form look like

---

INSTRUCTIONS TO APPLICANTS

Furnish all the information requested on these cards. The attached card will be returned to you with sample questions and necessary instructions, including the time and place of the written test.

TYPEWRITE OR PRINT IN INK. DO NOT SEPARATE THESE CARDS. FOLD ONLY AT PERFORATION.

MAIL OR TAKE THIS FORM–BOTH PARTS--TO THE POSTMASTER OF THE POST OFFICE WHERE YOU WISH TO BE EMPLOYED.

Third: Mail the form as soon as you can. (Part of it will be returned to you, telling you when and where to report for the test.)

HOW DO YOU FILL OUT THE APPLICATION FORM?

The application form is in two parts connected by a perforated line. Do NOT tear apart the form; both parts must be mailed. At the bottom of the left side of the form is printed PS Form 2479A Mar. 1975 APPLICATION CARD.

The Application Card, Part A, looks like this.

```
LAST NAME                    FIRST NAME              MIDDLE INITIAL



ADDRESS (House Number and Street)



CITY                              STATE              ZIP CODE



BIRTH DATE (Mo., Day, Year)                   DO NOT WRITE IN
                                              THIS SPACE
DATE OF THIS APPLICATION   TELEPHONE NUMBER



TITLE OF EXAMINATION



WHERE DO YOU WISH TO TAKE WRITTEN TEST (City & State)


PS Form 2479A Mar. 1975      APPLICATION CARD
```

Print or type the following information:

1. On the first line, enter your last name, first name, and middle initial.

2. On the second line, enter your address - house number and street.

3. On the third line, enter your city, state, and zip code.

4. On the fourth line, enter your birth date - month, day, and year.

5. On the fifth line, enter in the first block today's date and enter in the second block your telephone number.

6. On the sixth line, enter the title of the examination. If you want a job as postal clerk or carrier, enter Clerk/Carrier.

7. On the seventh line, enter the city and state where you wish to take the written test.

At the bottom of the right side of the form is printed PS Form 2479B Mar. 1975 ADMISSION CARD.

The Admission Card, Part B, looks like this:

TITLE OF EXAMINATION	DATE OF THIS APPLICATION	WHERE DO YOU WISH TO TAKE WRITTEN TEST *(City & State)*
DATE OF BIRTH	SOCIAL SECURITY NUMBER	POST OFFICE APPLIED FOR

IF YOU HAVE PERFORMED ACTIVE DUTY IN THE ARMED FORCES OF THE UNITED STATES AND WERE SEPARATED UNDER HONORABLE CONDITIONS INDICATE PERIODS OF SERVICE FROM *(Mo., Day, Yr.)* TO: *(Mo., Day, Yr.)*

DO NOT WRITE IN THIS SPACE

DO YOU CLAIM VETERAN PREFERENCE? ☐ NO ☐ YES IF YES, BASED ON:

☐ (1) ACTIVE DUTY IN THE ARMED FORCES OF THE U.S. DURING WORLD WAR I OR THE PERIOD DECEMBER 7, 1941, THROUGH JULY 1, 1955, (2) MORE THAN 180 CONSECUTIVE DAYS OF ACTIVE DUTY (OTHER THAN FOR TRAINING) IN THE ARMED FORCES OF THE U.S. AFTER JANUARY 31, 1955, OR (3) AWARD OF A CAMPAIGN BADGE OR SERVICE MEDAL.

☐ YOUR STATUS AS: (1) A DISABLED VETERAN OR A VETERAN WHO WAS AWARDED THE PURPLE HEART FOR WOUNDS OR INJURIES RECEIVED IN ACTION, (2) A VETERAN'S WIDOW WHO HAS NOT REMARRIED, (3) THE WIFE OF AN EX-SERVICEMAN WHO HAS A SERVICE-CONNECTED DISABILITY WHICH DISQUALIFIES HIM FOR CIVIL SERVICE APPOINTMENT, OR (4) THE WIDOWED, DIVORCED OR SEPARATED MOTHER OF AN EX-SERVICE SON OR DAUGHTER WHO DIED IN ACTION OR WHO IS TOTALLY AND PERMANENTLY DISABLED.

PRINT OR TYPE YOUR NAME AND ADDRESS

FIRST, MIDDLE, MAIDEN, IF ANY, AND LAST NAME

NUMBER AND STREET, OR R.D., OR POST OFFICE BOX NO.

CITY, STATE, AND ZIP CODE (ZIP CODE MUST BE INCLUDED)

THIS CARD WILL BE RETURNED TO YOU. BRING IT WITH YOU WHEN YOU REPORT FOR THE WRITTEN TEST.

PS Form 2479B Mar. 1975   ADMISSION CARD

Print or type the following information just as you did on Part A:

1. The title of the examination - Clerk/Carrier

2. The date of the application - today's date

3. Where you wish to take the written test - city and state

4. Your date of birth - month, day, and year

5. Your social security number. Enter one number in each block

6. The city and state where you wish to take the written test

7. Enter the two dates; month, day and year, if you have performed active duty in the armed forces of the United States and were separated under honorable conditions.

8. Mark the NO or YES box if you claim veteran preference. If you mark the YES box, then mark one of the descriptive boxes.

9. Enter your name and address in the last box.

After you have mailed in your Application Form, you will get back the right side of the form which will tell you WHEN and WHERE to take the examination. When this portion of the form is returned to you bring it with you when you report for the written test.

OF COURSE, IF YOU DID NOT PUT DOWN YOUR CORRECT ADDRESS, OR IF YOU FORGOT TO PUT IN YOUR NAME, YOU WILL NOT HEAR FROM ANYBODY.

DO IT RIGHT!

HOW TO MARK YOUR ANSWER SHEET

The Answer Sheet is where you mark your answers. Your score on the test depends on the marks you make on your Answer Sheet. Therefore, you must mark it exactly the way you are told in the examination room. Some advice on how to use the Answer Sheet is given below.

Here is an example of the wrong way and the correct way to mark your answer sheet.

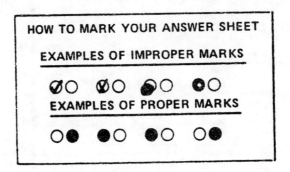

Don't take a long time to make your marks. Make a heavy pencil mark and move on to the next question.

For practice, mark the circles for the following number-letter combinations on the Answer Sheet on the next page. The first four in PART A have been done to show how; you do the rest of PART A--

PART A

1.	A	6.	A
2.	A	7.	D
3.	D	8.	A
4.	A	9.	A
5.	D	10.	D

Now mark the circles for the following number-letter combinations in PART B.

PART B

1.	B	6.	E
2.	C	7.	A
3.	A	8.	E
4.	D	9.	D
5	E	10.	D

Remember--make a neat, dark mark and move on to the next question. Use the rest of the Answer Sheet to practice making marks.

PART—A

1 ● Ⓓ	21 Ⓐ Ⓓ	46 Ⓐ Ⓓ	71 Ⓐ Ⓓ
2 ● Ⓓ	22 Ⓐ Ⓓ	47 Ⓐ Ⓓ	72 Ⓐ Ⓓ
3 Ⓐ ●	23 Ⓐ Ⓓ	48 Ⓐ Ⓓ	73 Ⓐ Ⓓ
4 ● Ⓓ	24 Ⓐ Ⓓ	49 Ⓐ Ⓓ	74 Ⓐ Ⓓ
5 Ⓐ Ⓓ	25 Ⓐ Ⓓ	50 Ⓐ Ⓓ	75 Ⓐ Ⓓ
6 Ⓐ Ⓓ	26 Ⓐ Ⓓ	51 Ⓐ Ⓓ	76 Ⓐ Ⓓ
7 Ⓐ Ⓓ	27 Ⓐ Ⓓ	52 Ⓐ Ⓓ	77 Ⓐ Ⓓ
8 Ⓐ Ⓓ	28 Ⓐ Ⓓ	53 Ⓐ Ⓓ	78 Ⓐ Ⓓ
9 Ⓐ Ⓓ	29 Ⓐ Ⓓ	54 Ⓐ Ⓓ	79 Ⓐ Ⓓ
10 Ⓐ Ⓓ	30 Ⓐ Ⓓ	55 Ⓐ Ⓓ	80 Ⓐ Ⓓ

PART—B

1 Ⓐ Ⓑ Ⓒ Ⓓ Ⓔ	31 Ⓐ Ⓑ Ⓒ Ⓓ Ⓔ	61 Ⓐ Ⓑ Ⓒ Ⓓ Ⓔ
2 Ⓐ Ⓑ Ⓒ Ⓓ Ⓔ	32 Ⓐ Ⓑ Ⓒ Ⓓ Ⓔ	62 Ⓐ Ⓑ Ⓒ Ⓓ Ⓔ
3 Ⓐ Ⓑ Ⓒ Ⓓ Ⓔ	33 Ⓐ Ⓑ Ⓒ Ⓓ Ⓔ	63 Ⓐ Ⓑ Ⓒ Ⓓ Ⓔ
4 Ⓐ Ⓑ Ⓒ Ⓓ Ⓔ	34 Ⓐ Ⓑ Ⓒ Ⓓ Ⓔ	64 Ⓐ Ⓑ Ⓒ Ⓓ Ⓔ
5 Ⓐ Ⓑ Ⓒ Ⓓ Ⓔ	35 Ⓐ Ⓑ Ⓒ Ⓓ Ⓔ	65 Ⓐ Ⓑ Ⓒ Ⓓ Ⓔ
6 Ⓐ Ⓑ Ⓒ Ⓓ Ⓔ	36 Ⓐ Ⓑ Ⓒ Ⓓ Ⓔ	66 Ⓐ Ⓑ Ⓒ Ⓓ Ⓔ
7 Ⓐ Ⓑ Ⓒ Ⓓ Ⓔ	37 Ⓐ Ⓑ Ⓒ Ⓓ Ⓔ	67 Ⓐ Ⓑ Ⓒ Ⓓ Ⓔ
8 Ⓐ Ⓑ Ⓒ Ⓓ Ⓔ	38 Ⓐ Ⓑ Ⓒ Ⓓ Ⓔ	68 Ⓐ Ⓑ Ⓒ Ⓓ Ⓔ
9 Ⓐ Ⓑ Ⓒ Ⓓ Ⓔ	39 Ⓐ Ⓑ Ⓒ Ⓓ Ⓔ	69 Ⓐ Ⓑ Ⓒ Ⓓ Ⓔ
10 Ⓐ Ⓑ Ⓒ Ⓓ Ⓔ	40 Ⓐ Ⓑ Ⓒ Ⓓ Ⓔ	70 Ⓐ Ⓑ Ⓒ Ⓓ Ⓔ

WHAT IS IN THE EXAMINATION

Clerk-Carrier Examination

The test for Clerk-Carrier has two parts. They are:

Part A: Address Checking

How quickly can you spot whether two addresses are alike or different? (See practice questions and tests starting on page 22.)

Part B: Memory for Addresses

How well can you memorize several groups of names and locations? (See practice questions and test starting on page 32.)

After you have passed this test, you will be placed on a list of eligibles on the basis of your score. If you are entitled to veterans' preference, you will be given the extra credit. (The higher your score the nearer the top of the list you will be.)

FILLING OUT THE ANSWER SHEET GRIDS

Filling out the answer sheet grids is very important. If the grids are filled out correctly, your answer sheet will be graded faster than if there are mistakes on the grids. Listed below is an explanation of how to complete the answer sheet grids correctly.

Before you begin to practice answering the sample questions, look at the Sample Answer Sheet Grids on page 13. Tear out one of the sample grid sheets and complete it according to the following instructions.

Let us assume the following:

1. Your name is James K. Certified.

2. You are taking the Clerk-Carrier Exam.

3. You would like to be hired as a Clerk.

4. You are a 5-point veteran.

5. Your social security number is 437-24-7424.

6. The date of the examination is March 15, 1978.

7. You were born in April 1935.

8. You are taking series number 402.

9. You would like to work in West Fishhook Falls, Montana – Installation Finance Number 537021.

In the top left hand corner of the grids, note that there are 20 blank spaces at the top of the NAME GRID. Under each space, every letter of the alphabet is contained in a circle. Now to complete the name: First, print the last name starting with box 1; if you have made the entry correctly, box 1 should have the letter C, box 2 letter E, box 3 letter R, etc. After printing the last name, skip a box (the box should be box 10). Then print the first name, starting with box 11. If you have made the entry correctly, box 11 should have a J, box 12 an A, box 13 an M, etc. Skip a box after completing the first name (which is box 16), and print the middle initial. Now darken the circle which contains the same letter as each box in which an entry has been made. In the number 1 box is a C, therefore the circle in column 1 containing C should be darkened; under column 2, the circle containing an E should be darkened; under column 3, the circle containing R should be darkened; etc., until all of the circles containing the same letters as the letters at the top of the grid are darkened. The blank circles under the skipped boxes must also be darkened.

Next fill in the EXAMINATION TITLE grid. You are taking the Clerk-Carrier Examination. Therefore, darken the blank circle beside Clerk-Carrier in the EXAMINATION TITLE box.

Next fill in YOUR JOB CHOICE grid. You would like to be hired as a Clerk. Therefore, darken the blank circle beside Clerk (only) in the JOB CHOICE box.

Next fill in VETERAN PREFERENCE grid. You are a 5-point veteran. Therefore, darken the blank circle beside 5 points (Tentative) in the VETERAN PREFERENCE box.

Next is the SOCIAL SECURITY NUMBER grid. Note that under the heading there are nine blank boxes and under the blank boxes are columns with circles containing numbers in them. To complete this grid, fill in the social security number 4 3 7 2 4 7 4 2 4, put one number in each blank box. Do not put in the two dashes. Next darken the circle in each column that has the same number as in the box above the column.

Then we have the DATE OF EXAMINATION grid. You will note the heading MO for month, DAY, and YEAR. Under each heading are two blank boxes and under the blank boxes are columns with circles containing numbers in them. To complete this grid, enter March 15, 1978 in this way. March is the third month, a single number month, but you have two empty blank boxes under the column heading MO. Therefore enter a zero in the first box and a three in the second box. In the two boxes under DAY, enter a one in the first box and a five in the second box. In the two boxes under YEAR, enter the last two numbers of the year 1978. Enter a seven in the first box and an eight in the second box. Next darken the circle in each column containing the same number as in the box above the column.

Next is the DATE OF BIRTH grid. It works the same way as the date of examination, except that there is no space for the day. Note the heading MO for month and YR for year. As Mr. Certified, you were born in April 1935. You would enter a zero and a four in the spaces for MO. April is the fourth month and the four is a single number so it must have a zero in front of it. In the boxes for year, enter the last two numbers of the year, 1935. Enter a three in the first space and a five in the second space. Next darken the circle in each column containing the same number as in the box.

Following that is the TEST SERIES grid. In the example, the test series is 402. Enter 402 in the blank boxes and then darken the correct circles.

INSTALLATION FINANCE NUMBER is next. To complete this grid, enter the installation finance number 537021 in the blank boxes and darken the circle with the same number as in the box. You will be told the finance number in the test room.

When you have finished, check that the darkened circles are correct. Check that the letters and numbers you have darkened are the same as those in the boxes at the top of the column. Then turn to page 19 which has a Completed Sample Grid. Check that you have completed yours in the same way.

Now tear out another of the sample answer sheet grids. This time use your own name, birth date, social security number, etc. Fill out the form just as you would in the test room. Make up your own date of examination, test series, and installation finance number.

Be sure to keep your pencil marks within the circles when you are darkening the circles. If you make a mistake, erase it completely.

As already noted, these pages are part of the booklet issued by the Postal Service. In order to keep the numbering and sequence of those pages, we have included this and four more sheets that are blank in that booklet. Thus, these random remarks are not part of the Postal Service booklet but are Ken-Book material -- why have blank pages when we might be saying something that might be useful to you?

We believe that the most useful material to occupy these pages would be added suggestions on passing these tests.

Consider first, Address Checking. It looks easy but it is easy to overlook something. Remember, however, that no one is expected to complete this test in the time allowed. Thus -- even though you may be penalized for wrong answers -- don't look back. Plunge ahead! But just be sure that you look carefully at every letter, number, capitalization, and punctuation mark! They are very tricky.

And of course -- as we remark elsewhere in our consideration of how to take civil service examinations -- see particularly, page KB-126 -- be sure that blacken the right circle on the answer sheet. If you get off the track and start putting the answer for 17 on space 16, you are pretty much washed up if keep it up for very long. While answers may be erased, there is no time for that in these speed tests.

(Continued on page KB-28)

SAMPLE ANSWER SHEET GRID

In the boxes below, print your last name first. Skip a box and print your first name. Skip a box, then print your middle initial. Below each box, blacken the circle that is lettered the same as the letter in the box. For each blank letter box, blacken the circle at the top of that column.

EXAMINATION TITLE

- ○ CLERK–CARRIER
- ○ MAIL–HANDLER

YOUR JOB CHOICE

- ○ CLERK (Only)
- ○ CARRIER (Only)
- ○ CLERK & CARRIER

VETERAN PREFERENCE

- ○ 5 POINTS (Tentative)
- ○ 10 POINTS (Compensable)
- ○ 10 POINTS (Other)

SOCIAL SECURITY NUMBER

DATE OF EXAMINATION
MO. | DAY | YEAR

BIRTH DATE
MO. | YEAR

TEST SERIES

INSTALLATION FINANCE NUMBER

MAKE NO MARKS HERE

Now as to Memory for Addresses -- sometimes referred to as Address Coding. This is generally given in two parts; in one you may refer back to the key boxes and in the second part you may not. This is not easy. If you have a photographic memory, you have it made. We have some specific suggestions for remembering the addresses on page KB-47. You might also look at the Postal Service suggestions on page KB-45. Remember again that no one is expected to finish this test either; it is just a matter of getting as many right answers down as possible. So, again, don't look back. We feel that this is the most difficult part of these examinations, so spend plenty of time on practice. (This test is not used in the Mail Handler examination.)

Then there is Meaning of Words. If you have a good vocabulary, this one should be duck soup for you. If not, you might practice. At present, this is only on the Mail Handler examination. There are a number of suggestions on improving your vocabulary on page KB-102. The words used in these examinations are not the easiest; you will not be asked what "money" means -- but they are not the hardest either; you will not be asked about jaw-breakers that are usually uttered only by college professors. We have nine pages of practice for this; they should give you a good idea of the range of words used in the examinations.

Number Series are difficult for most people; we have several pages of explanation and 72 questions on this. Remember that there is always a relationship among the numbers given that carries over to the ones not given. There may be addition, subtraction, multiplication, or division, going up or down -- and there may be alternating series.

(Continued on page KB-30.)

KB-29

In the boxes below, print your last name first. Skip a box and print your first name. Skip a box, then print your middle initial. Below each box, blacken the circle that is lettered the same as the letter in the box. For each blank letter box, blacken the circle at the top of that column.

EXAMINATION TITLE
○ CLERK—CARRIER
○ MAIL—HANDLER

YOUR JOB CHOICE
○ CLERK (Only)
○ CARRIER (Only)
○ CLERK & CARRIER

VETERAN PREFERENCE
○ 5 POINTS
     (Tentative)
○ 10 POINTS
     (Compensable)
○ 10 POINTS (Other)

SOCIAL SECURITY NUMBER

DATE OF EXAMINATION

MO.	DAY	YEAR

BIRTH DATE

MO.	YEAR

TEST SERIES

INSTALLATION FINANCE NUMBER

MAKE NO MARKS HERE

To prepare for the Following Oral Directions test, it is essential that you have someone to help you. We have placed this at the very end of the book (except for some spare answer sheets) so that you can cut out the directions. Ask him or her to read over the preliminary instructions ahead of time. They must be read to you at the proper speed.

These jobs that we discuss here are the three main jobs in the Postal Service; there must be distribution clerks to sort the mail out or run machines that do so; there must be mail handlers to run it from place to place; above all, there must be clerks to man the windows at the post offices and, under the same classification, the carriers who deliver the mail. They are satisfying jobs but they are not easy jobs. Consider the multitude of questions that people at the windows must be prepared to answer. By themselves or with aid of their supervisors -- and perhaps of the Postal Manual -- they must be able to tell you about rates, classes of mail, what is and is not mailable -- and how you can send a money order to Nepal (or can you?).

A comedian is always good for a laugh if he can get out a gag about slow mail. However, when one considers the billions of pieces of mail that go through the system, we suggest that it is remarkable how few of them get lost or delayed. In our business of selling The Ken-Books, failure of the Postal Service to deliver them is rare.

(Continued on page KB-32)

SAMPLE ANSWER SHEET GRID

In the boxes below, print your last name first. Skip a box and print your first name. Skip a box, then print your middle initial. Below each box, blacken the circle that is lettered the same as the letter in the box. For each blank letter box, blacken the circle at the top of that column.

EXAMINATION TITLE
- CLERK–CARRIER
- MAIL–HANDLER

YOUR JOB CHOICE
- CLERK (Only)
- CARRIER (Only)
- CLERK & CARRIER

VETERAN PREFERENCE
- 5 POINTS (Tentative)
- 10 POINTS (Compensable)
- 10 POINTS (Other)

SOCIAL SECURITY NUMBER

| DATE OF EXAMINATION | | | BIRTH DATE | | TEST SERIES | INSTALLATION FINANCE NUMBER | MAKE NO MARKS HERE |
| MO. | DAY | YEAR | MO. | YEAR | | | |

With the responsibility that it has for handling these billions of pieces of mail, the Postal Service must be sure that it is hiring competent people.

The applicants -- you -- who get these jobs will have lifetime jobs at good pay with the usual "perks" of public employment: vacation, holidays, insurance, retirement, etc.

Thus, you should give your preparation for the examination the same time and care that you would give to any other examination that could lead to a satisfactory lifetime career. If you are a genius, you might be able to pass it cold -- but there are not many geniuses among us. Each of the five types of tests requires a particular ability that only careful preparation can sharpen and enhance.

Study!

In the boxes below, print your last name first. Skip a box and print your first name. Skip a box, then print your middle initial. Below each box, blacken the circle that is lettered the same as the letter in the box. For each blank letter box, blacken the circle at the top of that column.

CERTIFIED JAMES K

EXAMINATION TITLE
● CLERK–CARRIER
○ MAIL–HANDLER

YOUR JOB CHOICE
● CLERK (Only)
○ CARRIER (Only)
○ CLERK & CARRIER

VETERAN PREFERENCE
● 5 POINTS (Tentative)
○ 10 POINTS (Compensable)
○ 10 POINTS (Other)

SOCIAL SECURITY NUMBER
437 24 7424

DATE OF EXAMINATION			BIRTH DATE		TEST SERIES	INSTALLATION FINANCE NUMBER	MAKE NO MARKS HERE
MO.	DAY	YEAR	MO.	YEAR			
03	15	78	04	35	402	537021	

THE FOLLOWING JOB LISTING COVERS SIX PAGES AND WILL BE FOUND INTERSPERSED THROUGHOUT THE BOOK. FOR CONTINUATION, SEE DIRECTIONS AT BOTTOM OF EACH SUCCESSIVE PAGE. - ED.

ALPHABETICAL LIST OF POSITION TITLES

Position Title	Level	Position No.	Occ Code	Craft
Accountable Paper Supply Clerk	5	SP 2-42	0530-05xx	C
Accounting Clerk	5	SP 2-23	0520-01xx	C
Accounting Technician (Cost Ascertainment)	6	SP 1-63	0525-32xx	C
Accounting Technician	6	SP 2-443	0525-31xx	C
Administrative Clerk, VMF	6	SP 5-43	0301-09xx	MV
Area Maintenance Technician	8	SP 6-77	4801-20xx	M
Area Maintenance Specialist	7	SP 6-78	4801-21xx	M
Assignment Clerk	6	SP 2-10	0212-05xx	C
Assistant Engineman	5	SP 6-11	5309-01xx	M
Automated Personnel Paperwork Technician	6	SP 2-505	0203-32xx	C
Automotive Mechanic	6	KP-14	5823-03xx	MV
Automotive Painter	6	SP 5-54	4155-01xx	MV
Billing & Coding Clerk, AMF	6	SP 2-17	2330-10xx	C
Body & Fender Repairman	7	SP 5-55	3809-02xx	MV
Blacksmith-Welder	6	SP 6-43	3704-02xx	M
Bulk Mail Clerk	5	SP 2-44	2320-15xx	C
Bulk Mail Dock Clerk	6	SP 2-615	2315-99xx	C
Bulk Mail Technician	6	SP 2-387	2320-28xx	C
Carpenter	6	SP 6-6	4607-02xx	M
Carrier, City or Special	5	KP-11	2310-01xx	CA
Carrier, Special Delivery Messenger	5	KP-11	2310-53xx	SD
Carrier Technician	6	SP 2-261	2310-02xx	CA

Continued on Page KB-44

PRACTICE TESTS

HOW TO USE THESE PRACTICE TESTS

On the following pages, you will find questions just like the ones used in the examinations for the job of Clerk-Carrier in the Postal Service. Each type of question is explained separately. Study the samples and then do the practice tests.

Each practice test is timed. Have a friend watch the time for you.

When you have finished each practice test, go back and check your answers to find out what your score is. Then compare your score with the scale that goes with the test to determine how well you did. This will help you to find out where you need more practice.

Be sure to do the practice questions before you try the Clerk-Carrier tests, which start on page 48. These tests are exactly like the ones you will have to take in the examination. The time limit for each part and the types of questions in each part are exactly as they are in the examination.

Address Checking

DESCRIPTION OF THE TEST AND SAMPLE QUESTIONS

Every member of the Postal work force is responsible for seeing that every letter reaches the right address. If one worker makes an error in reading an address, it can cause a serious delay in getting the letter to where it is supposed to go.

The Clerk-Carrier Examination includes a test of address checking. For this test you are to determine whether or not two addresses are alike or different. It is as easy as that. But how fast can you do it accurately? Look at the sample questions below. Each question consists of a pair of addresses like this -

762 W 18th St   762 W 18th St

     Are they Alike or Different? They are exactly Alike.

9486 Hillsdale Rd   9489 Hillsdale Rd

     Alike or Different? They are Different. Do you see why?

1242 Regal St   1242 Regel St

     Alike or Different?

Remember that this test measures both speed and accuracy. So work as fast as you can without making any mistakes. Have a friend time you while you are working on the practice tests--you may find that you get faster as you become used to this type of question.

Hints for Answering Address-Checking Questions

- Do not spend too much time on any one question

- The difference may not be noticeable at first, so be sure to check

  - all numbers (are they alike and in the same order or are they different)

  - abbreviations, such as St, Rd, NW, N Y (are they alike or are they different)

  - spellings of street, city, and state names

- Do not get nervous about the time limit. (In the official test no one is expected to do all the questions in the time allowed.)

- Make sure that you have marked the correct circle for each question.

Address Checking--Sample Questions

Starting now, if the two addresses are ALIKE darken the circle marked A
on the Sample Answer Sheet below. If the two addresses are DIFFERENT
in any way darken the circle marked D. Answer every question.

1 ...	239 Windell Ave		239 Windell Ave
	Alike or Different?	Alike.	Mark circle A for question 1.
2 ...	4667 Edgeworth Rd		4677 Edgeworth Rd
	Alike or Different?	Different.	Mark circle D for question 2.
3 ...	2661 Kennel St SE		2661 Kennel St SW
4 ...	3709 Columbine St		3707 Columbine St
5 ...	969 W 14th St NW		969 W 14th St NW
6 ...	4439 Frederick Pkwy		4439 Frederick Pkwy
7 ...	77 Summers St		77 Summers St
8 ...	828 N Franklin Pl		828 S Franklin Pl

Check your answers with the correct answers. If you have any wrong
answers, be sure you see why before you go on.

SAMPLE ANSWER
SHEET
1 Ⓐ Ⓓ
2 Ⓐ Ⓓ
3 Ⓐ Ⓓ
4 Ⓐ Ⓓ
5 Ⓐ Ⓓ
6 Ⓐ Ⓓ
7 Ⓐ Ⓓ
8 Ⓐ Ⓓ

CORRECT
ANSWERS
1 ● Ⓓ
2 Ⓐ ●
3 Ⓐ ●
4 Ⓐ ●
5 ● Ⓓ
6 ● Ⓓ
7 ● Ⓓ
8 Ⓐ ●

The addresses in the Practice Tests are like the ones you will have to
check in the examination. The ones in Practice Test 1 are easy with
only the city, state, and sometimes a ZIP Code. Work as fast as you can,
but be careful because you will lose points for making mistakes. Be
sure to take no more than the correct time for each test. Check your
answers with the answers at the end of each test.

ADDRESS CHECKING—PRACTICE TEST 1

Work exactly *3 minutes*. No more. No less. If you finish before the 3 minutes are up, go over your answers again. Be sure to mark your answers on the Sample Answer Sheet on the next page.

1 ...	Purdin Mo	Purdon Mo
2 ...	Hobart Ind 46342	Hobart Ind 46342
3 ...	Kuna Idaho	Kuna Idaho
4 ...	Janesville Calif 96114	Janesville Calif 96119
5 ...	Sioux Falls S Dak	Sioux Falls S Dak
6 ...	Homewood Miss	Homewood Miss
7 ...	Kaweah Calif	Kawaeh Calif
8 ...	Unionport Ohio	Unionport Ohio
9 ...	Meyersdale Pa	Meyersdale Va
10 ...	Coquille Oreg 97423	Coqville Oreg 97423
11 ...	Milan Wis	Milam Wis
12 ...	Prospect Ky	Prospect Ky
13 ...	Cloversville N Y	Cloverville N Y
14 ...	Locate Mont 59340	Locate Mont 59340
15 ...	Bozman Md	Bozeman Md
16 ...	Orient Ill	Orient Ill
17 ...	Yosemite Ky 42566	Yosemite Ky 42566
18 ...	Camden Miss 39045	Camden Miss 39054
19 ...	Bennington Vt	Bennington Vt
20 ...	La Farge Wis	La Farge Wis
21 ...	Fairfield N Y	Fairfield N C
22 ...	Wynot Nebr	Wynot Nebr
23 ...	Arona Pa	Aroda Pa
24 ...	Thurman N C 28683	Thurmond N C 28683
25 ...	Zenda Kans	Zenba Kans
26 ...	Pike N H	Pike N H
27 ...	Gorst Wash 98337	Gorst Wash 98837
28 ...	Joiner Ark	Joiner Ark
29 ...	Normangee Tex	Normangee Tex
30 ...	Toccoa Ga	Tococa Ga
31 ...	Small Point Maine 04567	Small Point Maine 04567
32 ...	Eagan Tenn	Eagar Tenn
33 ...	Belfield N Dak	Belford N Dak
34 ...	De Ridder La 70634	De Ridder La 70634
35 ...	Van Meter Iowa	Van Meter Iowa
36 ...	Valparaiso Fla	Valparaiso Ind
37 ...	Souris N Dak	Souris N Dak
38 ...	Robbinston Maine	Robbinstown Maine
39 ...	Dawes W Va 25054	Dawes W Va 25054
40 ...	Goltry Okla	Goltrey Okla

SAMPLE ANSWER SHEET PART A

1 Ⓐ Ⓓ	21 Ⓐ Ⓓ
2 Ⓐ Ⓓ	22 Ⓐ Ⓓ
3 Ⓐ Ⓓ	23 Ⓐ Ⓓ
4 Ⓐ Ⓓ	24 Ⓐ Ⓓ
5 Ⓐ Ⓓ	25 Ⓐ Ⓓ
6 Ⓐ Ⓓ	26 Ⓐ Ⓓ
7 Ⓐ Ⓓ	27 Ⓐ Ⓓ
8 Ⓐ Ⓓ	28 Ⓐ Ⓓ
9 Ⓐ Ⓓ	29 Ⓐ Ⓓ
10 Ⓐ Ⓓ	30 Ⓐ Ⓓ
11 Ⓐ Ⓓ	31 Ⓐ Ⓓ
12 Ⓐ Ⓓ	32 Ⓐ Ⓓ
13 Ⓐ Ⓓ	33 Ⓐ Ⓓ
14 Ⓐ Ⓓ	34 Ⓐ Ⓓ
15 Ⓐ Ⓓ	35 Ⓐ Ⓓ
16 Ⓐ Ⓓ	36 Ⓐ Ⓓ
17 Ⓐ Ⓓ	37 Ⓐ Ⓓ
18 Ⓐ Ⓓ	38 Ⓐ Ⓓ
19 Ⓐ Ⓓ	39 Ⓐ Ⓓ
20 Ⓐ Ⓓ	40 Ⓐ Ⓓ

CORRECT ANSWERS PART A

KB-39

1 Ⓐ ●	21 Ⓐ ●
2 ● Ⓓ	22 ● Ⓓ
3 ● Ⓓ	23 Ⓐ ●
4 Ⓐ ●	24 Ⓐ ●
5 ● Ⓓ	25 Ⓐ ●
6 ● Ⓓ	26 ● Ⓓ
7 Ⓐ ●	27 Ⓐ ●
8 ● Ⓓ	28 ● Ⓓ
9 Ⓐ ●	29 ● Ⓓ
10 Ⓐ ●	30 Ⓐ ●
11 Ⓐ ●	31 ● Ⓓ
12 ● Ⓓ	32 Ⓐ ●
13 Ⓐ ●	33 Ⓐ ●
14 ● Ⓓ	34 ● Ⓓ
15 Ⓐ ●	35 ● Ⓓ
16 ● Ⓓ	36 Ⓐ ●
17 ● Ⓓ	37 ● Ⓓ
18 Ⓐ ●	38 Ⓐ ●
19 ● Ⓓ	39 ● Ⓓ
20 ● Ⓓ	40 Ⓐ ●

Now check your answers. Compare them with the correct answers in the next column. Count how many you got right, and write that number on this line_____→ Number Right _____

Now count how many you got wrong, and write that number on this line_____→ Number Wrong _____

Subtract the Number Wrong from the Number Right, and write the Difference on this line_____→ Total Score _____

Meaning of Test Score

If your Total Score is *26 or more,* you have a Good score.

If your Total Score is from *16 to 25,* you have a Fair score.

If your Total Score is *15 or less,* you are not doing too well.
   You may be going too slowly, or you may be making too many mistakes.
   You need more practice.

ADDRESS CHECKING—PRACTICE TEST 2

These addresses are a little harder.

Remember to work as fast as you can but be careful. Work exactly *3 minutes*. No more. No less. If you finish before the 3 minutes are up, go over your answers again. Be sure to mark your answers on the Sample Answer Sheet on the next page.

1 ... 7961 Eastern Ave SE   7961 Eastern Ave SE
2 ... 3809 20th Rd N   3309 20th Rd N
3 ... Smicksburg Pa   Smithsburg Pa
4 ... Sherman Conn   Sherman Conn
5 ... Richland Ga   Richland La
6 ... 8520 Leesburg Pike SE   8520 Leesburg Pike SE
7 ... Genevia Ark   Geneva Ark
8 ... 104 W Jefferson St   104 W Jefferson St
9 ... Meandor W Va   Meander W Va
10 ... 6327 W Mari Ct   6327 W Mari Ct
11 ... 3191 Draper Dr SE   3191 Draper Dr SW
12 ... 1415 W Green Spring Rd   1415 W Green Spring Rd
13 ... Parr Ind   Parr Ind
14 ... East Falmouth Mass 02536   East Falmouth Miss 02536
15 ... 3016 N St NW   3016 M St NW

16 ... Yukon Mo   Yukon Mo
17 ... 7057 Brookfield Plaza   7057 Brookfield Plaza
18 ... Bethel Ohio 45106   Bethel Ohio 45106
19 ... Littleton N H   Littleton N C
20 ... 8909 Bowie Dr   8909 Bowie Dr
21 ... Colmar Ill   Colmar Ill
22 ... 784 Matthews Dr NE   784 Matthews Dr NE
23 ... 2923 John Marshall Dr   2932 John Marshall Dr
24 ... 6023 Woodmont Rd   6023 Woodmount Rd
25 ... Nolan Tex   Noland Tex
26 ... 342 E Lincolnia Rd   342 E Lincolnia Dr
27 ... Jane Calif   Jane Calif
28 ... 4921 Seminary Rd   4912 Seminary Rd
29 ... Ulmers S C   Ullmers S C
30 ... 4804 Montgomery Lane SW   4804 Montgomery Lane SW
31 ... 210 E Fairfax Dr   210 W Fairfax Dr

32 ... Hanapepe Hawaii   Hanapepe Hawaii
33 ... 450 La Calle del Punto   450 La Calle del Punto
34 ... Walland Tenn 37886   Walland Tenn 37836
35 ... Villamont Va   Villamont Va
36 ... 4102 Georgia Ave NW   4102 Georgia Rd NW
37 ... Aroch Oreg   Aroch Oreg
38 ... 6531 N Walton Ave   6531 N Waldon Ave
39 ... Jeff Ky   Jeff Ky
40 ... Delphos Iowa   Delphis Iowa

SAMPLE ANSWER SHEET PART A

1 Ⓐ Ⓓ	21 Ⓐ Ⓓ
2 Ⓐ Ⓓ	22 Ⓐ Ⓓ
3 Ⓐ Ⓓ	23 Ⓐ Ⓓ
4 Ⓐ Ⓓ	24 Ⓐ Ⓓ
5 Ⓐ Ⓓ	25 Ⓐ Ⓓ
6 Ⓐ Ⓓ	26 Ⓐ Ⓓ
7 Ⓐ Ⓓ	27 Ⓐ Ⓓ
8 Ⓐ Ⓓ	28 Ⓐ Ⓓ
9 Ⓐ Ⓓ	29 Ⓐ Ⓓ
10 Ⓐ Ⓓ	30 Ⓐ Ⓓ
11 Ⓐ Ⓓ	31 Ⓐ Ⓓ
12 Ⓐ Ⓓ	32 Ⓐ Ⓓ
13 Ⓐ Ⓓ	33 Ⓐ Ⓓ
14 Ⓐ Ⓓ	34 Ⓐ Ⓓ
15 Ⓐ Ⓓ	35 Ⓐ Ⓓ
16 Ⓐ Ⓓ	36 Ⓐ Ⓓ
17 Ⓐ Ⓓ	37 Ⓐ Ⓓ
18 Ⓐ Ⓓ	38 Ⓐ Ⓓ
19 Ⓐ Ⓓ	39 Ⓐ Ⓓ
20 Ⓐ Ⓓ	40 Ⓐ Ⓓ

CORRECT ANSWERS PART A

1 ● Ⓓ	21 ● Ⓓ
2 Ⓐ ●	22 ● Ⓓ
3 Ⓐ ●	23 Ⓐ ●
4 ● Ⓓ	24 Ⓐ ●
5 Ⓐ ●	25 Ⓐ ●
6 ● Ⓓ	26 Ⓐ ●
7 Ⓐ ●	27 ● Ⓓ
8 ● Ⓓ	28 Ⓐ ●
9 Ⓐ ●	29 Ⓐ ●
10 ● Ⓓ	30 ● Ⓓ
11 Ⓐ ●	31 Ⓐ ●
12 ● Ⓓ	32 ● Ⓓ
13 ● Ⓓ	33 ● Ⓓ
14 Ⓐ ●	34 Ⓐ ●
15 Ⓐ ●	35 ● Ⓓ
16 ● Ⓓ	36 Ⓐ ●
17 ● Ⓓ	37 ● Ⓓ
18 ● Ⓓ	38 Ⓐ ●
19 Ⓐ ●	39 ● Ⓓ
20 ● Ⓓ	40 Ⓐ ●

Now check your answers. Compare them with the correct answers in the next column. Count how many you got right, and write that number on this line_____→ Number Right _____

Now count how many you got wrong, and write that number on this line_____→ Number Wrong _____

Subtract the Number Wrong from the Number Right, and write the Difference on this line_____→ Total Score _____

Meaning of Test Score

If your Total Score is *26 or more,* you have a Good score.

If your Total Score is from *16 to 25,* you have a Fair score.

If your Total Score is *15 or less,* you are not doing too well.
    You may be going too slowly, or you may be making too many mistakes.
    You need more practice.

ADDRESS CHECKING—PRACTICE TEST 3

These addresses are exactly like the ones in the Clerk-Carrier examination.

Work as fast as you can without making too many errors. Work exactly *3 minutes*. No more. No less. If you finish before the 3 minutes are up, go over your answers again. Mark your answers on the Sample Answer Sheet on the next page.

1 ...	2134 S 20th St	2134 S 20th St
2 ...	4608 N Warnock St	4806 N Warnock St
3 ...	1202 W Girard Dr	1202 W Girard Rd
4 ...	3120 S Harcourt St	3120 S Harcourt St
5 ...	4618 W Addison St	4618 E Addison St
6 ...	Sessums Miss	Sessoms Miss
7 ...	6425 N Delancey	6425 N Delancey
8 ...	5407 Columbia Rd	5407 Columbia Rd
9 ...	2106 Southern Ave	2106 Southern Ave
10 ...	Highfalls N C 27259	Highlands NC 27259
11 ...	2873 Pershing Dr	2873 Pershing Dr
12 ...	1329 N H Ave NW	1329 N J Ave NW
13 ...	1316 N Quinn St	1316 N Quinn St
14 ...	7507 Wyngate Dr	7505 Wyngate Dr
15 ...	2918 Colesville Rd	2918 Colesvale Rd
16 ...	2071 E Belvedere Dr	2071 E Belvedere Dr
17 ...	Palmer Wash	Palmer Mich
18 ...	2106 16th St SW	2106 16th St SW
19 ...	2207 Markland Ave	2207 Markham Ave
20 ...	5345 16th St SW	5345 16th St SE
21 ...	239 Summit Pl NE	239 Summit Pl NE
22 ...	152 Continental Pkwy	152 Continental Blvd
23 ...	8092 13th Rd S	8029 13th Rd S
24 ...	3906 Queensbury Rd	3906 Queensbury Rd
25 ...	4719 Linnean Ave NW	4719 Linnean Ave NE
26 ...	Bradford Me	Bradley Me
27 ...	Parrott Ga 31777	Parrott Ga 31177
28 ...	4312 Lowell Lane	4312 Lowell Lane
29 ...	6929 W 135th Place	6929 W 135th Plaza
30 ...	5143 Somerset Cir	5143 Somerset Cir
31 ...	8501 Kennedy St	8501 Kennedy St
32 ...	2164 E McLean Ave	2164 E McLean Ave
33 ...	7186 E St NW	7186 F St NW
34 ...	2121 Beechcrest Rd	2121 Beechcroft Rd
35 ...	3609 E Montrose St	3609 E Montrose St
36 ...	324 S Alvadero St	324 S Alverado St
37 ...	2908 Plaza de las Estrellas	2908 Plaza de las Estrellas
38 ...	223 Great Falls Rd SE	223 Great Falls Dr SE
39 ...	Kelton S C 29354	Kelton S C 29354
40 ...	3201 Landover Rd	3201 Landover Rd

```
┌─────────────────────────┐          ┌─────────────────────────┐
│   SAMPLE ANSWER SHEET    │          │     CORRECT ANSWERS     │
│         PART A           │          │         PART A          │
│                          │          │                         │
│   1 Ⓐ Ⓓ   21 Ⓐ Ⓓ        │          │   1 ● Ⓓ   21 ● Ⓓ        │
│   2 Ⓐ Ⓓ   22 Ⓐ Ⓓ        │          │   2 Ⓐ ●   22 Ⓐ ●        │
│   3 Ⓐ Ⓓ   23 Ⓐ Ⓓ        │          │   3 Ⓐ ●   23 Ⓐ ●        │
│   4 Ⓐ Ⓓ   24 Ⓐ Ⓓ        │          │   4 ● Ⓓ   24 ● Ⓓ        │
│   5 Ⓐ Ⓓ   25 Ⓐ Ⓓ        │          │   5 Ⓐ ●   25 Ⓐ ●        │
│   6 Ⓐ Ⓓ   26 Ⓐ Ⓓ        │          │   6 Ⓐ ●   26 Ⓐ ●        │
│   7 Ⓐ Ⓓ   27 Ⓐ Ⓓ        │          │   7 ● Ⓓ   27 Ⓐ ●        │
│   8 Ⓐ Ⓓ   28 Ⓐ Ⓓ        │          │   8 ● Ⓓ   28 ● Ⓓ        │
│   9 Ⓐ Ⓓ   29 Ⓐ Ⓓ        │          │   9 ● Ⓓ   29 Ⓐ ●        │
│  10 Ⓐ Ⓓ   30 Ⓐ Ⓓ        │          │  10 Ⓐ ●   30 ● Ⓓ        │
│  11 Ⓐ Ⓓ   31 Ⓐ Ⓓ        │          │  11 ● Ⓓ   31 ● Ⓓ        │
│  12 Ⓐ Ⓓ   32 Ⓐ Ⓓ        │          │  12 Ⓐ ●   32 ● Ⓓ        │
│  13 Ⓐ Ⓓ   33 Ⓐ Ⓓ        │          │  13 ● Ⓓ   33 Ⓐ ●        │
│  14 Ⓐ Ⓓ   34 Ⓐ Ⓓ        │          │  14 Ⓐ ●   34 Ⓐ ●        │
│  15 Ⓐ Ⓓ   35 Ⓐ Ⓓ        │          │  15 Ⓐ ●   35 ● Ⓓ        │
│  16 Ⓐ Ⓓ   36 Ⓐ Ⓓ        │          │  16 ● Ⓓ   36 Ⓐ ●        │
│  17 Ⓐ Ⓓ   37 Ⓐ Ⓓ        │          │  17 Ⓐ ●   37 ● Ⓓ        │
│  18 Ⓐ Ⓓ   38 Ⓐ Ⓓ        │          │  18 ● Ⓓ   38 Ⓐ ●        │
│  19 Ⓐ Ⓓ   39 Ⓐ Ⓓ        │          │  19 Ⓐ ●   39 ● Ⓓ        │
│  20 Ⓐ Ⓓ   40 Ⓐ Ⓓ        │          │  20 Ⓐ ●   40 ● Ⓓ        │
└─────────────────────────┘          └─────────────────────────┘
```

Now check your answers. Compare them with the correct answers in the next column. Count how many you got right, and write that number on this line_____→ Number Right _____

Now count how many you got wrong, and write that number on this line_____→ Number Wrong _____

Subtract the Number Wrong from the Number Right, and write the Difference on this line_____→ Total Score _____

Meaning of Test Score

If your Total Score is *26 or more,* you have a Good score.

If your Total Score is from *16 to 25,* you have a Fair score.

If your Total Score is *15 or less,* you are not doing too well.
    You may be going too slowly, or you may be making too many mistakes.
    You need more practice.

Position Title	Level	Position No.	Occ Code	Craft
Distribution and Window Clerk	5	SP 2-1	2340-02xx	C
Distribution Window & Markup Clerk	5	SP 2-629	2340-80xx	C
Drafting Clerk	5	SP 1-17	0818-01xx	C&M
Driver-Instructor & Examiner	6	SP 5-24	5752-01xx	MV
Electronics Technician Trainee (Bulk Mail)	7	SP 6-84	0856-04xx	M
Electronics Technician	8	SP 6-75	0856-01xx	M
Electronics Technician	9	SP 6-80	0856-01xx	M
Electronics Technician	10	SP 6-76	0856-01xx	M
Elevator Mechanic	7	SP 6-12	5313-03xx	M
Elevator Operator	3	KP-2	5438-01xx	M
Elevator Starter	4	SP 6-3	5438-02xx	M
Employee Accounts Clerk	5	SP 2-6	0590-02xx	C
Engineman	6	SP 6-45	5309-02xx	M
Examination Specialist	6	SP 2-188	0203-19xx	C, SD, M, CA, MH, & MV
Express Mail Service Clerk	6	SP 2-617	2330-77xx	C
File Clerk	4	KP-6	0305-03xx	C
Fireman	4	SP 6-14	5402-01xx	M
Fireman-Laborer	4	SP 6-4	5402-02xx	M
Flat Sorting Machine Operator	5	SP 2-27	2315-20xx	C
Flat Sorting Machine Operator	6	SP 2-28	2315-21xx	C
Foreign Container Inventory Clerk	5	SP 2-22	2040-04xx	C
Fork Lift Operator	5	SP 7-15	5704-02xx	
Garageman	4	KP-9	6955-02xx	MV
General Clerk	5	SP 2-45	2340-01xx	C
General Clerk, VMF	5	SP 5-42	0301-48xx	MV

Continued on Page KB-56

MEMORY FOR ADDRESSES

DESCRIPTION OF THE TEST AND SAMPLE QUESTIONS

This test is part of the Clerk-Carrier examination. All Clerks in the Postal Service have to learn a scheme during their training period. The Clerk uses the scheme to sort the mail to where it is going. He must have a good memory in order to learn the scheme. Carriers also need good memories.

In this test you will be given 25 addresses to remember. The addresses are divided into five groups. Each group of five addresses is in a box such as those on the next page. Each box has a letter--A, B, C, D, or E. You will have to learn which letter goes with each address. You will be given time to study in the examination room. In order to practice for this test, you need to be timed.

While you are doing the practice test, find out what is the best way for you to memorize which letter goes with each address. Some people learn best by studying the addresses in one box; then covering it and seeing whether they can say the addresses to themselves. If they can say them, they then try to learn the next box. If they cannot, they study the names in the first box again; and then try to say the names with the box covered. They do this for all the boxes. Other people learn best by studying across the page. Still others do best by memorizing everything at once. If you do not know your best way, try different ways and see which one is best for you. Do not try to memorize the names by writing them down because you won't be allowed to write them in the official examination.

Hints for Memory for Addresses Test

° Be sure to spend the study period studying.

° Be sure to try to learn which letter goes with each address. It is to your advantage to learn as many as you can.

° Do not spend too much time on any one question.

° Do not get nervous about the time limit. (In the official test no one is expected to do all the questions in the time allowed.)

° If you are not sure of an answer, guess.

Sample Questions for Memory for Addresses

In this test you will have five boxes labeled A, B, C, D, and E. Each box contains five addresses. Three of the five are groups of street addresses like 1700-2599 Wood, 8500-8699 Lang, and 6200-6399 James, and two are names of places. They are different in each box.

You will also be given two lists of names. You will have to decide which box each name belongs in. When you are working on the first list, you will have the boxes with the names in front of you. When you are working on the second list, you will not be able to look at the boxes.

The addresses you will use for the Practice Test are given in the boxes below.

A	B	C	D	E
1700-2599 Wood Dushore 8500-8699 Lang Lott 6200-6399 James	2700-3299 Wood Jeriel 8700-9399 Lang Vanna 5700-6199 James	1300-1699 Wood Levering 9400-9499 Lang Ekron 6400-6499 James	3300-3599 Wood Bair 8000-8499 Lang Viborg 5000-5699 James	2600-2699 Wood Danby 9500-9999 Lang Lycan 4700-4999 James

Questions 1 through 5 show the way the questions look. You have to decide in which lettered box (A, B, C, D, or E) the address belongs and then mark that answer on the Sample Answer Sheet on this page.

1. Levering
   This address is in box C. So darken circle C on the Sample Answer Sheet.
2. 2700-3299 Wood
   This address is in box B. So darken circle B on the Sample Answer Sheet.
3. Vanna
   This address is in box B. So darken circle B on the Sample Answer Sheet.
4. 6200-6399 James
5. Bair

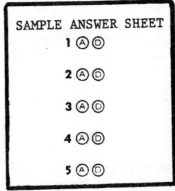

The answers for samples 4 and 5 are 4A and 5D.

Your practice test starts on the next page.

MEMORY FOR ADDRESSES--PRACTICE TEST

STUDY--3 minutes

Now go back to page 32 and spend 3 minutes memorizing the addresses in the boxes. TRY TO LEARN THE LOCATION OF AS MANY ADDRESSES AS YOU CAN. Cover each box with your hand and see if you can repeat, to yourself, the addresses in that box.

When the 3 minutes for studying are up, turn to page 34 and continue with the practice.

READ THE FOLLOWING AFTER YOU HAVE DONE THE TESTS FOR THE BOXES ON PAGE KB-46 AND THEN TRY THIS SYSTEM FOR OTHER TESTS OF THIS TYPE.

KEN-BOOK SUGGESTIONS FOR THE MEMORY FOR ADDRESSES TEST:
Some people find it helpful in remembering the single-name part of this test at least to use some trick combinations of letters that will help to recall the box-letter that is to follow.   This is particularly helpful if there is only one letter of a kind. To illustrate:
Using the boxes in this test: Remember Dua and Lotta -- dua lotta work; then when you see these, you will remember A for Dushore and Lott. Many cartoons, etc., refer to the boss as J.B. or maybe, V.B. for Very Bad -- as a way to recall B for Jeriel and Vanna.   For Levering, think of a C in front --Clever and for Ekron note that it would be pronounced the same way if there were a C in it -- Ecktron.   For Bair -- Bad spells just that and for Viborg -- Vid stands for video.   For Danby think of Dan-E -- Danny Boy and for Lycan -- LycE -- lice.   Some of these might sound foolish but such a system can be a big help in remembering for the short period of the examination.
The numbers with the names are more difficult but sometimes you can recall a few of them by noting where the high and low numbers are: the lowest number in the boxes is 1300 -- try to remember 13C. Note that the highest -- 9999 is at the right end.

List 1

WORK—*3 minutes*

For each question, mark the Sample Answer Sheet on the next page to show the letter of the box in which the address belongs. Try to remember the location of as many addresses as you can. If you are not sure of an address, guess. Work only 3 minutes.

A	B	C	D	E
1700–2599 Wood Dushore 8500–8699 Lang Lott 6200–6399 James	2700–3299 Wood Jeriel 8700–9399 Lang Vanna 5700–6199 James	1300–1699 Wood Levering 9400–9499 Lang Ekron 6400–6499 James	3300–3599 Wood Bair 8000–8499 Lang Viborg 5000–5699 James	2600–2699 Wood Danby 9500–9999 Lang Lycan 4700–4999 James

1. 6200–6399 James
2. 1700–2599 Wood
3. Bair
4. 1700–2599 Wood
5. Ekron
6. Viborg
7. Danby
8. 8500–8699 Lang

9. Lycan
10. 8000–8499 Lang
11. 4700–4999 James
12. 9400–9499 Lang
13. 2700–3299 Wood
14. Jeriel
15. 9500–9999 Lang
16. 1300–1699 Wood

17. 8700–9399 Lang
18. Levering
19. Vanna
20. 6400–6499 James
21. 3300–3599 Wood
22. Dushore
23. Lycan
24. 5700–6199 James

25. Lott
26. Viborg
27. Jeriel
28. 5000–5699 James
29. 2600–2699 Wood
30. 4700–4999 James
31. 2700–3299 Wood
32. 8000–8499 Lang

33. Ekron
34. 3300–3599 Wood
35. 9400–9499 Lang
36. 6200–6399 James
37. 2600–2699 Wood
38. 8500–8699 Lang
39. Levering
40. Lott

41. Bair
42. 1700–2599 Wood
43. 6400–6499 James
44. 9500–9999 Lang
45. Jeriel
46. 4700–4999 James
47. Dushore
48. Lycan

49. 1700–2599 Wood
50. 6200–6399 James
51. Vanna
52. Ekron
53. 8700–9399 Lang
54. Bair
55. 2600–2699 Wood
56. Dushore

57. 5700–6199 James
58. 1300–1699 Wood
59. Levering
60. Lott
61. Jeriel
62. 2600–2699 Wood
63. Lott
64. 4700–4999 James

65. Dushore
66. Danby
67. 8500–8699 Lang
68. Vanna
69. 2700–3299 Wood
70. 9500–9999 Lang
71. Viborg
72. Ekron

73. 6200–6399 James
74. 2600–2699 Wood
75. Levering
76. Lott
77. 1300–1699 Wood
78. Bair
79. Lycan
80. 5700–6199 James

81. Levering
82. 8700–9399 Lang
83. 5000–5699 James
84. 1700–2599 Wood
85. Jeriel
86. 6200–6399 James
87. Ekron
88. 2700–3299 Wood

STOP.

If you finish before the 3 minutes are up, go back and check your answers for the questions on this page for the rest of the 3 minutes.

When the 3 minutes are up, go on to page 36.

1 Ⓐ Ⓑ Ⓒ Ⓓ Ⓔ 31 Ⓐ Ⓑ Ⓒ Ⓓ Ⓔ 61 Ⓐ Ⓑ Ⓒ Ⓓ Ⓔ
2 Ⓐ Ⓑ Ⓒ Ⓓ Ⓔ 32 Ⓐ Ⓑ Ⓒ Ⓓ Ⓔ 62 Ⓐ Ⓑ Ⓒ Ⓓ Ⓔ
3 Ⓐ Ⓑ Ⓒ Ⓓ Ⓔ 33 Ⓐ Ⓑ Ⓒ Ⓓ Ⓔ 63 Ⓐ Ⓑ Ⓒ Ⓓ Ⓔ
4 Ⓐ Ⓑ Ⓒ Ⓓ Ⓔ 34 Ⓐ Ⓑ Ⓒ Ⓓ Ⓔ 64 Ⓐ Ⓑ Ⓒ Ⓓ Ⓔ
5 Ⓐ Ⓑ Ⓒ Ⓓ Ⓔ 35 Ⓐ Ⓑ Ⓒ Ⓓ Ⓔ 65 Ⓐ Ⓑ Ⓒ Ⓓ Ⓔ
6 Ⓐ Ⓑ Ⓒ Ⓓ Ⓔ 36 Ⓐ Ⓑ Ⓒ Ⓓ Ⓔ 66 Ⓐ Ⓑ Ⓒ Ⓓ Ⓔ
7 Ⓐ Ⓑ Ⓒ Ⓓ Ⓔ 37 Ⓐ Ⓑ Ⓒ Ⓓ Ⓔ 67 Ⓐ Ⓑ Ⓒ Ⓓ Ⓔ
8 Ⓐ Ⓑ Ⓒ Ⓓ Ⓔ 38 Ⓐ Ⓑ Ⓒ Ⓓ Ⓔ 68 Ⓐ Ⓑ Ⓒ Ⓓ Ⓔ
9 Ⓐ Ⓑ Ⓒ Ⓓ Ⓔ 39 Ⓐ Ⓑ Ⓒ Ⓓ Ⓔ 69 Ⓐ Ⓑ Ⓒ Ⓓ Ⓔ
10 Ⓐ Ⓑ Ⓒ Ⓓ Ⓔ 40 Ⓐ Ⓑ Ⓒ Ⓓ Ⓔ 70 Ⓐ Ⓑ Ⓒ Ⓓ Ⓔ
11 Ⓐ Ⓑ Ⓒ Ⓓ Ⓔ 41 Ⓐ Ⓑ Ⓒ Ⓓ Ⓔ 71 Ⓐ Ⓑ Ⓒ Ⓓ Ⓔ
12 Ⓐ Ⓑ Ⓒ Ⓓ Ⓔ 42 Ⓐ Ⓑ Ⓒ Ⓓ Ⓔ 72 Ⓐ Ⓑ Ⓒ Ⓓ Ⓔ
13 Ⓐ Ⓑ Ⓒ Ⓓ Ⓔ 43 Ⓐ Ⓑ Ⓒ Ⓓ Ⓔ 73 Ⓐ Ⓑ Ⓒ Ⓓ Ⓔ
14 Ⓐ Ⓑ Ⓒ Ⓓ Ⓔ 44 Ⓐ Ⓑ Ⓒ Ⓓ Ⓔ 74 Ⓐ Ⓑ Ⓒ Ⓓ Ⓔ
15 Ⓐ Ⓑ Ⓒ Ⓓ Ⓔ 45 Ⓐ Ⓑ Ⓒ Ⓓ Ⓔ 75 Ⓐ Ⓑ Ⓒ Ⓓ Ⓔ
16 Ⓐ Ⓑ Ⓒ Ⓓ Ⓔ 46 Ⓐ Ⓑ Ⓒ Ⓓ Ⓔ 76 Ⓐ Ⓑ Ⓒ Ⓓ Ⓔ
17 Ⓐ Ⓑ Ⓒ Ⓓ Ⓔ 47 Ⓐ Ⓑ Ⓒ Ⓓ Ⓔ 77 Ⓐ Ⓑ Ⓒ Ⓓ Ⓔ
18 Ⓐ Ⓑ Ⓒ Ⓓ Ⓔ 48 Ⓐ Ⓑ Ⓒ Ⓓ Ⓔ 78 Ⓐ Ⓑ Ⓒ Ⓓ Ⓔ
19 Ⓐ Ⓑ Ⓒ Ⓓ Ⓔ 49 Ⓐ Ⓑ Ⓒ Ⓓ Ⓔ 79 Ⓐ Ⓑ Ⓒ Ⓓ Ⓔ
20 Ⓐ Ⓑ Ⓒ Ⓓ Ⓔ 50 Ⓐ Ⓑ Ⓒ Ⓓ Ⓔ 80 Ⓐ Ⓑ Ⓒ Ⓓ Ⓔ
21 Ⓐ Ⓑ Ⓒ Ⓓ Ⓔ 51 Ⓐ Ⓑ Ⓒ Ⓓ Ⓔ 81 Ⓐ Ⓑ Ⓒ Ⓓ Ⓔ
22 Ⓐ Ⓑ Ⓒ Ⓓ Ⓔ 52 Ⓐ Ⓑ Ⓒ Ⓓ Ⓔ 82 Ⓐ Ⓑ Ⓒ Ⓓ Ⓔ
23 Ⓐ Ⓑ Ⓒ Ⓓ Ⓔ 53 Ⓐ Ⓑ Ⓒ Ⓓ Ⓔ 83 Ⓐ Ⓑ Ⓒ Ⓓ Ⓔ
24 Ⓐ Ⓑ Ⓒ Ⓓ Ⓔ 54 Ⓐ Ⓑ Ⓒ Ⓓ Ⓔ 84 Ⓐ Ⓑ Ⓒ Ⓓ Ⓔ
25 Ⓐ Ⓑ Ⓒ Ⓓ Ⓔ 55 Ⓐ Ⓑ Ⓒ Ⓓ Ⓔ 85 Ⓐ Ⓑ Ⓒ Ⓓ Ⓔ
26 Ⓐ Ⓑ Ⓒ Ⓓ Ⓔ 56 Ⓐ Ⓑ Ⓒ Ⓓ Ⓔ 86 Ⓐ Ⓑ Ⓒ Ⓓ Ⓔ
27 Ⓐ Ⓑ Ⓒ Ⓓ Ⓔ 57 Ⓐ Ⓑ Ⓒ Ⓓ Ⓔ 87 Ⓐ Ⓑ Ⓒ Ⓓ Ⓔ
28 Ⓐ Ⓑ Ⓒ Ⓓ Ⓔ 58 Ⓐ Ⓑ Ⓒ Ⓓ Ⓔ 88 Ⓐ Ⓑ Ⓒ Ⓓ Ⓔ
29 Ⓐ Ⓑ Ⓒ Ⓓ Ⓔ 59 Ⓐ Ⓑ Ⓒ Ⓓ Ⓔ
30 Ⓐ Ⓑ Ⓒ Ⓓ Ⓔ 60 Ⓐ Ⓑ Ⓒ Ⓓ Ⓔ

List 2

WORK—*3 minutes*

Now do these questions without looking back at the boxes with the addresses in them.

For each question, mark your answer on the Sample Answer Sheet on the next page. If you are not sure of an answer, guess.

1. Jeriel	25. 2700–3299 Wood	49. Bair	73. Dushore
2. Dushore	26. 5700–6199 James	50. 8700–9399 Lang	74. 8000–8499 Lang
3. 5000–5699 James	27. Levering	51. 6200–6399 James	75. Bair
4. 1300–1699 Wood	28. 9500–9999 Lang	52. 9400–9499 Lang	76. Ekron
5. 8500–8699 Lang	29. 2600–2699 Wood	53. Viborg	77. 6200–6399 James
6. Bair	30. 3300–3599 Wood	54. 8000–8499 Lang	78. 3300–3599 Wood
7. 5700–6199 James	31. Viborg	55. 4700–4999 James	79. 8700–9399 Lang
8. Levering	32. 9400–9499 Lang	56. Lycan	80. Viborg
9. Danby	33. Jeriel	57. Vanna	81. 4700–4999 James
10. Viborg	34. Bair	58. Danby	82. Lycan
11. 8000–8499 Lang	35. 8500–8699 Lang	59. 5700–6199 James	83. 1700–2599 Wood
12. 2700–3299 Wood	36. 1700–2599 Wood	60. Lott	84. 8500–8699 Lang
13. 9400–9499 Lang	37. 8000–8499 Lang	61. 2700–3299 Wood	85. 1300–1699 Wood
14. 3300–3599 Wood	38. Danby	62. 5000–5699 James	86. Jeriel
15. 4700–4999 James	39. Ekron	63. 1700–2599 Wood	87. Danby
16. 9500–9999 Lang	40. 4700–4999 James	64. 8000–8499 Lang	88. 6400–6499 James
17. Ekron	41. Dushore	65. 9400–9499 Lang	
18. 1300–1699 Wood	42. Vanna	66. Jeriel	**STOP.**
19. Vanna	43. 5000–5699 James	67. 9500–9999 Lang	
20. Lycan	44. Lott	68. Dushore	If you finish before the
21. 8700–9399 Lang	45. 1300–1699 Wood	69. 2600–2699 Wood	end of 3 minutes, go back
22. Dushore	46. Levering	70. 8500–8699 Lang	and be sure that you
23. 6200–6399 James	47. 5700–6199 James	71. Levering	are satisfied with your
24. Lott	48. 9500–9999 Lang	72. 5000–5699 James	answers.

Second Study

STUDY—*5 minutes*

You can see that memory is important in this test.

Now turn back to page 32 and spend 5 minutes memorizing the addresses in the boxes. TRY TO MEMORIZE THE LOCATION OF AS MANY ADDRESSES AS YOU CAN. Cover each box with your hand and see if you can repeat, to yourself, the addresses in that box.

When the 5 minutes for studying are up, turn to page 38 and continue with the practice.

SAMPLE ANSWER SHEET
PART—B

1 Ⓐ Ⓑ Ⓒ Ⓓ Ⓔ   31 Ⓐ Ⓑ Ⓒ Ⓓ Ⓔ   61 Ⓐ Ⓑ Ⓒ Ⓓ Ⓔ

2 Ⓐ Ⓑ Ⓒ Ⓓ Ⓔ   32 Ⓐ Ⓑ Ⓒ Ⓓ Ⓔ   62 Ⓐ Ⓑ Ⓒ Ⓓ Ⓔ

3 Ⓐ Ⓑ Ⓒ Ⓓ Ⓔ   33 Ⓐ Ⓑ Ⓒ Ⓓ Ⓔ   63 Ⓐ Ⓑ Ⓒ Ⓓ Ⓔ

4 Ⓐ Ⓑ Ⓒ Ⓓ Ⓔ   34 Ⓐ Ⓑ Ⓒ Ⓓ Ⓔ   64 Ⓐ Ⓑ Ⓒ Ⓓ Ⓔ

5 Ⓐ Ⓑ Ⓒ Ⓓ Ⓔ   35 Ⓐ Ⓑ Ⓒ Ⓓ Ⓔ   65 Ⓐ Ⓑ Ⓒ Ⓓ Ⓔ

6 Ⓐ Ⓑ Ⓒ Ⓓ Ⓔ   36 Ⓐ Ⓑ Ⓒ Ⓓ Ⓔ   66 Ⓐ Ⓑ Ⓒ Ⓓ Ⓔ

7 Ⓐ Ⓑ Ⓒ Ⓓ Ⓔ   37 Ⓐ Ⓑ Ⓒ Ⓓ Ⓔ   67 Ⓐ Ⓑ Ⓒ Ⓓ Ⓔ

8 Ⓐ Ⓑ Ⓒ Ⓓ Ⓔ   38 Ⓐ Ⓑ Ⓒ Ⓓ Ⓔ   68 Ⓐ Ⓑ Ⓒ Ⓓ Ⓔ

9 Ⓐ Ⓑ Ⓒ Ⓓ Ⓔ   39 Ⓐ Ⓑ Ⓒ Ⓓ Ⓔ   69 Ⓐ Ⓑ Ⓒ Ⓓ Ⓔ

10 Ⓐ Ⓑ Ⓒ Ⓓ Ⓔ   40 Ⓐ Ⓑ Ⓒ Ⓓ Ⓔ   70 Ⓐ Ⓑ Ⓒ Ⓓ Ⓔ

11 Ⓐ Ⓑ Ⓒ Ⓓ Ⓔ   41 Ⓐ Ⓑ Ⓒ Ⓓ Ⓔ   71 Ⓐ Ⓑ Ⓒ Ⓓ Ⓔ

12 Ⓐ Ⓑ Ⓒ Ⓓ Ⓔ   42 Ⓐ Ⓑ Ⓒ Ⓓ Ⓔ   72 Ⓐ Ⓑ Ⓒ Ⓓ Ⓔ

13 Ⓐ Ⓑ Ⓒ Ⓓ Ⓔ   43 Ⓐ Ⓑ Ⓒ Ⓓ Ⓔ   73 Ⓐ Ⓑ Ⓒ Ⓓ Ⓔ

14 Ⓐ Ⓑ Ⓒ Ⓓ Ⓔ   44 Ⓐ Ⓑ Ⓒ Ⓓ Ⓔ   74 Ⓐ Ⓑ Ⓒ Ⓓ Ⓔ

15 Ⓐ Ⓑ Ⓒ Ⓓ Ⓔ   45 Ⓐ Ⓑ Ⓒ Ⓓ Ⓔ   75 Ⓐ Ⓑ Ⓒ Ⓓ Ⓔ

16 Ⓐ Ⓑ Ⓒ Ⓓ Ⓔ   46 Ⓐ Ⓑ Ⓒ Ⓓ Ⓔ   76 Ⓐ Ⓑ Ⓒ Ⓓ Ⓔ

17 Ⓐ Ⓑ Ⓒ Ⓓ Ⓔ   47 Ⓐ Ⓑ Ⓒ Ⓓ Ⓔ   77 Ⓐ Ⓑ Ⓒ Ⓓ Ⓔ

18 Ⓐ Ⓑ Ⓒ Ⓓ Ⓔ   48 Ⓐ Ⓑ Ⓒ Ⓓ Ⓔ   78 Ⓐ Ⓑ Ⓒ Ⓓ Ⓔ

19 Ⓐ Ⓑ Ⓒ Ⓓ Ⓔ   49 Ⓐ Ⓑ Ⓒ Ⓓ Ⓔ   79 Ⓐ Ⓑ Ⓒ Ⓓ Ⓔ

20 Ⓐ Ⓑ Ⓒ Ⓓ Ⓔ   50 Ⓐ Ⓑ Ⓒ Ⓓ Ⓔ   80 Ⓐ Ⓑ Ⓒ Ⓓ Ⓔ

21 Ⓐ Ⓑ Ⓒ Ⓓ Ⓔ   51 Ⓐ Ⓑ Ⓒ Ⓓ Ⓔ   81 Ⓐ Ⓑ Ⓒ Ⓓ Ⓔ

22 Ⓐ Ⓑ Ⓒ Ⓓ Ⓔ   52 Ⓐ Ⓑ Ⓒ Ⓓ Ⓔ   82 Ⓐ Ⓑ Ⓒ Ⓓ Ⓔ

23 Ⓐ Ⓑ Ⓒ Ⓓ Ⓔ   53 Ⓐ Ⓑ Ⓒ Ⓓ Ⓔ   83 Ⓐ Ⓑ Ⓒ Ⓓ Ⓔ

24 Ⓐ Ⓑ Ⓒ Ⓓ Ⓔ   54 Ⓐ Ⓑ Ⓒ Ⓓ Ⓔ   84 Ⓐ Ⓑ Ⓒ Ⓓ Ⓔ

25 Ⓐ Ⓑ Ⓒ Ⓓ Ⓔ   55 Ⓐ Ⓑ Ⓒ Ⓓ Ⓔ   85 Ⓐ Ⓑ Ⓒ Ⓓ Ⓔ

26 Ⓐ Ⓑ Ⓒ Ⓓ Ⓔ   56 Ⓐ Ⓑ Ⓒ Ⓓ Ⓔ   86 Ⓐ Ⓑ Ⓒ Ⓓ Ⓔ

27 Ⓐ Ⓑ Ⓒ Ⓓ Ⓔ   57 Ⓐ Ⓑ Ⓒ Ⓓ Ⓔ   87 Ⓐ Ⓑ Ⓒ Ⓓ Ⓔ

28 Ⓐ Ⓑ Ⓒ Ⓓ Ⓔ   58 Ⓐ Ⓑ Ⓒ Ⓓ Ⓔ   88 Ⓐ Ⓑ Ⓒ Ⓓ Ⓔ

29 Ⓐ Ⓑ Ⓒ Ⓓ Ⓔ   59 Ⓐ Ⓑ Ⓒ Ⓓ Ⓔ

List 1—Second Time

WORK—*5 minutes*

For each question, mark your answer on the Sample Answer Sheet on the next page. Try to remember the location of as many addresses as you can.

A	B	C	D	E
1700–2599 Wood Dushore 8500–8699 Lang Lott 6200–6399 James	2700–3299 Wood Jeriel 8700–9399 Lang Vanna 5700–6199 James	1300–1699 Wood Levering 9400–9499 Lang Ekron 6400–6499 James	3300–3599 Wood Bair 8000–8499 Lang Viborg 5000–5699 James	2600–2699 Wood Danby 9500–9999 Lang Lycan 4700–4999 James

1. 6200–6399 James
2. 1700–2599 Wood
3. Bair
4. 1700–2599 Wood
5. Ekron
6. Viborg
7. Danby
8. 8500–8699 Lang

9. Lycan
10. 8000–8499 Lang
11. 4700–4999 James
12. 9400–9499 Lang
13. 2700–3299 Wood
14. Jeriel
15. 9500–9999 Lang
16. 1300–1699 Wood

17. 8700–9399 Lang
18. Levering
19. Vanna
20. 6400–6499 James
21. 3300–3599 Wood
22. Dushore
23. Lycan
24. 5700–6199 James

25. Lott
26. Viborg
27. Jeriel
28. 5000–5699 James
29. 2600–2699 Wood
30. 4700–4999 James
31. 2700–3299 Wood
32. 8000–8499 Lang

33. Ekron
34. 3300–3599 Wood
35. 9400–9499 Lang
36. 6200–6399 James
37. 2600–2699 Wood
38. 8500–8699 Lang
39. Levering
40. Lott

41. Bair
42. 1700–2599 Wood
43. 6400–6499 James
44. 9500–9999 Lang
45. Jeriel
46. 4700–4999 James
47. Dushore
48. Lycan

49. 1700–2599 Wood
50. 6200–6399 James
51. Vanna
52. Ekron
53. 8700–9399 Lang
54. Bair
55. 2600–2699 Wood
56. Dushore

57. 5700–6199 James
58. 1300–1699 Wood
59. Levering
60. Lott
61. Jeriel
62. 2600–2699 Wood
63. Lott
64. 4700–4999 James

65. Dushore
66. Danby
67. 8500–8699 Lang
68. Vanna
69. 2700–3299 Wood
70. 9500–9999 Lang
71. Viborg
72. Ekron

73. 6200–6399 James
74. 2600–2699 Wood
75. Levering
76. Lott
77. 1300–1699 Wood
78. Bair
79. Lycan
80. 5700–6199 James

81. Levering
82. 8700–9399 Lang
83. 5000–5699 James
84. 1700–2599 Wood
85. Jeriel
86. 6200–6399 James
87. Ekron
88. 2700–3299 Wood

STOP.

If you finish before the 5 minutes are up, go back and check your answers for the questions on this page.

At the end of 5 minutes, turn to page 40.

1 Ⓐ Ⓑ Ⓒ Ⓓ Ⓔ   31 Ⓐ Ⓑ Ⓒ Ⓓ Ⓔ   61 Ⓐ Ⓑ Ⓒ Ⓓ Ⓔ

2 Ⓐ Ⓑ Ⓒ Ⓓ Ⓔ   32 Ⓐ Ⓑ Ⓒ Ⓓ Ⓔ   62 Ⓐ Ⓑ Ⓒ Ⓓ Ⓔ

3 Ⓐ Ⓑ Ⓒ Ⓓ Ⓔ   33 Ⓐ Ⓑ Ⓒ Ⓓ Ⓔ   63 Ⓐ Ⓑ Ⓒ Ⓓ Ⓔ

4 Ⓐ Ⓑ Ⓒ Ⓓ Ⓔ   34 Ⓐ Ⓑ Ⓒ Ⓓ Ⓔ   64 Ⓐ Ⓑ Ⓒ Ⓓ Ⓔ

5 Ⓐ Ⓑ Ⓒ Ⓓ Ⓔ   35 Ⓐ Ⓑ Ⓒ Ⓓ Ⓔ   65 Ⓐ Ⓑ Ⓒ Ⓓ Ⓔ

6 Ⓐ Ⓑ Ⓒ Ⓓ Ⓔ   36 Ⓐ Ⓑ Ⓒ Ⓓ Ⓔ   66 Ⓐ Ⓑ Ⓒ Ⓓ Ⓔ

7 Ⓐ Ⓑ Ⓒ Ⓓ Ⓔ   37 Ⓐ Ⓑ Ⓒ Ⓓ Ⓔ   67 Ⓐ Ⓑ Ⓒ Ⓓ Ⓔ

8 Ⓐ Ⓑ Ⓒ Ⓓ Ⓔ   38 Ⓐ Ⓑ Ⓒ Ⓓ Ⓔ   68 Ⓐ Ⓑ Ⓒ Ⓓ Ⓔ

9 Ⓐ Ⓑ Ⓒ Ⓓ Ⓔ   39 Ⓐ Ⓑ Ⓒ Ⓓ Ⓔ   69 Ⓐ Ⓑ Ⓒ Ⓓ Ⓔ

10 Ⓐ Ⓑ Ⓒ Ⓓ Ⓔ   40 Ⓐ Ⓑ Ⓒ Ⓓ Ⓔ   70 Ⓐ Ⓑ Ⓒ Ⓓ Ⓔ

11 Ⓐ Ⓑ Ⓒ Ⓓ Ⓔ   41 Ⓐ Ⓑ Ⓒ Ⓓ Ⓔ   71 Ⓐ Ⓑ Ⓒ Ⓓ Ⓔ

12 Ⓐ Ⓑ Ⓒ Ⓓ Ⓔ   42 Ⓐ Ⓑ Ⓒ Ⓓ Ⓔ   72 Ⓐ Ⓑ Ⓒ Ⓓ Ⓔ

13 Ⓐ Ⓑ Ⓒ Ⓓ Ⓔ   43 Ⓐ Ⓑ Ⓒ Ⓓ Ⓔ   73 Ⓐ Ⓑ Ⓒ Ⓓ Ⓔ

14 Ⓐ Ⓑ Ⓒ Ⓓ Ⓔ   44 Ⓐ Ⓑ Ⓒ Ⓓ Ⓔ   74 Ⓐ Ⓑ Ⓒ Ⓓ Ⓔ

15 Ⓐ Ⓑ Ⓒ Ⓓ Ⓔ   45 Ⓐ Ⓑ Ⓒ Ⓓ Ⓔ   75 Ⓐ Ⓑ Ⓒ Ⓓ Ⓔ

16 Ⓐ Ⓑ Ⓒ Ⓓ Ⓔ   46 Ⓐ Ⓑ Ⓒ Ⓓ Ⓔ   76 Ⓐ Ⓑ Ⓒ Ⓓ Ⓔ

17 Ⓐ Ⓑ Ⓒ Ⓓ Ⓔ   47 Ⓐ Ⓑ Ⓒ Ⓓ Ⓔ   77 Ⓐ Ⓑ Ⓒ Ⓓ Ⓔ

18 Ⓐ Ⓑ Ⓒ Ⓓ Ⓔ   48 Ⓐ Ⓑ Ⓒ Ⓓ Ⓔ   78 Ⓐ Ⓑ Ⓒ Ⓓ Ⓔ

19 Ⓐ Ⓑ Ⓒ Ⓓ Ⓔ   49 Ⓐ Ⓑ Ⓒ Ⓓ Ⓔ   79 Ⓐ Ⓑ Ⓒ Ⓓ Ⓔ

20 Ⓐ Ⓑ Ⓒ Ⓓ Ⓔ   50 Ⓐ Ⓑ Ⓒ Ⓓ Ⓔ   80 Ⓐ Ⓑ Ⓒ Ⓓ Ⓔ

21 Ⓐ Ⓑ Ⓒ Ⓓ Ⓔ   51 Ⓐ Ⓑ Ⓒ Ⓓ Ⓔ   81 Ⓐ Ⓑ Ⓒ Ⓓ Ⓔ

22 Ⓐ Ⓑ Ⓒ Ⓓ Ⓔ   52 Ⓐ Ⓑ Ⓒ Ⓓ Ⓔ   82 Ⓐ Ⓑ Ⓒ Ⓓ Ⓔ

23 Ⓐ Ⓑ Ⓒ Ⓓ Ⓔ   53 Ⓐ Ⓑ Ⓒ Ⓓ Ⓔ   83 Ⓐ Ⓑ Ⓒ Ⓓ Ⓔ

24 Ⓐ Ⓑ Ⓒ Ⓓ Ⓔ   54 Ⓐ Ⓑ Ⓒ Ⓓ Ⓔ   84 Ⓐ Ⓑ Ⓒ Ⓓ Ⓔ

25 Ⓐ Ⓑ Ⓒ Ⓓ Ⓔ   55 Ⓐ Ⓑ Ⓒ Ⓓ Ⓔ   85 Ⓐ Ⓑ Ⓒ Ⓓ Ⓔ

26 Ⓐ Ⓑ Ⓒ Ⓓ Ⓔ   56 Ⓐ Ⓑ Ⓒ Ⓓ Ⓔ   86 Ⓐ Ⓑ Ⓒ Ⓓ Ⓔ

27 Ⓐ Ⓑ Ⓒ Ⓓ Ⓔ   57 Ⓐ Ⓑ Ⓒ Ⓓ Ⓔ   87 Ⓐ Ⓑ Ⓒ Ⓓ Ⓔ

28 Ⓐ Ⓑ Ⓒ Ⓓ Ⓔ   58 Ⓐ Ⓑ Ⓒ Ⓓ Ⓔ   88 Ⓐ Ⓑ Ⓒ Ⓓ Ⓔ

29 Ⓐ Ⓑ Ⓒ Ⓓ Ⓔ   59 Ⓐ Ⓑ Ⓒ Ⓓ Ⓔ

30 Ⓐ Ⓑ Ⓒ Ⓓ Ⓔ   60 Ⓐ Ⓑ Ⓒ Ⓓ Ⓔ

List 2—Second Time

WORK—*5 minutes*

This is the section that counts. The other times were to help you learn the addresses.

Do these questions without looking back at the boxes with the addresses in them. Work for 5 minutes.

For each question, mark the Sample Answer Sheet on the next page to show the letter of the box in which the address belongs.

1. Jeriel
2. Dushore
3. 5000–5699 James
4. 1300–1699 Wood
5. 8500–8699 Lang
6. Bair
7. 5700–6199 James
8. Levering

9. Danby
10. Viborg
11. 8000–8499 Lang
12. 2700–3299 Wood
13. 9400–9499 Lang
14. 3300–3599 Wood
15. 4700–4999 James
16. 9500–9999 Lang

17. Ekron
18. 1300–1699 Wood
19. Vanna
20. Lycan
21. 8700–9399 Lang
22. Dushore
23. 6200–6399 James
24. Lott

25. 2700–3299 Wood
26. 5700–6199 James
27. Levering
28. 9500–9999 Lang
29. 2600–2699 Wood
30. 3300–3599 Wood
31. Viborg
32. 9400–9499 Lang

33. Jeriel
34. Bair
35. 8500–8699 Lang
36. 1700–2599 Wood
37. 8000–8499 Lang
38. Danby
39. Ekron
40. 4700–4999 James

41. Dushore
42. Vanna
43. 5000–5699 James
44. Lott
45. 1300–1699 Wood
46. Levering
47. 5700–6199 James
48. 9500–9999 Lang

49. Bair
50. 8700–9399 Lang
51. 6200–6399 James
52. 9400–9499 Lang
53. Viborg
54. 8000–8499 Lang
55. 4700–4999 James
56. Lycan

57. Vanna
58. Danby
59. 5700–6199 James
60. Lott
61. 2700–3299 Wood
62. 5000–5699 James
63. 1700–2599 Wood
64. 8000–8499 Lang

65. 9400–9499 Lang
66. Jeriel
67. 9500–9999 Lang
68. Dushore
69. 2600–2699 Wood
70. 8500–8699 Lang
71. Levering
72. 5000–5699 James

73. Dushore
74. 8000–8499 Lang
75. Bair
76. Ekron
77. 6200–6399 James
78. 3300–3599 Wood
79. 8700–9399 Lang
80. Viborg

81. 4700–4999 James
82. Lycan
83. 1700–2599 Wood
84. 8500–8699 Lang
85. 1300–1699 Wood
86. Jeriel
87. Danby
88. 6400–6499 James

STOP.

If you finish before the 5 minutes are up, go back and check your answers.

At the end of the 5 minutes, compare your answers with those given in the Correct Answers for sample questions on page 43.

SAMPLE ANSWER SHEET
PART-B

1 Ⓐ Ⓑ Ⓒ Ⓓ Ⓔ	31 Ⓐ Ⓑ Ⓒ Ⓓ Ⓔ	61 Ⓐ Ⓑ Ⓒ Ⓓ Ⓔ
2 Ⓐ Ⓑ Ⓒ Ⓓ Ⓔ	32 Ⓐ Ⓑ Ⓒ Ⓓ Ⓔ	62 Ⓐ Ⓑ Ⓒ Ⓓ Ⓔ
3 Ⓐ Ⓑ Ⓒ Ⓓ Ⓔ	33 Ⓐ Ⓑ Ⓒ Ⓓ Ⓔ	63 Ⓐ Ⓑ Ⓒ Ⓓ Ⓔ
4 Ⓐ Ⓑ Ⓒ Ⓓ Ⓔ	34 Ⓐ Ⓑ Ⓒ Ⓓ Ⓔ	64 Ⓐ Ⓑ Ⓒ Ⓓ Ⓔ
5 Ⓐ Ⓑ Ⓒ Ⓓ Ⓔ	35 Ⓐ Ⓑ Ⓒ Ⓓ Ⓔ	65 Ⓐ Ⓑ Ⓒ Ⓓ Ⓔ
6 Ⓐ Ⓑ Ⓒ Ⓓ Ⓔ	36 Ⓐ Ⓑ Ⓒ Ⓓ Ⓔ	66 Ⓐ Ⓑ Ⓒ Ⓓ Ⓔ
7 Ⓐ Ⓑ Ⓒ Ⓓ Ⓔ	37 Ⓐ Ⓑ Ⓒ Ⓓ Ⓔ	67 Ⓐ Ⓑ Ⓒ Ⓓ Ⓔ
8 Ⓐ Ⓑ Ⓒ Ⓓ Ⓔ	38 Ⓐ Ⓑ Ⓒ Ⓓ Ⓔ	68 Ⓐ Ⓑ Ⓒ Ⓓ Ⓔ
9 Ⓐ Ⓑ Ⓒ Ⓓ Ⓔ	39 Ⓐ Ⓑ Ⓒ Ⓓ Ⓔ	69 Ⓐ Ⓑ Ⓒ Ⓓ Ⓔ
10 Ⓐ Ⓑ Ⓒ Ⓓ Ⓔ	40 Ⓐ Ⓑ Ⓒ Ⓓ Ⓔ	70 Ⓐ Ⓑ Ⓒ Ⓓ Ⓔ
11 Ⓐ Ⓑ Ⓒ Ⓓ Ⓔ	41 Ⓐ Ⓑ Ⓒ Ⓒ Ⓔ	71 Ⓐ Ⓑ Ⓒ Ⓓ Ⓔ
12 Ⓐ Ⓑ Ⓒ Ⓓ Ⓔ	42 Ⓐ Ⓑ Ⓒ Ⓓ Ⓔ	72 Ⓐ Ⓑ Ⓒ Ⓓ Ⓔ
13 Ⓐ Ⓑ Ⓒ Ⓓ Ⓔ	43 Ⓐ Ⓑ Ⓒ Ⓓ Ⓔ	73 Ⓐ Ⓑ Ⓒ Ⓓ Ⓔ
14 Ⓐ Ⓑ Ⓒ Ⓓ Ⓔ	44 Ⓐ Ⓑ Ⓒ Ⓓ Ⓔ	74 Ⓐ Ⓑ Ⓒ Ⓓ Ⓔ
15 Ⓐ Ⓑ Ⓒ Ⓓ Ⓔ	45 Ⓐ Ⓑ Ⓒ Ⓓ Ⓔ	75 Ⓐ Ⓑ Ⓒ Ⓓ Ⓔ
16 Ⓐ Ⓑ Ⓒ Ⓓ Ⓔ	46 Ⓐ Ⓑ Ⓒ Ⓓ Ⓔ	76 Ⓐ Ⓑ Ⓒ Ⓓ Ⓔ
17 Ⓐ Ⓑ Ⓒ Ⓓ Ⓔ	47 Ⓐ Ⓑ Ⓒ Ⓓ Ⓔ	77 Ⓐ Ⓑ Ⓒ Ⓓ Ⓔ
18 Ⓐ Ⓑ Ⓒ Ⓓ Ⓔ	48 Ⓐ Ⓑ Ⓒ Ⓓ Ⓔ	78 Ⓐ Ⓑ Ⓒ Ⓓ Ⓔ
19 Ⓐ Ⓑ Ⓒ Ⓓ Ⓔ	49 Ⓐ Ⓑ Ⓒ Ⓓ Ⓔ	79 Ⓐ Ⓑ Ⓒ Ⓓ Ⓔ
20 Ⓐ Ⓑ Ⓒ Ⓓ Ⓔ	50 Ⓐ Ⓑ Ⓒ Ⓓ Ⓔ	80 Ⓐ Ⓑ Ⓒ Ⓓ Ⓔ
21 Ⓐ Ⓑ Ⓒ Ⓓ Ⓔ	51 Ⓐ Ⓑ Ⓒ Ⓓ Ⓔ	81 Ⓐ Ⓑ Ⓒ Ⓓ Ⓔ
22 Ⓐ Ⓑ Ⓒ Ⓓ Ⓔ	52 Ⓐ Ⓑ Ⓒ Ⓓ Ⓔ	82 Ⓐ Ⓑ Ⓒ Ⓓ Ⓔ
23 Ⓐ Ⓑ Ⓒ Ⓓ Ⓔ	53 Ⓐ Ⓑ Ⓒ Ⓓ Ⓔ	83 Ⓐ Ⓑ Ⓒ Ⓓ Ⓔ
24 Ⓐ Ⓑ Ⓒ Ⓓ Ⓔ	54 Ⓐ Ⓑ Ⓒ Ⓓ Ⓔ	84 Ⓐ Ⓑ Ⓒ Ⓓ Ⓔ
25 Ⓐ Ⓑ Ⓒ Ⓓ Ⓔ	55 Ⓐ Ⓑ Ⓒ Ⓓ Ⓔ	85 Ⓐ Ⓑ Ⓒ Ⓓ Ⓔ
26 Ⓐ Ⓑ Ⓒ Ⓓ Ⓔ	56 Ⓐ Ⓑ Ⓒ Ⓓ Ⓔ	86 Ⓐ Ⓑ Ⓒ Ⓓ Ⓔ
27 Ⓐ Ⓑ Ⓒ Ⓓ Ⓔ	57 Ⓐ Ⓑ Ⓒ Ⓓ Ⓔ	87 Ⓐ Ⓑ Ⓒ Ⓓ Ⓔ
28 Ⓐ Ⓑ Ⓒ Ⓓ Ⓔ	58 Ⓐ Ⓑ Ⓒ Ⓒ Ⓔ	88 Ⓐ Ⓑ Ⓒ Ⓓ Ⓔ
29 Ⓐ Ⓑ Ⓒ Ⓓ Ⓔ	59 Ⓐ Ⓑ Ⓒ Ⓒ Ⓔ	
30 Ⓐ Ⓑ Ⓒ Ⓒ Ⓔ	60 Ⓐ Ⓑ Ⓒ Ⓒ Ⓔ	

Position Title	Level	Position No.	Occ Code	Craft
Laborer-Custodial	3	SP 6-13	3502-03xx	M
Laborer, Materials Handling	3	SP 1-11	3502-02xx	M&MH
Lead Automotive Mechanic	7	SP 5-65	5823-10xx	MV
Leather Worker	5	SP 7-43	3102-03xx	
Letter Box Mechanic (Shop)	6	SP 6-46	3843-02xx	M
Lock Box Equipment Repairman	5	SP 7-44	5311-09xx	
Lock Assembler	3	SP 7-4	5311-01xx	
Lockmaker	5	SP 7-3	5311-02xx	
Machine Operator	3	SP 7-5	3401-01xx	
Machine Operator	4	SP 7-6	3401-01xx	
Machine Operator (A)	6	SP 7-42	3401-02xx	
Machine Operator (B)	6	SP 7-41	3401-03xx	
Machinist	7	SP 6-18	3414-02xx	M
Machinist (MES)	8	SP 7-52	3414-03xx	
Mail Classification Clerk (MSC)	7	SP 2-465	2345-52xx	C
Mail Classification Clerk (MSC)	6	SP 2-464	2345-52xx	C
Mail Equipment Handler	4	SP 7-21	3502-01xx	
Mail Equipment Handler	4	SP 2-247	3502-01xx	MH
Mail Handler	4	KP-8	2315-01xx	MH
Mail Handler Equipment Operator	5	SP 2-21	5704-03xx	MH
Mail Handler Technician	5	SP 2-498	2315-62xx	MH
Mail Processing Machine Operator	5	SP 2-354	2340-45xx	MH
Mail Processing Machine Operator	5	SP 2-470	2340-45xx	MH
Mail Rewrapper	4	SP 2-9	2340-27xx	MH
Mailing Requirements Clerk	6	SP 2-468	2345-32xx	C
Mailing Requirements Clerk	5	SP 2-469	2345-32xx	C

Continued on Page KB-61

PART—B

Check your answers by comparing your answers with the correct answers.

#	Ans		#	Ans		#	Ans
1	B		31	D		61	B
2	A		32	C		62	D
3	D		33	B		63	A
4	C		34	D		64	D
5	A		35	A		65	C
6	D		36	A		66	B
7	B		37	D		67	E
8	C		38	E		68	A
9	E		39	C		69	E
10	D		40	E		70	A
11	D		41	A		71	C
12	B		42	B		72	D
13	C		43	D		73	A
14	D		44	A		74	D
15	E		45	C		75	D
16	E		46	C		76	C
17	C		47	B		77	A
18	C		48	E		78	D
19	B		49	D		79	B
20	E		50	B		80	D
21	B		51	A		81	E
22	A		52	C		82	E
23	A		53	D		83	A
24	A		54	D		84	A
25	B		55	E		85	C
26	B		56	E		86	B
27	C		57	B		87	E
28	E		58	E		88	C
29	E		59	B			
30	D		60	A			

Count how many you got right, and write that number on this line ————————————————————————————————→ Number Right _____

Now count how many you got wrong, and write that number on this line ——————————————————→ Number Wrong _____

Divide the Number Wrong by 4, and write the answer on this line ——————————————————————————————→ 1/4 Number Wrong _____

Subtract the 1/4 Number Wrong from the Number Right, and write the Difference on this line ——————————————→ Total Score _____

Meaning of Test Score

If your Total Score is *44 or more*, you have a Good score.

If your Total Score is from *26 to 43*, you have a Fair score.

If your Total Score is *25 or less*, you are not doing too well.

You may be going too slowly, or you may be making too many mistakes. You need more practice.

SAMPLE TESTS

Now that you have studied the instructions and taken the practice tests in this book, you are ready to take the Sample Tests for Clerk-Carrier. The Sample Tests are exactly like the ones you will have to take in the examinations. The time allowances and the numbers of questions are the same as they are in the real tests.

At the back of the book you will find some answer sheets to use. These answer sheets are like the ones you will use in the examinations.

When you are ready to try a Sample Test, tear out an answer sheet from the back of the book. Then do what the instructions tell you to do. Remember that in the address-checking and memory for addresses sections you will lose credit for wrong answers. In the address-checking section it will be better not to guess.

It is a good idea to have a friend tell you when the time is up for each set of sample questions and each part of the test. (There are sample questions for each part.)

After you have finished answering the questions for a sample test, compare your answers with the correct answers for that test and see how well you did.

CLERK-CARRIER TEST

Time Required for Each Part

Part A

Samples	3 minutes
Test	6 minutes

Part B

Samples and Study	6 minutes (Approximately)
Test-List 1 Practice	3 minutes
Test-List 2 Practice	3 minutes
Study	5 minutes
Test-List 1	5 minutes
Test-List 2	5 minutes

INTERPRETATION OF TEST SCORES ON SAMPLE CLERK-CARRIER TEST

After you have taken a Part of the test or after you have finished the test, compare your answers with those given in the Correct Answers to Sample Test. You will find them on pages 61 and 62.

For the Address Checking (Part A), count the number that you got right and the number that you got wrong. (If you didn't mark anything for a question, it doesn't get counted.)

From the number right
Subtract the number wrong
This number (the difference) is your score_____→

The meaning of the score is as follows:

52 or higher---------------------------------- Good.
Between 32 and 51---------------------------- Fair.
Below 32----------------------------------- You need more practice.

Go back and see where you made your mistakes. Were you careless? Did you work too slowly?

In the Memory for Addresses (Part B), only Test-List 2, which you recorded on your answer sheet, counts. For that Part, count the number that you got right and the number that you got wrong. (If you didn't mark anything for a question, it doesn't get counted.)

Divide the number wrong by 4. _____

From the number right
Subtract 1/4 the number wrong
This number (the difference) is your score _____→

The meaning of the score is as follows:

44 or higher------------------------------- Good.
Between 26 and 43-------------------------- Fair.
Below 26----------------------------------- You need more practice.

Go back and see where you made your mistakes. Were you careless? Did you work too slowly? Try to find out what is the best way for you to memorize. Go to page 48.

Position Title	Level	Position No.	Occ Code	Craft
Money Orders & Special Items Supply Clerk	5	SP 7-55	2040-19xx	
Motor Vehicle Operator	5	KP-10	5703-02xx	MV
OCR Operator	5	SP 2-528	2315-78xx	C
Office Appliance Repairman	5	SP 6-22	4806-04xx	M
Office Clerk	4	SP 1-12	0301-01xx	C
Office Clerk, Custodial	5	SP 6-55	0301-05xx	M
Office Clerk Mailbag Facility	5	SP 7-59	0301-35xx	
Office Clerk Supply Center	5	SP 7-58	0301-03xx	
Office Clerk, Vehicle Operations	5	SP 5-23	0301-04xx	MV
Office Machine Operator	5	SP 1-35	0350-01xx	
Office Services Clerk (WASC)	4	SP 7-61	0301-06xx	
Office Staff Assistant or Secretary	5	SP 2-534	0318-01xx	C
Office Staff Secretary (Steno)	5	SP 2-540	0318-04xx	C
Office Staff Assistant or Secretary (Typist)	5	SP 2-546	0318-05xx	C
Oiler, Mail Processing Equipment	4	SP 6-62	5323-01xx	M
Operator, Sewing Machine (Repair)	4	SP 7-26	3111-02xx	
Operator, Sewing Machine (Shops)	4	SP 7-1	3111-01xx	
Operator-Varityper	5	SP 7-10	4401-08xx	
Overhaul Specialist	8	SP 6-82	5342-11xx	M
Packer-in-Charge	5	SP 7-8	7002-02xx	
Packer-Shipper	4	SP 2-581	7002-03xx	MH
Packer Warehouseman	4	SP 7-32	6907-02xx	
Painter	6	SP 6-5	4102-02xx	M
Parcel Post Distributor (Machine)	5	SP 2-439	2315-06xx	C
Parcel Post Distributor (Machine)	6	SP 2-362	2315-06xx	C
Personnel Clerk	5	SP 1-10	0203-14xx	C

Continued on Page KB-72

SAMPLE CLERK-CARRIER TEST

There are two parts to this test. It is best to have a friend to
watch the time for you. The correct time limit for each part is given
on page 45. Be careful not to take any more time than given in the
instructions for each part.

Tear out an answer sheet from the back of the book and use it to
mark your answers for each part of this test.

Directions and Samples for Part A

In this Part you will be given addresses to compare. On your
answer sheet darken the circle marked A if the two addresses are exactly
Alike in every way. Darken the circle marked D if they are *Different*.

Here are some sample questions for you to do. Mark your answers
to them on the Sample Answer Sheet on the next page. You should not take
more than *3 minutes* to read and study the material on these two pages of
the test.

Show your answer to a question by darkening completely the circle
corresponding to the letter that is the same as the letter of your
answer. You must keep your mark within the circle. If you have to
erase a mark, be sure to erase it completely. Mark only one answer for
each question.

```
1 ... 2134 S 20th St              2134 S 20th St
    Since the two addresses are exactly alike, mark A for question 1
    on the Sample Answer Sheet.
2 ... 4608 N Warnock St           4806 N Warnock St
3 ... 1202 W Girard Dr            1202 W Girard Rd
4 ... Chappaqua N Y 10514         Chappaqua N Y 10514
5 ... 2207 Markland Ave           2207 Markham Ave
```

SAMPLE ANSWER SHEET		CORRECT ANSWERS	
1 (A) (D)		1 ● (D)	
2 (A) (D)		2 (A) ●	
3 (A) (D)		3 (A) ●	
4 (A) (D)		4 ● (D)	
5 (A) (D)		5 (A) ●	

Now compare your answers with the Correct Answers. If your answers are not the same as the correct answers shown, go back and study the samples to see where you made a mistake.

It will be to your advantage to work as quickly and accurately as possible since your score on this part of the test will be based on the number of wrong answers as well as the number of right answers. It is not expected that you will be able to finish all the questions in the time allowed.

Be sure to use a pencil so that you can make erasures.

Look at your answer sheet. The answers to this part of the examination must be marked in Part A of the answer sheet. Notice also that the answer spaces are numbered down the page. Mark the answer for question 1 in space 1.

When you begin the test, work as fast as you can without making mistakes. Do as many questions as you can in the time allowed.

You will have *6 minutes* to answer as many of the 95 questions as you can.

DO NOT TURN THIS PAGE UNTIL YOU ARE READY TO BEGIN THE TEST.

PART A

REMEMBER: Mark your answers on the separate answer sheet. Use "A" for "Alike" and "D" for "Different." Work as quickly as you can.

1	405 Winter Rd NW	405 Winter Rd NW
2	607 S Calaveras Rd	607 S Calaveras Rd
3	8406 La Casa St	8406 La Cosa St
4	121 N Rippon St	121 N Rippon St
5	Wideman Ark	Wiseman Ark
6	Sodus N Y 14551	Sodus N Y 14551
7	3429 Hermosa Dr	3429 Hermoso Dr
8	3628 S Zeeland St	3268 S Zeeland St
9	1330 Cheverly Ave NE	1330 Cheverly Ave NE
10	1689 N Derwood Dr	1689 N Derwood Dr
11	3886 Sunrise Ct	3886 Sunrise Ct
12	635 La Calle Mayor	653 La Calle Mayor
13	2560 Lansford Pl	2560 Lansford St
14	4631 Central Ave	4631 Central Ave
15	Mason City Iowa 50401	Mason City Iowa 50401

16	758 Los Arboles Ave SE	758 Los Arboles Ave SW
17	3282 E Downington St	3282 E Dunnington St
18	7117 N Burlingham Ave	7117 N Burlingham Ave
19	32 Oaklawn Blvd	32 Oakland Blvd
20	1274 Manzana Rd	1274 Manzana Rd
21	4598 E Kenilworth Dr	4598 E Kenilworth Dr
22	Dayton Okla 73449	Dagton Okla 73449
23	1172 W 83rd Ave	1127 W 83rd Ave
24	6434 E Pulaski St	6434 E Pulaski Ct
25	2764 N Rutherford Pl	2764 N Rutherford Pl
26	565 Greenville Blvd SE	565 Greenview Blvd SE
27	Washington D C 20013	Washington D C 20018
28	3824 Massasoit St	3824 Massasoit St
29	22 Sagnaw Pkwy	22 Saganaw Pkwy
30	Byram Conn 10573	Byram Conn 10573
31	1928 S Fairfield Ave	1928 S Fairfield St

32	36218 Overhills Dr	36218 Overhills Dr
33	516 Avenida de Las Americas NW	516 Avenida de Las Americas NW
34	7526 Naraganset Pl SW	7526 Naraganset Pl SW
35	52626 W Ogelsby Dr	52626 W Ogelsby Dr
36	1003 Winchester Rd	1003 Westchester Rd
37	3478 W Cavanaugh Ct	3478 W Cavenaugh Ct
38	Kendall Calif 90551	Kendell Calif 90551
39	225 El Camino Blvd	225 El Camino Ave
40	7310 Via de los Pisos	7310 Via de los Pinos
41	1987 Wellington Ave SW	1987 Wellington Ave SW
42	3124 S 71st St	3142 S 71st St
43	729 Lincolnwood Blvd	729 Lincolnwood Blvd
44	1166 N Beaumont Dr	1166 S Beaumont Dr
45	3224 W Winecona Pl	3224 W Winecona Pl
46	608 La Calle Bienvenida	607 La Calle Bienvenida
47	La Molte Iowa 52045	La Molte Iowa 52045

GO ON TO NUMBER 48 ON THE NEXT PAGE.

48 ... 8625 Armitage Ave NW		8625 Armitage Ave NW
49 ... 2343 Broadview Ave		2334 Broadview Ave
50 ... 4279 Sierra Grande Ave NE		4279 Sierra Grande Dr NE
51 ... 165 32d Ave		165 32d Ave
52 ... 12742 N Deerborn St		12724 N Deerborn St
53 ... 114 Estancia Ave		141 Estancia Ave
54 ... 351 S Berwyn Rd		351 S Berwyn Pl
55 ... 7732 Avenida Manana SW		7732 Avenida Manana SW
56 ... 6337 C St SW		6337 G St SW
57 ... 57895 E Drexyl Ave		58795 E Drexyl Ave
58 ... Altro Tex 75923		Altra Tex 75923
59 ... 3465 S Nashville St		3465 N Nashville St
60 ... 1226 Odell Blvd NW		1226 Oddell Blvd NW
61 ... 94002 Chappel Ct		94002 Chappel Ct
62 ... 512 La Vega Dr		512 La Veta Dr
63 ... 8774 W Winona Pl		8774 E Winona Pl
64 ... 6431 Ingleside St SE		6431 Ingleside St SE
65 ... 2270 N Leanington St		2270 N Leanington St
66 ... 235 Calle de Los Vecinos		235 Calle de Los Vecinos
67 ... 3987 E Westwood Ave		3987 W Westwood Ave
68 ... Skamokawa Wash		Skamohawa Wash
69 ... 2674 E Champlain Cir		2764 E Champlain Cir
70 ... 8751 Elmhurst Blvd		8751 Elmwood Blvd
71 ... 6649 Solano Dr		6649 Solana Dr
72 ... 4423 S Escenaba St		4423 S Escenaba St
73 ... 1198 N St NW		1198 M St NW
74 ... Sparta Ga		Sparta Va
75 ... 96753 Wrightwood Ave		96753 Wrightwood Ave
76 ... 2445 Sangamow Ave SE		2445 Sangamow Ave SE
77 ... 5117 E 67 Pl		5171 E 67 Pl
78 ... 847 Mesa Grande Pl		847 Mesa Grande Ct
79 ... 1100 Cermaken St		1100 Cermaker St
80 ... 321 Tijeras Ave NW		321 Tijeras Ave NW
81 ... 3405 Prospect St		3405 Prospect St
82 ... 6643 Burlington Pl		6643 Burlingtown Pl
83 ... 851 Esperanza Blvd		851 Esperanza Blvd
84 ... Jenkinjones W Va		Jenkinjones W Va
85 ... 1008 Pennsylvania Ave SE		1008 Pennsylvania Ave SW
86 ... 2924 26th St N		2929 26th St N
87 ... 7115 Highland Dr		7115 Highland Dr
88 ... Chaptico Md		Chaptica Md
89 ... 3508 Camron Mills Rd		3508 Camron Mills Rd
90 ... 67158 Capston Dr		67158 Capston Dr
91 ... 3613 S Taylor Ave		3631 S Taylor Ave
92 ... 2421 Menokin Dr		2421 Menokin Dr
93 ... 3226 M St NW		3226 N St NW
94 ... 1201 S Court House Rd		1201 S Court House Rd
95 ... Findlay Ohio 45840		Findley Ohio 45840

STOP.

If you finish before the time is up, check your answers for Part A.
Do not go to any other part.

When the time is up, turn to page 52 .

Samples for Part B

Part B has five boxes labeled A, B, C, D, and E. Each box contains five addresses. Three of the five addresses are groups of street addresses like 2100-2799 Mall, 4800-4999 Cliff and 1900-2299 Laurel, and two are names of places. They are different in each box. You will be given two lists of addresses. For each street address or name in the list, you are to decide in which lettered box (A, B, C, D, or E) it belongs and then mark that circle on the answer sheet. For List 1, the boxes will be shown on the same page with the addresses. While you are working on List 2, you will not be able to look at the boxes. Then you will have to match the addresses with the correct box from memory. Try to memorize the location of as many addresses as you can.

A	B	C	D	E
2100-2799 Mall Ceres 4800-4999 Cliff Natoma 1900-2299 Laurel	3900-4399 Mall Cedar 4000-4299 Cliff Foster 2300-2999 Laurel	4400-4599 Mall Niles 3300-3999 Cliff Dexter 3200-3799 Laurel	3400-3899 Mall Cicero 4500-4799 Cliff Pearl 3000-3199 Laurel	2800-3399 Mall Delhi 4300-4499 Cliff Magnet 1500-1899 Laurel

Sample Questions:

1. 3300-3999 Cliff--This address is in box C. So you would darken circle C.
2. Natoma--This name is in box A. So you would darken circle A.
3. Foster
4. 1500-1899 Laurel
5. 3900-4399 Mall
6. Pearl
7. 3200-3799 Laurel

```
SAMPLE ANSWER
    SHEET
1 Ⓐ Ⓑ Ⓒ Ⓓ Ⓔ

2 Ⓐ Ⓑ Ⓒ Ⓓ Ⓔ

3 Ⓐ Ⓑ Ⓒ Ⓓ Ⓔ

4 Ⓐ Ⓑ Ⓒ Ⓓ Ⓔ

5 Ⓐ Ⓑ Ⓒ Ⓓ Ⓔ

6 Ⓐ Ⓑ Ⓒ Ⓓ Ⓔ

7 Ⓐ Ⓑ Ⓒ Ⓓ Ⓔ
```

The answers to samples 3 to 7 are:
3B, 4E, 5B, 6D, and 7C.

In List 1 the boxes with the addresses will be before your eyes. Therefore you will be able to check your answers by looking at the top of the
page. However, checking takes time and the more you remember, the faster
you will be able to work. On List 2 the boxes with the addresses will
not be shown. Then you will have only your memory to depend on when
answering the questions. Thus, memory will be very important in this
test.

Different people study in different ways. Many people find it easier to
learn the addresses in one box at a time than to learn all the addresses
at once.

You will now have *3 minutes* to study the addresses and letters so that
you will have a good idea of the letter that goes with each address. Do
not spend more than 3 minutes studying the addresses.

Now memorize the addresses in the boxes. These are the addresses that
will be in the test. TRY TO LEARN THE LOCATION OF AS MANY ADDRESSES AS
YOU CAN. Cover each box with your hand and see if you can repeat, to
yourself, the addresses in that box.

DO NOT TURN THIS PAGE UNTIL THE TIME IS UP. THEN TURN TO PAGE 54.

PART B

List 1

For each question, mark the   answer sheet on the next page to show the letter of the box in which the address belongs. Try to remember the location of as many addresses as you can. You will now have *3 minutes* for List 1. If you are not sure of an answer you should guess.

A	B	C	D	E
2100–2799 Mall Ceres 4800–4999 Cliff Natoma 1900–2299 Laurel	3900–4399 Mall Cedar 4000–4299 Cliff Foster 2300–2999 Laurel	4400–4599 Mall Niles 3300–3999 Cliff Dexter 3200–3799 Laurel	3400–3899 Mall Cicero 4500–4799 Cliff Pearl 3000–3199 Laurel	2800–3399 Mall Delhi 4300–4499 Cliff Magnet 1500–1899 Laurel

1. Magnet
2. Niles
3. 3400–3899 Mall
4. 1900–2299 Laurel
5. Cicero
6. Dexter
7. 2300–2999 Laurel
8. 3300–3999 Cliff

9. 3200–3799 Laurel
10. 2100–2799 Mall
11. Pearl
12. 3200–3799 Laurel
13. Ceres
14. 4500–4799 Cliff
15. 3900–4399 Mall
16. Delhi

17. 4300–4499 Cliff
18. 3000–3199 Laurel
19. Ceres
20. Foster
21. Natoma
22. 4400–4599 Mall
23. Cedar
24. 2300–2999 Laurel

25. 1500–1899 Laurel
26. 4000–4299 Cliff
27. Dexter
28. Magnet
29. 3300–3999 Cliff
30. 3400–3899 Mall
31. Niles
32. 2100–2799 Mall

33. 1900–2299 Laurel
34. Cedar
35. Pearl
36. 2800–3399 Mall
37. 4800–4999 Cliff
38. 3900–4399 Mall
39. Foster
40. 3000–3199 Laurel

41. Ceres
42. Niles
43. 3400–3899 Mall
44. Delhi
45. 2300–2999 Laurel
46. 4500–4799 Cliff
47. Dexter
48. Magnet

49. 3300–3999 Cliff
50. Cicero
51. 4300–4499 Cliff
52. 3900–4399 Mall
53. Natoma
54. 3200–3799 Laurel
55. Pearl
56. 4000–4299 Cliff

57. 4500–4799 Cliff
58. 2100–2799 Mall
59. Foster
60. 4400–4599 Mall
61. 4800–4999 Cliff
62. Ceres
63. 2800–3399 Mall
64. 1500–1899 Laurel

65. Natoma
66. 3000–3199 Laurel
67. 4000–4299 Cliff
68. Niles
69. 2300–2999 Laurel
70. Magnet
71. Delhi
72. 4400–4599 Mall

73. Cicero
74. Cedar
75. 2800–3399 Mall
76. 1900–2299 Laurel
77. Dexter
78. Pearl
79. 4300–4499 Cliff
80. 3900–4399 Mall

81. Foster
82. 4800–4999 Cliff
83. Delhi
84. Ceres
85. 1500–1899 Laurel
86. Natoma
87. 2800–3399 Mall
88. Niles

STOP.

If you finish before the time is up, go back and check your answers for the questions on this page. Do not go to any other page until the time is up.

1 Ⓐ Ⓑ Ⓒ Ⓓ Ⓔ	31 Ⓐ Ⓑ Ⓒ Ⓓ Ⓔ	61 Ⓐ Ⓑ Ⓒ Ⓓ Ⓔ
2 Ⓐ Ⓑ Ⓒ Ⓓ Ⓔ	32 Ⓐ Ⓑ Ⓒ Ⓓ Ⓔ	62 Ⓐ Ⓑ Ⓒ Ⓓ Ⓔ
3 Ⓐ Ⓑ Ⓒ Ⓓ Ⓔ	33 Ⓐ Ⓑ Ⓒ Ⓓ Ⓔ	63 Ⓐ Ⓑ Ⓒ Ⓓ Ⓔ
4 Ⓐ Ⓑ Ⓒ Ⓓ Ⓔ	34 Ⓐ Ⓑ Ⓒ Ⓓ Ⓔ	64 Ⓐ Ⓑ Ⓒ Ⓓ Ⓔ
5 Ⓐ Ⓑ Ⓒ Ⓓ Ⓔ	35 Ⓐ Ⓑ Ⓒ Ⓓ Ⓔ	65 Ⓐ Ⓑ Ⓒ Ⓓ Ⓔ
6 Ⓐ Ⓑ Ⓒ Ⓓ Ⓔ	36 Ⓐ Ⓑ Ⓒ Ⓓ Ⓔ	66 Ⓐ Ⓑ Ⓒ Ⓓ Ⓔ
7 Ⓐ Ⓑ Ⓒ Ⓓ Ⓔ	37 Ⓐ Ⓑ Ⓒ Ⓓ Ⓔ	67 Ⓐ Ⓑ Ⓒ Ⓓ Ⓔ
8 Ⓐ Ⓑ Ⓒ Ⓓ Ⓔ	38 Ⓐ Ⓑ Ⓒ Ⓓ Ⓔ	68 Ⓐ Ⓑ Ⓒ Ⓓ Ⓔ
9 Ⓐ Ⓑ Ⓒ Ⓓ Ⓔ	39 Ⓐ Ⓑ Ⓒ Ⓓ Ⓔ	69 Ⓐ Ⓑ Ⓒ Ⓓ Ⓔ
10 Ⓐ Ⓑ Ⓒ Ⓓ Ⓔ	40 Ⓐ Ⓑ Ⓒ Ⓓ Ⓔ	70 Ⓐ Ⓑ Ⓒ Ⓓ Ⓔ
11 Ⓐ Ⓑ Ⓒ Ⓓ Ⓔ	41 Ⓐ Ⓑ Ⓒ Ⓓ Ⓔ	71 Ⓐ Ⓑ Ⓒ Ⓓ Ⓔ
12 Ⓐ Ⓑ Ⓒ Ⓓ Ⓔ	42 Ⓐ Ⓑ Ⓒ Ⓓ Ⓔ	72 Ⓐ Ⓑ Ⓒ Ⓓ Ⓔ
13 Ⓐ Ⓑ Ⓒ Ⓓ Ⓔ	43 Ⓐ Ⓑ Ⓒ Ⓓ Ⓔ	73 Ⓐ Ⓑ Ⓒ Ⓓ Ⓔ
14 Ⓐ Ⓑ Ⓒ Ⓓ Ⓔ	44 Ⓐ Ⓑ Ⓒ Ⓓ Ⓔ	74 Ⓐ Ⓑ Ⓒ Ⓓ Ⓔ
15 Ⓐ Ⓑ Ⓒ Ⓓ Ⓔ	45 Ⓐ Ⓑ Ⓒ Ⓓ Ⓔ	75 Ⓐ Ⓑ Ⓒ Ⓓ Ⓔ
16 Ⓐ Ⓑ Ⓒ Ⓓ Ⓔ	46 Ⓐ Ⓑ Ⓒ Ⓓ Ⓔ	76 Ⓐ Ⓑ Ⓒ Ⓓ Ⓔ
17 Ⓐ Ⓑ Ⓒ Ⓓ Ⓔ	47 Ⓐ Ⓑ Ⓒ Ⓓ Ⓔ	77 Ⓐ Ⓑ Ⓒ Ⓓ Ⓔ
18 Ⓐ Ⓑ Ⓒ Ⓓ Ⓔ	48 Ⓐ Ⓑ Ⓒ Ⓓ Ⓔ	78 Ⓐ Ⓑ Ⓒ Ⓓ Ⓔ
19 Ⓐ Ⓑ Ⓒ Ⓓ Ⓔ	49 Ⓐ Ⓑ Ⓒ Ⓓ Ⓔ	79 Ⓐ Ⓑ Ⓒ Ⓓ Ⓔ
20 Ⓐ Ⓑ Ⓒ Ⓓ Ⓔ	50 Ⓐ Ⓑ Ⓒ Ⓓ Ⓔ	80 Ⓐ Ⓑ Ⓒ Ⓓ Ⓔ
21 Ⓐ Ⓑ Ⓒ Ⓓ Ⓔ	51 Ⓐ Ⓑ Ⓒ Ⓓ Ⓔ	81 Ⓐ Ⓑ Ⓒ Ⓓ Ⓔ
22 Ⓐ Ⓑ Ⓒ Ⓓ Ⓔ	52 Ⓐ Ⓑ Ⓒ Ⓓ Ⓔ	82 Ⓐ Ⓑ Ⓒ Ⓓ Ⓔ
23 Ⓐ Ⓑ Ⓒ Ⓓ Ⓔ	53 Ⓐ Ⓑ Ⓒ Ⓓ Ⓔ	83 Ⓐ Ⓑ Ⓒ Ⓓ Ⓔ
24 Ⓐ Ⓑ Ⓒ Ⓓ Ⓔ	54 Ⓐ Ⓑ Ⓒ Ⓓ Ⓔ	84 Ⓐ Ⓑ Ⓒ Ⓓ Ⓔ
25 Ⓐ Ⓑ Ⓒ Ⓓ Ⓔ	55 Ⓐ Ⓑ Ⓒ Ⓓ Ⓔ	85 Ⓐ Ⓑ Ⓒ Ⓓ Ⓔ
26 Ⓐ Ⓑ Ⓒ Ⓓ Ⓔ	56 Ⓐ Ⓑ Ⓒ Ⓓ Ⓔ	86 Ⓐ Ⓑ Ⓒ Ⓓ Ⓔ
27 Ⓐ Ⓑ Ⓒ Ⓓ Ⓔ	57 Ⓐ Ⓑ Ⓒ Ⓓ Ⓔ	87 Ⓐ Ⓑ Ⓒ Ⓓ Ⓔ
28 Ⓐ Ⓑ Ⓒ Ⓓ Ⓔ	58 Ⓐ Ⓑ Ⓒ Ⓓ Ⓔ	88 Ⓐ Ⓑ Ⓒ Ⓓ Ⓔ
29 Ⓐ Ⓑ Ⓒ Ⓓ Ⓔ	59 Ⓐ Ⓑ Ⓒ Ⓓ Ⓔ	
30 Ⓐ Ⓑ Ⓒ Ⓓ Ⓔ	60 Ⓐ Ⓑ Ⓒ Ⓓ Ⓔ	

List 2

For each question, mark·the answer sheet on the next page to show the letter of the box in which the address belongs. If you are not sure of an answer, you should guess. You will record your answers on the next page. While you are working on List 2, do not turn to any other page. You will have *3 minutes* to do this list.

1. Cedar
2. 4300–4499 Cliff
3. 4400–4599 Mall
4. Natoma
5. 2300–2999 Laurel
6. 4500–4799 Cliff
7. Ceres
8. 3400–3899 Mall

9. Delhi
10. Dexter
11. 1900–2299 Laurel
12. 3300–3999 Cliff
13. Cicero
14. 4000–4299 Cliff
15. 2100–2799 Mall
16. Foster

17. Magnet
18. Ceres
19. 2800–3399 Mall
20. 3200–3799 Laurel
21. 4300–4499 Cliff
22. Pearl
23. 3900–4399 Mall
24. Natoma

25. 4800–4999 Cliff
26. 1500–1899 Laurel
27. Cedar
28. 4400–4599 Mall
29. 4500–4799 Cliff
30. Dexter
31. 3000–3199 Laurel
32. Niles

33. Delhi
34. 3900–4399 Mall
35. Cicero
36. Dexter
37. 4800–4999 Cliff
38. 2300–2999 Laurel
39. 2100–2799 Mall
40. 3300–3999 Cliff

41. 3400–3899 Mall
42. 4300–4499 Cliff
43. Ceres
44. Foster
45. Magnet
46. 3200–3799 Laurel
47. Pearl
48. 1500–1899 Laurel

49. 4500–4799 Cliff
50. 1900–2299 Laurel
51. Niles
52. 3300–3999 Cliff
53. 2800–3399 Mall
54. Cicero
55. Delhi
56. 4000–4299 Cliff

57. Dexter
58. Magnet
59. 3000–3199 Laurel
60. 3900–4399 Mall
61. Natoma
62. 3000–3199 Laurel
63. 4300–4499 Cliff
64. Cedar

65. 4400–4599 Mall
66. 1500–1899 Laurel
67. 4800–4999 Cliff
68. Delhi
69. Pearl
70. 2300–2999 Laurel
71. 4500–4799 Cliff
72. Niles

73. 4000–4299 Cliff
74. 3400–3899 Mall
75. 1900–2299 Laurel
76. 2800–3399 Mall
77. Ceres
78. Magnet
79. Cicero
80. 3200–3799 Laurel

81. 3000–3199 Laurel
82. 3900–4399 Mall
83. Natoma
84. 3300–3999 Cliff
85. 3400–3899 Mall
86. Foster
87. 2100–2799 Mall
88. 4300–4499 Cliff

If you finish before the time is· up, go back and check your answers to this part only. When the time is up turn back to page 52 and study the boxes again. You will have 5 minutes to restudy the addresses. When that time is up, go to page 54 and do that list again, using the answer sheet on page 59. You will have 5 minutes to do List 1 again. When that time is up turn to page 60 and read the instructions.

1 Ⓐ Ⓑ Ⓒ Ⓓ Ⓔ	31 Ⓐ Ⓑ Ⓒ Ⓓ Ⓔ	61 Ⓐ Ⓑ Ⓒ Ⓓ Ⓔ
2 Ⓐ Ⓑ Ⓒ Ⓓ Ⓔ	32 Ⓐ Ⓑ Ⓒ Ⓓ Ⓔ	62 Ⓐ Ⓑ Ⓒ Ⓓ Ⓔ
3 Ⓐ Ⓑ Ⓒ Ⓓ Ⓔ	33 Ⓐ Ⓑ Ⓒ Ⓓ Ⓔ	63 Ⓐ Ⓑ Ⓒ Ⓓ Ⓔ
4 Ⓐ Ⓑ Ⓒ Ⓓ Ⓔ	34 Ⓐ Ⓑ Ⓒ Ⓓ Ⓔ	64 Ⓐ Ⓑ Ⓒ Ⓓ Ⓔ
5 Ⓐ Ⓑ Ⓒ Ⓓ Ⓔ	35 Ⓐ Ⓑ Ⓒ Ⓓ Ⓔ	65 Ⓐ Ⓑ Ⓒ Ⓓ Ⓔ
6 Ⓐ Ⓑ Ⓒ Ⓓ Ⓔ	36 Ⓐ Ⓑ Ⓒ Ⓓ Ⓔ	66 Ⓐ Ⓑ Ⓒ Ⓓ Ⓔ
7 Ⓐ Ⓑ Ⓒ Ⓓ Ⓔ	37 Ⓐ Ⓑ Ⓒ Ⓓ Ⓔ	67 Ⓐ Ⓑ Ⓒ Ⓓ Ⓔ
8 Ⓐ Ⓑ Ⓒ Ⓓ Ⓔ	38 Ⓐ Ⓑ Ⓒ Ⓓ Ⓔ	68 Ⓐ Ⓑ Ⓒ Ⓓ Ⓔ
9 Ⓐ Ⓑ Ⓒ Ⓓ Ⓔ	39 Ⓐ Ⓑ Ⓒ Ⓓ Ⓔ	69 Ⓐ Ⓑ Ⓒ Ⓓ Ⓔ
10 Ⓐ Ⓑ Ⓒ Ⓓ Ⓔ	40 Ⓐ Ⓑ Ⓒ Ⓓ Ⓔ	70 Ⓐ Ⓑ Ⓒ Ⓓ Ⓔ
11 Ⓐ Ⓑ Ⓒ Ⓓ Ⓔ	41 Ⓐ Ⓑ Ⓒ Ⓓ Ⓔ	71 Ⓐ Ⓑ Ⓒ Ⓓ Ⓔ
12 Ⓐ Ⓑ Ⓒ Ⓓ Ⓔ	42 Ⓐ Ⓑ Ⓒ Ⓓ Ⓔ	72 Ⓐ Ⓑ Ⓒ Ⓓ Ⓔ
13 Ⓐ Ⓑ Ⓒ Ⓓ Ⓔ	43 Ⓐ Ⓑ Ⓒ Ⓓ Ⓔ	73 Ⓐ Ⓑ Ⓒ Ⓓ Ⓔ
14 Ⓐ Ⓑ Ⓒ Ⓓ Ⓔ	44 Ⓐ Ⓑ Ⓒ Ⓓ Ⓔ	74 Ⓐ Ⓑ Ⓒ Ⓓ Ⓔ
15 Ⓐ Ⓑ Ⓒ Ⓓ Ⓔ	45 Ⓐ Ⓑ Ⓒ Ⓓ Ⓔ	75 Ⓐ Ⓑ Ⓒ Ⓓ Ⓔ
16 Ⓐ Ⓑ Ⓒ Ⓓ Ⓔ	46 Ⓐ Ⓑ Ⓒ Ⓓ Ⓔ	76 Ⓐ Ⓑ Ⓒ Ⓓ Ⓔ
17 Ⓐ Ⓑ Ⓒ Ⓓ Ⓔ	47 Ⓐ Ⓑ Ⓒ Ⓓ Ⓔ	77 Ⓐ Ⓑ Ⓒ Ⓓ Ⓔ
18 Ⓐ Ⓑ Ⓒ Ⓓ Ⓔ	48 Ⓐ Ⓑ Ⓒ Ⓓ Ⓔ	78 Ⓐ Ⓑ Ⓒ Ⓓ Ⓔ
19 Ⓐ Ⓑ Ⓒ Ⓓ Ⓔ	49 Ⓐ Ⓑ Ⓒ Ⓓ Ⓔ	79 Ⓐ Ⓑ Ⓒ Ⓓ Ⓔ
20 Ⓐ Ⓑ Ⓒ Ⓓ Ⓔ	50 Ⓐ Ⓑ Ⓒ Ⓓ Ⓔ	80 Ⓐ Ⓑ Ⓒ Ⓓ Ⓔ
21 Ⓐ Ⓑ Ⓒ Ⓓ Ⓔ	51 Ⓐ Ⓑ Ⓒ Ⓓ Ⓔ	81 Ⓐ Ⓑ Ⓒ Ⓓ Ⓔ
22 Ⓐ Ⓑ Ⓒ Ⓓ Ⓔ	52 Ⓐ Ⓑ Ⓒ Ⓓ Ⓔ	82 Ⓐ Ⓑ Ⓒ Ⓓ Ⓔ
23 Ⓐ Ⓑ Ⓒ Ⓓ Ⓔ	53 Ⓐ Ⓑ Ⓒ Ⓓ Ⓔ	83 Ⓐ Ⓑ Ⓒ Ⓓ Ⓔ
24 Ⓐ Ⓑ Ⓒ Ⓓ Ⓔ	54 Ⓐ Ⓑ Ⓒ Ⓓ Ⓔ	84 Ⓐ Ⓑ Ⓒ Ⓓ Ⓔ
25 Ⓐ Ⓑ Ⓒ Ⓓ Ⓔ	55 Ⓐ Ⓑ Ⓒ Ⓓ Ⓔ	85 Ⓐ Ⓑ Ⓒ Ⓓ Ⓔ
26 Ⓐ Ⓑ Ⓒ Ⓓ Ⓔ	56 Ⓐ Ⓑ Ⓒ Ⓓ Ⓔ	86 Ⓐ Ⓑ Ⓒ Ⓓ Ⓔ
27 Ⓐ Ⓑ Ⓒ Ⓓ Ⓔ	57 Ⓐ Ⓑ Ⓒ Ⓓ Ⓔ	87 Ⓐ Ⓑ Ⓒ Ⓓ Ⓔ
28 Ⓐ Ⓑ Ⓒ Ⓓ Ⓔ	58 Ⓐ Ⓑ Ⓒ Ⓓ Ⓔ	88 Ⓐ Ⓑ Ⓒ Ⓓ Ⓔ
29 Ⓐ Ⓑ Ⓒ Ⓓ Ⓔ	59 Ⓐ Ⓑ Ⓒ Ⓓ Ⓔ	
30 Ⓐ Ⓑ Ⓒ Ⓓ Ⓔ	60 Ⓐ Ⓑ Ⓒ Ⓓ Ⓔ	

Position Title	Level	Position No.	Occ Code	Craft
Schemes and Schedules Clerk	6	SP 2-14	2350-08xx	C
Schemes Clerk	5	SP 1-51	2350-01xx	C
Schemes Examiner	6	SP 2-4	1712-04xx	C
Schedule Clerk, Foreign Mail	6	SP 2-158	2350-06xx	C
Self Service Postal Unit Technician	6	SP 2-433	2340-48xx	C
Senior Lockmaker	6	SP 7-45	5311-03xx	
Senior Philatelic Clerk	6	SP 2-631	2345-05xx	C
Senior Postal Source Data Technician	7	SP 2-568	0301-84xx	C
Setup Pressman (MES)	6	SP 7-40	3803-02xx	
Sewing Machine Mechanic	6	SP 7-51	5312-01xx	
Shipping Clerk	4	SP 7-56	2040-13xx	
Sign Painter—Illustrator	6	SP 2-18	1020-05xx	C
Sign Painter—Letterer	5	SP 2-19	4104-04xx	C
Special Delivery Messenger	5	KP-11	2310-53xx	SD
Special Postal Clerk	6	SP 2-157	2315-08xx	C
Special Postal Clerk	6	SP 2-157	2320-31xx	C
Special Transfer Clerk	7	SP 2-331	2330-02xx	C
Special Transfer Clerk, Airmail	7	SP 2-386	2330-43xx	C
Stamp Supply Clerk	6	SP 2-156	2320-03xx	C
Stationary Engineer	7	SP 6-81	5415-01xx	M
Storekeeper (A)	5	SP 7-50	2040-10xx	
Storekeeper (B)	5	SP 7-49	2040-18xx	
Storekeeper, Automotive Parts	7	SP 5-47	2040-11xx	MV
Storekeeper, Automotive Parts	6	SP 5-46	2040-11xx	MV
Supply Clerk	4	SP 1-4	2040-07xx	C&M
Telephone Operator	4	SP 1-3	0382-01xx	M

Continued on Page KB-85

1	Ⓐ Ⓑ Ⓒ Ⓓ Ⓔ		31	Ⓐ Ⓑ Ⓒ Ⓓ Ⓔ		61	Ⓐ Ⓑ Ⓒ Ⓓ Ⓔ										

1 Ⓐ Ⓑ Ⓒ Ⓓ Ⓔ   31 Ⓐ Ⓑ Ⓒ Ⓓ Ⓔ   61 Ⓐ Ⓑ Ⓒ Ⓓ Ⓔ

2 Ⓐ Ⓑ Ⓒ Ⓓ Ⓔ   32 Ⓐ Ⓑ Ⓒ Ⓓ Ⓔ   62 Ⓐ Ⓑ Ⓒ Ⓓ Ⓔ

3 Ⓐ Ⓑ Ⓒ Ⓓ Ⓔ   33 Ⓐ Ⓑ Ⓒ Ⓓ Ⓔ   63 Ⓐ Ⓑ Ⓒ Ⓓ Ⓔ

4 Ⓐ Ⓑ Ⓒ Ⓓ Ⓔ   34 Ⓐ Ⓑ Ⓒ Ⓓ Ⓔ   64 Ⓐ Ⓑ Ⓒ Ⓓ Ⓔ

5 Ⓐ Ⓑ Ⓒ Ⓓ Ⓔ   35 Ⓐ Ⓑ Ⓒ Ⓓ Ⓔ   65 Ⓐ Ⓑ Ⓒ Ⓓ Ⓔ

6 Ⓐ Ⓑ Ⓒ Ⓓ Ⓔ   36 Ⓐ Ⓑ Ⓒ Ⓓ Ⓔ   66 Ⓐ Ⓑ Ⓒ Ⓓ Ⓔ

7 Ⓐ Ⓑ Ⓒ Ⓓ Ⓔ   37 Ⓐ Ⓑ Ⓒ Ⓓ Ⓔ   67 Ⓐ Ⓑ Ⓒ Ⓓ Ⓔ

8 Ⓐ Ⓑ Ⓒ Ⓓ Ⓔ   38 Ⓐ Ⓑ Ⓒ Ⓓ Ⓔ   68 Ⓐ Ⓑ Ⓒ Ⓓ Ⓔ

9 Ⓐ Ⓑ Ⓒ Ⓓ Ⓔ   39 Ⓐ Ⓑ Ⓒ Ⓓ Ⓔ   69 Ⓐ Ⓑ Ⓒ Ⓓ Ⓔ

10 Ⓐ Ⓑ Ⓒ Ⓓ Ⓔ   40 Ⓐ Ⓑ Ⓒ Ⓓ Ⓔ   70 Ⓐ Ⓑ Ⓒ Ⓓ Ⓔ

11 Ⓐ Ⓑ Ⓒ Ⓓ Ⓔ   41 Ⓐ Ⓑ Ⓒ Ⓓ Ⓔ   71 Ⓐ Ⓑ Ⓒ Ⓓ Ⓔ

12 Ⓐ Ⓑ Ⓒ Ⓓ Ⓔ   42 Ⓐ Ⓑ Ⓒ Ⓓ Ⓔ   72 Ⓐ Ⓑ Ⓒ Ⓓ Ⓔ

13 Ⓐ Ⓑ Ⓒ Ⓓ Ⓔ   43 Ⓐ Ⓑ Ⓒ Ⓓ Ⓔ   73 Ⓐ Ⓑ Ⓒ Ⓓ Ⓔ

14 Ⓐ Ⓑ Ⓒ Ⓓ Ⓔ   44 Ⓐ Ⓑ Ⓒ Ⓓ Ⓔ   74 Ⓐ Ⓑ Ⓒ Ⓓ Ⓔ

15 Ⓐ Ⓑ Ⓒ Ⓓ Ⓔ   45 Ⓐ Ⓑ Ⓒ Ⓓ Ⓔ   75 Ⓐ Ⓑ Ⓒ Ⓓ Ⓔ

16 Ⓐ Ⓑ Ⓒ Ⓓ Ⓔ   46 Ⓐ Ⓑ Ⓒ Ⓓ Ⓔ   76 Ⓐ Ⓑ Ⓒ Ⓓ Ⓔ

17 Ⓐ Ⓑ Ⓒ Ⓓ Ⓔ   47 Ⓐ Ⓑ Ⓒ Ⓓ Ⓔ   77 Ⓐ Ⓑ Ⓒ Ⓓ Ⓔ

18 Ⓐ Ⓑ Ⓒ Ⓓ Ⓔ   48 Ⓐ Ⓑ Ⓒ Ⓓ Ⓔ   78 Ⓐ Ⓑ Ⓒ Ⓓ Ⓔ

19 Ⓐ Ⓑ Ⓒ Ⓓ Ⓔ   49 Ⓐ Ⓑ Ⓒ Ⓓ Ⓔ   79 Ⓐ Ⓑ Ⓒ Ⓓ Ⓔ

20 Ⓐ Ⓑ Ⓒ Ⓓ Ⓔ   50 Ⓐ Ⓑ Ⓒ Ⓓ Ⓔ   80 Ⓐ Ⓑ Ⓒ Ⓓ Ⓔ

21 Ⓐ Ⓑ Ⓒ Ⓓ Ⓔ   51 Ⓐ Ⓑ Ⓒ Ⓓ Ⓔ   81 Ⓐ Ⓑ Ⓒ Ⓓ Ⓔ

22 Ⓐ Ⓑ Ⓒ Ⓓ Ⓔ   52 Ⓐ Ⓑ Ⓒ Ⓓ Ⓔ   82 Ⓐ Ⓑ Ⓒ Ⓓ Ⓔ

23 Ⓐ Ⓑ Ⓒ Ⓓ Ⓔ   53 Ⓐ Ⓑ Ⓒ Ⓓ Ⓔ   83 Ⓐ Ⓑ Ⓒ Ⓓ Ⓔ

24 Ⓐ Ⓑ Ⓒ Ⓓ Ⓔ   54 Ⓐ Ⓑ Ⓒ Ⓓ Ⓔ   84 Ⓐ Ⓑ Ⓒ Ⓓ Ⓔ

25 Ⓐ Ⓑ Ⓒ Ⓓ Ⓔ   55 Ⓐ Ⓑ Ⓒ Ⓓ Ⓔ   85 Ⓐ Ⓑ Ⓒ Ⓓ Ⓔ

26 Ⓐ Ⓑ Ⓒ Ⓓ Ⓔ   56 Ⓐ Ⓑ Ⓒ Ⓓ Ⓔ   86 Ⓐ Ⓑ Ⓒ Ⓓ Ⓔ

27 Ⓐ Ⓑ Ⓒ Ⓓ Ⓔ   57 Ⓐ Ⓑ Ⓒ Ⓓ Ⓔ   87 Ⓐ Ⓑ Ⓒ Ⓓ Ⓔ

28 Ⓐ Ⓑ Ⓒ Ⓓ Ⓔ   58 Ⓐ Ⓑ Ⓒ Ⓓ Ⓔ   88 Ⓐ Ⓑ Ⓒ Ⓓ Ⓔ

29 Ⓐ Ⓑ Ⓒ Ⓓ Ⓔ   59 Ⓐ Ⓑ Ⓒ Ⓓ Ⓔ

30 Ⓐ Ⓑ Ⓒ Ⓓ Ⓔ   60 Ⓐ Ⓑ Ⓒ Ⓓ Ⓔ

Test-List 2

For each question, mark your answer sheet to show the letter of the box in which the address belongs. Be sure to mark your answers on the correct answer sheet. Your answers will go in the section labeled Part B. The first question is numbered 1. You will have *5 minutes* to do Test--List 2. During the 5 minutes for this list, **do not turn to** any other page.

1. Cedar
2. 4300–4499 Cliff
3. 4400–4599 Mall
4. Natoma
5. 2300–2999 Laurel
6. 4500–4799 Cliff
7. Ceres
8. 3400–3899 Mall

9. Delhi
10. Dexter
11. 1900–2299 Laurel
12. 3300–3999 Cliff
13. Cicero
14. 4000–4299 Cliff
15. 2100–2799 Mall
16. Foster

17. Magnet
18. Ceres
19. 2800–3399 Mall
20. 3200–3799 Laurel
21. 4300–4499 Cliff
22. Pearl
23. 3900–4399 Mall
24. Natoma

25. 4800–4999 Cliff
26. 1500–1899 Laurel
27. Cedar
28. 4400–4599 Mall
29. 4500–4799 Cliff
30. Dexter
31. 3000–3199 Laurel
32. Niles

33. Delhi
34. 3900–4399 Mall
35. Cicero
36. Dexter
37. 4800–4999 Cliff
38. 2300–2999 Laurel
39. 2100–2799 Mall
40. 3300–3999 Cliff

41. 3400–3899 Mall
42. 4300–4499 Cliff
43. Ceres
44. Foster
45. Magnet
46. 3200–3799 Laurel
47. Pearl
48. 1500–1899 Laurel

49. 4500–4799 Cliff
50. 1900–2299 Laurel
51. Niles
52. 3300–3999 Cliff
53. 2800–3399 Mall
54. Cicero
55. Delhi
56. 4000–4299 Cliff

57. Dexter
58. Magnet
59. 3000–3199 Laurel
60. 3900–4399 Mall
61. Natoma
62. 3000–3199 Laurel
63. 4300–4499 Cliff
64. Cedar

65. 4400–4599 Mall
66. 1500–1899 Laurel
67. 4800–4999 Cliff
68. Delhi
69. Pearl
70. 2300–2999 Laurel
71. 4500–4799 Cliff
72. Niles

73. 4000–4299 Cliff
74. 3400–3899 Mall
75. 1900–2299 Laurel
76. 2800–3399 Mall
77. Ceres
78. Magnet
79. Cicero
80. 3200–3799 Laurel

81. 3000–3199 Laurel
82. 3900–4399 Mall
83. Natoma
84. 3300–3999 Cliff
85. 3400–3899 Mall
86. Foster
87. 2100–2799 Mall
88. 4300–4499 Cliff

STOP.

If you finish before the time is up, go back and rework the questions on this page only.

CORRECT ANSWER FOR CLERK-CARRIER TEST

PART A

1 ● Ⓓ	21 ◯ Ⓓ	46 Ⓐ ●	71 Ⓐ ●
2 ● Ⓓ	22 Ⓐ ●	47 ● Ⓓ	72 ● Ⓓ
3 Ⓐ ●	23 Ⓐ ●	48 ● Ⓓ	73 Ⓐ ●
4 ● Ⓓ	24 Ⓐ ●	49 Ⓐ ●	74 Ⓐ ●
5 Ⓐ ●	25 ● Ⓓ	50 Ⓐ ●	75 ● Ⓓ
6 ● Ⓓ	26 Ⓐ ●	51 ● Ⓓ	76 ● Ⓓ
7 Ⓐ ●	27 Ⓐ ●	52 Ⓐ ●	77 Ⓐ ●
8 Ⓐ ●	28 ● Ⓓ	53 Ⓐ ●	78 Ⓐ ●
9 ● Ⓓ	29 Ⓐ ●	54 Ⓐ ●	79 Ⓐ ●
10 ● Ⓓ	30 ● Ⓓ	55 ● Ⓓ	80 ● Ⓓ
11 ● Ⓓ	31 Ⓐ ●	56 Ⓐ ●	81 ● Ⓓ
12 Ⓐ ●	32 ● Ⓓ	57 Ⓐ ●	82 Ⓐ ●
13 Ⓐ ●	33 ● Ⓓ	58 Ⓐ ●	83 ● Ⓓ
14 ● Ⓓ	34 ● Ⓓ	59 Ⓐ ●	84 ● Ⓓ
15 ● Ⓓ	35 ● Ⓓ	60 Ⓐ ●	85 Ⓐ ●
16 Ⓐ ●	36 Ⓐ ●	61 ● Ⓓ	86 Ⓐ ●
17 Ⓐ ●	37 Ⓐ ●	62 Ⓐ ●	87 ● Ⓓ
18 ● Ⓓ	38 Ⓐ ●	63 Ⓐ ●	88 Ⓐ ●
19 Ⓐ ●	39 Ⓐ ●	64 ● Ⓓ	89 ● Ⓓ
20 ● Ⓓ	40 Ⓐ ●	65 ● Ⓓ	90 ● Ⓓ
	41 ● Ⓓ	66 ● Ⓓ	91 Ⓐ ●
	42 Ⓐ ●	67 Ⓐ ●	92 ● Ⓓ
	43 ● Ⓓ	68 Ⓐ ●	93 Ⓐ ●
	44 Ⓐ ●	69 Ⓐ ●	94 ● Ⓓ
	45 ● Ⓓ	70 Ⓐ ●	95 Ⓐ ●

CORRECT ANSWERS FOR CLERK-CARRIER TEST
PART—B

#	Ans	#	Ans	#	Ans
1	B	31	D	61	A
2	E	32	C	62	D
3	C	33	E	63	E
4	A	34	B	64	B
5	B	35	D	65	C
6	D	36	C	66	E
7	A	37	A	67	A
8	D	38	B	68	E
9	E	39	A	69	D
10	C	40	C	70	B
11	A	41	D	71	D
12	C	42	E	72	C
13	D	43	A	73	B
14	B	44	B	74	D
15	A	45	E	75	A
16	B	46	C	76	E
17	E	47	D	77	A
18	A	48	E	78	E
19	E	49	D	79	D
20	C	50	A	80	C
21	E	51	C	81	D
22	D	52	C	82	B
23	B	53	E	83	A
24	A	54	D	84	C
25	A	55	E	85	D
26	E	56	B	86	B
27	B	57	C	87	A
28	C	58	E	88	E
29	D	59	D		
30	C	60	B		

ANSWER SHEET

PART—A

1 Ⓐ Ⓓ	21 Ⓐ Ⓓ	46 Ⓐ Ⓓ	71 Ⓐ Ⓓ
2 Ⓐ Ⓓ	22 Ⓐ Ⓓ	47 Ⓐ Ⓓ	72 Ⓐ Ⓓ
3 Ⓐ Ⓓ	23 Ⓐ Ⓓ	48 Ⓐ Ⓓ	73 Ⓐ Ⓓ
4 Ⓐ Ⓓ	24 Ⓐ Ⓓ	49 Ⓐ Ⓓ	74 Ⓐ Ⓓ
5 Ⓐ Ⓓ	25 Ⓐ Ⓓ	50 Ⓐ Ⓓ	75 Ⓐ Ⓓ
6 Ⓐ Ⓓ	26 Ⓐ Ⓓ	51 Ⓐ Ⓓ	76 Ⓐ Ⓓ
7 Ⓐ Ⓓ	27 Ⓐ Ⓓ	52 Ⓐ Ⓓ	77 Ⓐ Ⓓ
8 Ⓐ Ⓓ	28 Ⓐ Ⓓ	53 Ⓐ Ⓓ	78 Ⓐ Ⓓ
9 Ⓐ Ⓓ	29 Ⓐ Ⓓ	54 Ⓐ Ⓓ	79 Ⓐ Ⓓ
10 Ⓐ Ⓓ	30 Ⓐ Ⓓ	55 Ⓐ Ⓓ	80 Ⓐ Ⓓ
11 Ⓐ Ⓓ	31 Ⓐ Ⓓ	56 Ⓐ Ⓓ	81 Ⓐ Ⓓ
12 Ⓐ Ⓓ	32 Ⓐ Ⓓ	57 Ⓐ Ⓓ	82 Ⓐ Ⓓ
13 Ⓐ Ⓓ	33 Ⓐ Ⓓ	58 Ⓐ Ⓓ	83 Ⓐ Ⓓ
14 Ⓐ Ⓓ	34 Ⓐ Ⓓ	59 Ⓐ Ⓓ	84 Ⓐ Ⓓ
15 Ⓐ Ⓓ	35 Ⓐ Ⓓ	60 Ⓐ Ⓓ	85 Ⓐ Ⓓ
16 Ⓐ Ⓓ	36 Ⓐ Ⓓ	61 Ⓐ Ⓓ	86 Ⓐ Ⓓ
17 Ⓐ Ⓓ	37 Ⓐ Ⓓ	62 Ⓐ Ⓓ	87 Ⓐ Ⓓ
18 Ⓐ Ⓓ	38 Ⓐ Ⓓ	63 Ⓐ Ⓓ	88 Ⓐ Ⓓ
19 Ⓐ Ⓓ	39 Ⓐ Ⓓ	64 Ⓐ Ⓓ	89 Ⓐ Ⓓ
20 Ⓐ Ⓓ	40 Ⓐ Ⓓ	65 Ⓐ Ⓓ	90 Ⓐ Ⓓ
	41 Ⓐ Ⓓ	66 Ⓐ Ⓓ	91 Ⓐ Ⓓ
	42 Ⓐ Ⓓ	67 Ⓐ Ⓓ	92 Ⓐ Ⓓ
	43 Ⓐ Ⓓ	68 Ⓐ Ⓓ	93 Ⓐ Ⓓ
	44 Ⓐ Ⓓ	69 Ⓐ Ⓓ	94 Ⓐ Ⓓ
	45 Ⓐ Ⓓ	70 Ⓐ Ⓓ	95 Ⓐ Ⓓ

ANSWER SHEET
PART--B

1 Ⓐ Ⓑ Ⓒ Ⓓ Ⓔ	31 Ⓐ Ⓑ Ⓒ Ⓓ Ⓔ	61 Ⓐ Ⓑ Ⓒ Ⓓ Ⓔ
2 Ⓐ Ⓑ Ⓒ Ⓓ Ⓔ	32 Ⓐ Ⓑ Ⓒ Ⓓ Ⓔ	62 Ⓐ Ⓑ Ⓒ Ⓓ Ⓔ
3 Ⓐ Ⓑ Ⓒ Ⓓ Ⓔ	33 Ⓐ Ⓑ Ⓒ Ⓓ Ⓔ	63 Ⓐ Ⓑ Ⓒ Ⓓ Ⓔ
4 Ⓐ Ⓑ Ⓒ Ⓓ Ⓔ	34 Ⓐ Ⓑ Ⓒ Ⓓ Ⓔ	64 Ⓐ Ⓑ Ⓒ Ⓓ Ⓔ
5 Ⓐ Ⓑ Ⓒ Ⓓ Ⓔ	35 Ⓐ Ⓑ Ⓒ Ⓓ Ⓔ	65 Ⓐ Ⓑ Ⓒ Ⓓ Ⓔ
6 Ⓐ Ⓑ Ⓒ Ⓓ Ⓔ	36 Ⓐ Ⓑ Ⓒ Ⓓ Ⓔ	66 Ⓐ Ⓑ Ⓒ Ⓓ Ⓔ
7 Ⓐ Ⓑ Ⓒ Ⓓ Ⓔ	37 Ⓐ Ⓑ Ⓒ Ⓓ Ⓔ	67 Ⓐ Ⓑ Ⓒ Ⓓ Ⓔ
8 Ⓐ Ⓑ Ⓒ Ⓓ Ⓔ	38 Ⓐ Ⓑ Ⓒ Ⓓ Ⓔ	68 Ⓐ Ⓑ Ⓒ Ⓓ Ⓔ
9 Ⓐ Ⓑ Ⓒ Ⓓ Ⓔ	39 Ⓐ Ⓑ Ⓒ Ⓓ Ⓔ	69 Ⓐ Ⓑ Ⓒ Ⓓ Ⓔ
10 Ⓐ Ⓑ Ⓒ Ⓓ Ⓔ	40 Ⓐ Ⓑ Ⓒ Ⓓ Ⓔ	70 Ⓐ Ⓑ Ⓒ Ⓓ Ⓔ
11 Ⓐ Ⓑ Ⓒ Ⓓ Ⓔ	41 Ⓐ Ⓑ Ⓒ Ⓓ Ⓔ	71 Ⓐ Ⓑ Ⓒ Ⓓ Ⓔ
12 Ⓐ Ⓑ Ⓒ Ⓓ Ⓔ	42 Ⓐ Ⓑ Ⓒ Ⓓ Ⓔ	72 Ⓐ Ⓑ Ⓒ Ⓓ Ⓔ
13 Ⓐ Ⓑ Ⓒ Ⓓ Ⓔ	43 Ⓐ Ⓑ Ⓒ Ⓓ Ⓔ	73 Ⓐ Ⓑ Ⓒ Ⓓ Ⓔ
14 Ⓐ Ⓑ Ⓒ Ⓓ Ⓔ	44 Ⓐ Ⓑ Ⓒ Ⓓ Ⓔ	74 Ⓐ Ⓑ Ⓒ Ⓓ Ⓔ
15 Ⓐ Ⓑ Ⓒ Ⓓ Ⓔ	45 Ⓐ Ⓑ Ⓒ Ⓓ Ⓔ	75 Ⓐ Ⓑ Ⓒ Ⓓ Ⓔ
16 Ⓐ Ⓑ Ⓒ Ⓓ Ⓔ	46 Ⓐ Ⓑ Ⓒ Ⓓ Ⓔ	76 Ⓐ Ⓑ Ⓒ Ⓓ Ⓔ
17 Ⓐ Ⓑ Ⓒ Ⓓ Ⓔ	47 Ⓐ Ⓑ Ⓒ Ⓓ Ⓔ	77 Ⓐ Ⓑ Ⓒ Ⓓ Ⓔ
18 Ⓐ Ⓑ Ⓒ Ⓓ Ⓔ	48 Ⓐ Ⓑ Ⓒ Ⓓ Ⓔ	78 Ⓐ Ⓑ Ⓒ Ⓓ Ⓔ
19 Ⓐ Ⓑ Ⓒ Ⓓ Ⓔ	49 Ⓐ Ⓑ Ⓒ Ⓓ Ⓔ	79 Ⓐ Ⓑ Ⓒ Ⓓ Ⓔ
20 Ⓐ Ⓑ Ⓒ Ⓓ Ⓔ	50 Ⓐ Ⓑ Ⓒ Ⓓ Ⓔ	80 Ⓐ Ⓑ Ⓒ Ⓓ Ⓔ
21 Ⓐ Ⓑ Ⓒ Ⓓ Ⓔ	51 Ⓐ Ⓑ Ⓒ Ⓓ Ⓔ	81 Ⓐ Ⓑ Ⓒ Ⓓ Ⓔ
22 Ⓐ Ⓑ Ⓒ Ⓓ Ⓔ	52 Ⓐ Ⓑ Ⓒ Ⓓ Ⓔ	82 Ⓐ Ⓑ Ⓒ Ⓓ Ⓔ
23 Ⓐ Ⓑ Ⓒ Ⓓ Ⓔ	53 Ⓐ Ⓑ Ⓒ Ⓓ Ⓔ	83 Ⓐ Ⓑ Ⓒ Ⓓ Ⓔ
24 Ⓐ Ⓑ Ⓒ Ⓓ Ⓔ	54 Ⓐ Ⓑ Ⓒ Ⓓ Ⓔ	84 Ⓐ Ⓑ Ⓒ Ⓓ Ⓔ
25 Ⓐ Ⓑ Ⓒ Ⓓ Ⓔ	55 Ⓐ Ⓑ Ⓒ Ⓓ Ⓔ	85 Ⓐ Ⓑ Ⓒ Ⓓ Ⓔ
26 Ⓐ Ⓑ Ⓒ Ⓓ Ⓔ	56 Ⓐ Ⓑ Ⓒ Ⓓ Ⓔ	86 Ⓐ Ⓑ Ⓒ Ⓓ Ⓔ
27 Ⓐ Ⓑ Ⓒ Ⓓ Ⓔ	57 Ⓐ Ⓑ Ⓒ Ⓓ Ⓔ	87 Ⓐ Ⓑ Ⓒ Ⓓ Ⓔ
28 Ⓐ Ⓑ Ⓒ Ⓓ Ⓔ	58 Ⓐ Ⓑ Ⓒ Ⓓ Ⓔ	88 Ⓐ Ⓑ Ⓒ Ⓓ Ⓔ
29 Ⓐ Ⓑ Ⓒ Ⓓ Ⓔ	59 Ⓐ Ⓑ Ⓒ Ⓓ Ⓔ	
30 Ⓐ Ⓑ Ⓒ Ⓓ Ⓔ	60 Ⓐ Ⓑ Ⓒ Ⓓ Ⓔ	

ANSWER SHEET

PART—A

1 Ⓐ Ⓓ	21 Ⓐ Ⓓ	46 Ⓐ Ⓓ	71 Ⓐ Ⓓ
2 Ⓐ Ⓓ	22 Ⓐ Ⓓ	47 Ⓐ Ⓓ	72 Ⓐ Ⓓ
3 Ⓐ Ⓓ	23 Ⓐ Ⓓ	48 Ⓐ Ⓓ	73 Ⓐ Ⓓ
4 Ⓐ Ⓓ	24 Ⓐ Ⓓ	49 Ⓐ Ⓓ	74 Ⓐ Ⓓ
5 Ⓐ Ⓓ	25 Ⓐ Ⓓ	50 Ⓐ Ⓓ	75 Ⓐ Ⓓ
6 Ⓐ Ⓓ	26 Ⓐ Ⓓ	51 Ⓐ Ⓓ	76 Ⓐ Ⓓ
7 Ⓐ Ⓓ	27 Ⓐ Ⓓ	52 Ⓐ Ⓓ	77 Ⓐ Ⓓ
8 Ⓐ Ⓓ	28 Ⓐ Ⓓ	53 Ⓐ Ⓓ	78 Ⓐ Ⓓ
9 Ⓐ Ⓓ	29 Ⓐ Ⓓ	54 Ⓐ Ⓓ	79 Ⓐ Ⓓ
10 Ⓐ Ⓓ	30 Ⓐ Ⓓ	55 Ⓐ Ⓓ	80 Ⓐ Ⓓ
11 Ⓐ Ⓓ	31 Ⓐ Ⓓ	56 Ⓐ Ⓓ	81 Ⓐ Ⓓ
12 Ⓐ Ⓓ	32 Ⓐ Ⓓ	57 Ⓐ Ⓓ	82 Ⓐ Ⓓ
13 Ⓐ Ⓓ	33 Ⓐ Ⓓ	58 Ⓐ Ⓓ	83 Ⓐ Ⓓ
14 Ⓐ Ⓓ	34 Ⓐ Ⓓ	59 Ⓐ Ⓓ	84 Ⓐ Ⓓ
15 Ⓐ Ⓓ	35 Ⓐ Ⓓ	60 Ⓐ Ⓓ	85 Ⓐ Ⓓ
16 Ⓐ Ⓓ	36 Ⓐ Ⓓ	61 Ⓐ Ⓓ	86 Ⓐ Ⓓ
17 Ⓐ Ⓓ	37 Ⓐ Ⓓ	62 Ⓐ Ⓓ	87 Ⓐ Ⓓ
18 Ⓐ Ⓓ	38 Ⓐ Ⓓ	63 Ⓐ Ⓓ	88 Ⓐ Ⓓ
19 Ⓐ Ⓓ	39 Ⓐ Ⓓ	64 Ⓐ Ⓓ	89 Ⓐ Ⓓ
20 Ⓐ Ⓓ	40 Ⓐ Ⓓ	65 Ⓐ Ⓓ	90 Ⓐ Ⓓ
	41 Ⓐ Ⓓ	66 Ⓐ Ⓓ	91 Ⓐ Ⓓ
	42 Ⓐ Ⓓ	67 Ⓐ Ⓓ	92 Ⓐ Ⓓ
	43 Ⓐ Ⓓ	68 Ⓐ Ⓓ	93 Ⓐ Ⓓ
	44 Ⓐ Ⓓ	69 Ⓐ Ⓓ	94 Ⓐ Ⓓ
	45 Ⓐ Ⓓ	70 Ⓐ Ⓓ	95 Ⓐ Ⓓ

ANSWER SHEET
PART-B

1 Ⓐ Ⓑ Ⓒ Ⓓ Ⓔ	31 Ⓐ Ⓑ Ⓒ Ⓓ Ⓔ	61 Ⓐ Ⓑ Ⓒ Ⓓ Ⓔ
2 Ⓐ Ⓑ Ⓒ Ⓓ Ⓔ	32 Ⓐ Ⓑ Ⓒ Ⓓ Ⓔ	62 Ⓐ Ⓑ Ⓒ Ⓓ Ⓔ
3 Ⓐ Ⓑ Ⓒ Ⓓ Ⓔ	33 Ⓐ Ⓑ Ⓒ Ⓓ Ⓔ	63 Ⓐ Ⓑ Ⓒ Ⓓ Ⓔ
4 Ⓐ Ⓑ Ⓒ Ⓓ Ⓔ	34 Ⓐ Ⓑ Ⓒ Ⓓ Ⓔ	64 Ⓐ Ⓑ Ⓒ Ⓓ Ⓔ
5 Ⓐ Ⓑ Ⓒ Ⓓ Ⓔ	35 Ⓐ Ⓑ Ⓒ Ⓓ Ⓔ	65 Ⓐ Ⓑ Ⓒ Ⓓ Ⓔ
6 Ⓐ Ⓑ Ⓒ Ⓓ Ⓔ	36 Ⓐ Ⓑ Ⓒ Ⓓ Ⓔ	66 Ⓐ Ⓑ Ⓒ Ⓓ Ⓔ
7 Ⓐ Ⓑ Ⓒ Ⓓ Ⓔ	37 Ⓐ Ⓑ Ⓒ Ⓓ Ⓔ	67 Ⓐ Ⓑ Ⓒ Ⓓ Ⓔ
8 Ⓐ Ⓑ Ⓒ Ⓓ Ⓔ	38 Ⓐ Ⓑ Ⓒ Ⓓ Ⓔ	68 Ⓐ Ⓑ Ⓒ Ⓓ Ⓔ
9 Ⓐ Ⓑ Ⓒ Ⓓ Ⓔ	39 Ⓐ Ⓑ Ⓒ Ⓓ Ⓔ	69 Ⓐ Ⓑ Ⓒ Ⓓ Ⓔ
10 Ⓐ Ⓑ Ⓒ Ⓓ Ⓔ	40 Ⓐ Ⓑ Ⓒ Ⓓ Ⓔ	70 Ⓐ Ⓑ Ⓒ Ⓓ Ⓔ
11 Ⓐ Ⓑ Ⓒ Ⓓ Ⓔ	41 Ⓐ Ⓑ Ⓒ Ⓓ Ⓔ	71 Ⓐ Ⓑ Ⓒ Ⓓ Ⓔ
12 Ⓐ Ⓑ Ⓒ Ⓓ Ⓔ	42 Ⓐ Ⓑ Ⓒ Ⓓ Ⓔ	72 Ⓐ Ⓑ Ⓒ Ⓓ Ⓔ
13 Ⓐ Ⓑ Ⓒ Ⓓ Ⓔ	43 Ⓐ Ⓑ Ⓒ Ⓓ Ⓔ	73 Ⓐ Ⓑ Ⓒ Ⓓ Ⓔ
14 Ⓐ Ⓑ Ⓒ Ⓓ Ⓔ	44 Ⓐ Ⓑ Ⓒ Ⓓ Ⓔ	74 Ⓐ Ⓑ Ⓒ Ⓓ Ⓔ
15 Ⓐ Ⓑ Ⓒ Ⓓ Ⓔ	45 Ⓐ Ⓑ Ⓒ Ⓓ Ⓔ	75 Ⓐ Ⓑ Ⓒ Ⓓ Ⓔ
16 Ⓐ Ⓑ Ⓒ Ⓓ Ⓔ	46 Ⓐ Ⓑ Ⓒ Ⓓ Ⓔ	76 Ⓐ Ⓑ Ⓒ Ⓓ Ⓔ
17 Ⓐ Ⓑ Ⓒ Ⓓ Ⓔ	47 Ⓐ Ⓑ Ⓒ Ⓓ Ⓔ	77 Ⓐ Ⓑ Ⓒ Ⓓ Ⓔ
18 Ⓐ Ⓑ Ⓒ Ⓓ Ⓔ	48 Ⓐ Ⓑ Ⓒ Ⓓ Ⓔ	78 Ⓐ Ⓑ Ⓒ Ⓓ Ⓔ
19 Ⓐ Ⓑ Ⓒ Ⓓ Ⓔ	49 Ⓐ Ⓑ Ⓒ Ⓓ Ⓔ	79 Ⓐ Ⓑ Ⓒ Ⓓ Ⓔ
20 Ⓐ Ⓑ Ⓒ Ⓓ Ⓔ	50 Ⓐ Ⓑ Ⓒ Ⓓ Ⓔ	80 Ⓐ Ⓑ Ⓒ Ⓓ Ⓔ
21 Ⓐ Ⓑ Ⓒ Ⓓ Ⓔ	51 Ⓐ Ⓑ Ⓒ Ⓓ Ⓔ	81 Ⓐ Ⓑ Ⓒ Ⓓ Ⓔ
22 Ⓐ Ⓑ Ⓒ Ⓓ Ⓔ	52 Ⓐ Ⓑ Ⓒ Ⓓ Ⓔ	82 Ⓐ Ⓑ Ⓒ Ⓓ Ⓔ
23 Ⓐ Ⓑ Ⓒ Ⓓ Ⓔ	53 Ⓐ Ⓑ Ⓒ Ⓓ Ⓔ	83 Ⓐ Ⓑ Ⓒ Ⓓ Ⓔ
24 Ⓐ Ⓑ Ⓒ Ⓓ Ⓔ	54 Ⓐ Ⓑ Ⓒ Ⓓ Ⓔ	84 Ⓐ Ⓑ Ⓒ Ⓓ Ⓔ
25 Ⓐ Ⓑ Ⓒ Ⓓ Ⓔ	55 Ⓐ Ⓑ Ⓒ Ⓓ Ⓔ	85 Ⓐ Ⓑ Ⓒ Ⓓ Ⓔ
26 Ⓐ Ⓑ Ⓒ Ⓓ Ⓔ	56 Ⓐ Ⓑ Ⓒ Ⓓ Ⓔ	86 Ⓐ Ⓑ Ⓒ Ⓓ Ⓔ
27 Ⓐ Ⓑ Ⓒ Ⓓ Ⓔ	57 Ⓐ Ⓑ Ⓒ Ⓓ Ⓔ	87 Ⓐ Ⓑ Ⓒ Ⓓ Ⓔ
28 Ⓐ Ⓑ Ⓒ Ⓓ Ⓔ	58 Ⓐ Ⓑ Ⓒ Ⓓ Ⓔ	88 Ⓐ Ⓑ Ⓒ Ⓓ Ⓔ
29 Ⓐ Ⓑ Ⓒ Ⓓ Ⓔ	59 Ⓐ Ⓑ Ⓒ Ⓓ Ⓔ	
30 Ⓐ Ⓑ Ⓒ Ⓓ Ⓔ	60 Ⓐ Ⓑ Ⓒ Ⓓ Ⓔ	

ANSWER SHEET

PART-A

1 Ⓐ Ⓓ	21 Ⓐ Ⓓ	46 Ⓐ Ⓓ	71 Ⓐ Ⓓ
2 Ⓐ Ⓓ	22 Ⓐ Ⓓ	47 Ⓐ Ⓓ	72 Ⓐ Ⓓ
3 Ⓐ Ⓓ	23 Ⓐ Ⓓ	48 Ⓐ Ⓓ	73 Ⓐ Ⓓ
4 Ⓐ Ⓓ	24 Ⓐ Ⓓ	49 Ⓐ Ⓒ	74 Ⓐ Ⓓ
5 Ⓐ Ⓓ	25 Ⓐ Ⓓ	50 Ⓐ Ⓓ	75 Ⓐ Ⓓ
6 Ⓐ Ⓓ	26 Ⓐ Ⓓ	51 Ⓐ Ⓓ	76 Ⓐ Ⓓ
7 Ⓐ Ⓓ	27 Ⓐ Ⓓ	52 Ⓐ Ⓓ	77 Ⓐ Ⓓ
8 Ⓐ Ⓓ	28 Ⓐ Ⓓ	53 Ⓐ Ⓓ	78 Ⓐ Ⓓ
9 Ⓐ Ⓓ	29 Ⓐ Ⓓ	54 Ⓐ Ⓓ	79 Ⓐ Ⓓ
10 Ⓐ Ⓓ	30 Ⓐ Ⓓ	55 Ⓐ Ⓓ	80 Ⓐ Ⓓ
11 Ⓐ Ⓓ	31 Ⓐ Ⓓ	56 Ⓐ Ⓓ	81 Ⓐ Ⓓ
12 Ⓐ Ⓓ	32 Ⓐ Ⓓ	57 Ⓐ Ⓓ	82 Ⓐ Ⓓ
13 Ⓐ Ⓓ	33 Ⓐ Ⓓ	58 Ⓐ Ⓓ	83 Ⓐ Ⓓ
14 Ⓐ Ⓓ	34 Ⓐ Ⓓ	59 Ⓐ Ⓓ	84 Ⓐ Ⓓ
15 Ⓐ Ⓓ	35 Ⓐ Ⓓ	60 Ⓐ Ⓓ	85 Ⓐ Ⓓ
16 Ⓐ Ⓓ	36 Ⓐ Ⓓ	61 Ⓐ Ⓓ	86 Ⓐ Ⓓ
17 Ⓐ Ⓓ	37 Ⓐ Ⓓ	62 Ⓐ Ⓓ	87 Ⓐ Ⓓ
18 Ⓐ Ⓓ	38 Ⓐ Ⓓ	63 Ⓐ Ⓓ	88 Ⓐ Ⓓ
19 Ⓐ Ⓓ	39 Ⓐ Ⓓ	64 Ⓐ Ⓓ	89 Ⓐ Ⓓ
20 Ⓐ Ⓓ	40 Ⓐ Ⓓ	65 Ⓐ Ⓓ	90 Ⓐ Ⓓ
	41 Ⓐ Ⓓ	66 Ⓐ Ⓓ	91 Ⓐ Ⓓ
	42 Ⓐ Ⓓ	67 Ⓐ Ⓓ	92 Ⓐ Ⓓ
	43 Ⓐ Ⓓ	68 Ⓐ Ⓓ	93 Ⓐ Ⓓ
	44 Ⓐ Ⓓ	69 Ⓐ Ⓓ	94 Ⓐ Ⓓ
	45 Ⓐ Ⓓ	70 Ⓐ Ⓓ	95 Ⓐ Ⓓ

ANSWER SHEET
PART--B

1 Ⓐ Ⓑ Ⓒ Ⓓ Ⓔ	31 Ⓐ Ⓑ Ⓒ Ⓓ Ⓔ	61 Ⓐ Ⓑ Ⓒ Ⓓ Ⓔ
2 Ⓐ Ⓑ Ⓒ Ⓓ Ⓔ	32 Ⓐ Ⓑ Ⓒ Ⓓ Ⓔ	62 Ⓐ Ⓑ Ⓒ Ⓓ Ⓔ
3 Ⓐ Ⓑ Ⓒ Ⓓ Ⓔ	33 Ⓐ Ⓑ Ⓒ Ⓓ Ⓔ	63 Ⓐ Ⓑ Ⓒ Ⓓ Ⓔ
4 Ⓐ Ⓑ Ⓒ Ⓓ Ⓔ	34 Ⓐ Ⓑ Ⓒ Ⓓ Ⓔ	64 Ⓐ Ⓑ Ⓒ Ⓓ Ⓔ
5 Ⓐ Ⓑ Ⓒ Ⓓ Ⓔ	35 Ⓐ Ⓑ Ⓒ Ⓓ Ⓔ	65 Ⓐ Ⓑ Ⓒ Ⓓ Ⓔ
6 Ⓐ Ⓑ Ⓒ Ⓓ Ⓔ	36 Ⓐ Ⓑ Ⓒ Ⓓ Ⓔ	66 Ⓐ Ⓑ Ⓒ Ⓓ Ⓔ
7 Ⓐ Ⓑ Ⓒ Ⓓ Ⓔ	37 Ⓐ Ⓑ Ⓒ Ⓓ Ⓔ	67 Ⓐ Ⓑ Ⓒ Ⓓ Ⓔ
8 Ⓐ Ⓑ Ⓒ Ⓓ Ⓔ	38 Ⓐ Ⓑ Ⓒ Ⓓ Ⓔ	68 Ⓐ Ⓑ Ⓒ Ⓓ Ⓔ
9 Ⓐ Ⓑ Ⓒ Ⓓ Ⓔ	39 Ⓐ Ⓑ Ⓒ Ⓓ Ⓔ	69 Ⓐ Ⓑ Ⓒ Ⓓ Ⓔ
10 Ⓐ Ⓑ Ⓒ Ⓓ Ⓔ	40 Ⓐ Ⓑ Ⓒ Ⓓ Ⓔ	70 Ⓐ Ⓑ Ⓒ Ⓓ Ⓔ
11 Ⓐ Ⓑ Ⓒ Ⓓ Ⓔ	41 Ⓐ Ⓑ Ⓒ Ⓓ Ⓔ	71 Ⓐ Ⓑ Ⓒ Ⓓ Ⓔ
12 Ⓐ Ⓑ Ⓒ Ⓓ Ⓔ	42 Ⓐ Ⓑ Ⓒ Ⓓ Ⓔ	72 Ⓐ Ⓑ Ⓒ Ⓓ Ⓔ
13 Ⓐ Ⓑ Ⓒ Ⓓ Ⓔ	43 Ⓐ Ⓑ Ⓒ Ⓓ Ⓔ	73 Ⓐ Ⓑ Ⓒ Ⓓ Ⓔ
14 Ⓐ Ⓑ Ⓒ Ⓓ Ⓔ	44 Ⓐ Ⓑ Ⓒ Ⓓ Ⓔ	74 Ⓐ Ⓑ Ⓒ Ⓓ Ⓔ
15 Ⓐ Ⓑ Ⓒ Ⓓ Ⓔ	45 Ⓐ Ⓑ Ⓒ Ⓓ Ⓔ	75 Ⓐ Ⓑ Ⓒ Ⓓ Ⓔ
16 Ⓐ Ⓑ Ⓒ Ⓓ Ⓔ	46 Ⓐ Ⓑ Ⓒ Ⓓ Ⓔ	76 Ⓐ Ⓑ Ⓒ Ⓓ Ⓔ
17 Ⓐ Ⓑ Ⓒ Ⓓ Ⓔ	47 Ⓐ Ⓑ Ⓒ Ⓓ Ⓔ	77 Ⓐ Ⓑ Ⓒ Ⓓ Ⓔ
18 Ⓐ Ⓑ Ⓒ Ⓓ Ⓔ	48 Ⓐ Ⓑ Ⓒ Ⓓ Ⓔ	78 Ⓐ Ⓑ Ⓒ Ⓓ Ⓔ
19 Ⓐ Ⓑ Ⓒ Ⓓ Ⓔ	49 Ⓐ Ⓑ Ⓒ Ⓓ Ⓔ	79 Ⓐ Ⓑ Ⓒ Ⓓ Ⓔ
20 Ⓐ Ⓑ Ⓒ Ⓓ Ⓔ	50 Ⓐ Ⓑ Ⓒ Ⓓ Ⓔ	80 Ⓐ Ⓑ Ⓒ Ⓓ Ⓔ
21 Ⓐ Ⓑ Ⓒ Ⓓ Ⓔ	51 Ⓐ Ⓑ Ⓒ Ⓓ Ⓔ	81 Ⓐ Ⓑ Ⓒ Ⓓ Ⓔ
22 Ⓐ Ⓑ Ⓒ Ⓓ Ⓔ	52 Ⓐ Ⓑ Ⓒ Ⓓ Ⓔ	82 Ⓐ Ⓑ Ⓒ Ⓓ Ⓔ
23 Ⓐ Ⓑ Ⓒ Ⓓ Ⓔ	53 Ⓐ Ⓑ Ⓒ Ⓓ Ⓔ	83 Ⓐ Ⓑ Ⓒ Ⓓ Ⓔ
24 Ⓐ Ⓑ Ⓒ Ⓓ Ⓔ	54 Ⓐ Ⓑ Ⓒ Ⓓ Ⓔ	84 Ⓐ Ⓑ Ⓒ Ⓓ Ⓔ
25 Ⓐ Ⓑ Ⓒ Ⓓ Ⓔ	55 Ⓐ Ⓑ Ⓒ Ⓓ Ⓔ	85 Ⓐ Ⓑ Ⓒ Ⓓ Ⓔ
26 Ⓐ Ⓑ Ⓒ Ⓓ Ⓔ	56 Ⓐ Ⓑ Ⓒ Ⓓ Ⓔ	86 Ⓐ Ⓑ Ⓒ Ⓓ Ⓔ
27 Ⓐ Ⓑ Ⓒ Ⓓ Ⓔ	57 Ⓐ Ⓑ Ⓒ Ⓓ Ⓔ	87 Ⓐ Ⓑ Ⓒ Ⓓ Ⓔ
28 Ⓐ Ⓑ Ⓒ Ⓓ Ⓔ	58 Ⓐ Ⓑ Ⓒ Ⓓ Ⓔ	88 Ⓐ Ⓑ Ⓒ Ⓓ Ⓔ
29 Ⓐ Ⓑ Ⓒ Ⓓ Ⓔ	59 Ⓐ Ⓑ Ⓒ Ⓓ Ⓔ	
30 Ⓐ Ⓑ Ⓒ Ⓓ Ⓔ	60 Ⓐ Ⓑ Ⓒ Ⓓ Ⓔ	

ANSWER SHEET

PART—A

1 Ⓐ Ⓓ	21 Ⓐ Ⓓ	46 Ⓐ Ⓓ	71 Ⓐ Ⓓ
2 Ⓐ Ⓓ	22 Ⓐ Ⓓ	47 Ⓐ Ⓓ	72 Ⓐ Ⓓ
3 Ⓐ Ⓓ	23 Ⓐ Ⓓ	48 Ⓐ Ⓓ	73 Ⓐ Ⓓ
4 Ⓐ Ⓓ	24 Ⓐ Ⓓ	49 Ⓐ Ⓓ	74 Ⓐ Ⓓ
5 Ⓐ Ⓓ	25 Ⓐ Ⓓ	50 Ⓐ Ⓓ	75 Ⓐ Ⓓ
6 Ⓐ Ⓓ	26 Ⓐ Ⓓ	51 Ⓐ Ⓓ	76 Ⓐ Ⓓ
7 Ⓐ Ⓓ	27 Ⓐ Ⓓ	52 Ⓐ Ⓓ	77 Ⓐ Ⓓ
8 Ⓐ Ⓓ	28 Ⓐ Ⓓ	53 Ⓐ Ⓓ	78 Ⓐ Ⓓ
9 Ⓐ Ⓓ	29 Ⓐ Ⓓ	54 Ⓐ Ⓓ	79 Ⓐ Ⓓ
10 Ⓐ Ⓓ	30 Ⓐ Ⓓ	55 Ⓐ Ⓓ	80 Ⓐ Ⓓ
11 Ⓐ Ⓓ	31 Ⓐ Ⓓ	56 Ⓐ Ⓓ	81 Ⓐ Ⓓ
12 Ⓐ Ⓓ	32 Ⓐ Ⓓ	57 Ⓐ Ⓓ	82 Ⓐ Ⓓ
13 Ⓐ Ⓓ	33 Ⓐ Ⓓ	58 Ⓐ Ⓓ	83 Ⓐ Ⓓ
14 Ⓐ Ⓓ	34 Ⓐ Ⓓ	59 Ⓐ Ⓓ	84 Ⓐ Ⓓ
15 Ⓐ Ⓓ	35 Ⓐ Ⓓ	60 Ⓐ Ⓓ	85 Ⓐ Ⓓ
16 Ⓐ Ⓓ	36 Ⓐ Ⓓ	61 Ⓐ Ⓓ	86 Ⓐ Ⓓ
17 Ⓐ Ⓓ	37 Ⓐ Ⓓ	62 Ⓐ Ⓓ	87 Ⓐ Ⓓ
18 Ⓐ Ⓓ	38 Ⓐ Ⓓ	63 Ⓐ Ⓓ	88 Ⓐ Ⓓ
19 Ⓐ Ⓓ	39 Ⓐ Ⓓ	64 Ⓐ Ⓓ	89 Ⓐ Ⓓ
20 Ⓐ Ⓓ	40 Ⓐ Ⓓ	65 Ⓐ Ⓓ	90 Ⓐ Ⓓ
	41 Ⓐ Ⓓ	66 Ⓐ Ⓓ	91 Ⓐ Ⓓ
	42 Ⓐ Ⓓ	67 Ⓐ Ⓓ	92 Ⓐ Ⓓ
	43 Ⓐ Ⓓ	68 Ⓐ Ⓓ	93 Ⓐ Ⓓ
	44 Ⓐ Ⓓ	69 Ⓐ Ⓓ	94 Ⓐ Ⓓ
	45 Ⓐ Ⓓ	70 Ⓐ Ⓓ	95 Ⓐ Ⓓ

ANSWER SHEET
PART--B

1 Ⓐ Ⓑ Ⓒ Ⓓ Ⓔ	31 Ⓐ Ⓑ Ⓒ Ⓓ Ⓔ	61 Ⓐ Ⓑ Ⓒ Ⓓ Ⓔ
2 Ⓐ Ⓑ Ⓒ Ⓓ Ⓔ	32 Ⓐ Ⓑ Ⓒ Ⓓ Ⓔ	62 Ⓐ Ⓑ Ⓒ Ⓓ Ⓔ
3 Ⓐ Ⓑ Ⓒ Ⓓ Ⓔ	33 Ⓐ Ⓑ Ⓒ Ⓓ Ⓔ	63 Ⓐ Ⓑ Ⓒ Ⓓ Ⓔ
4 Ⓐ Ⓑ Ⓒ Ⓓ Ⓔ	34 Ⓐ Ⓑ Ⓒ Ⓓ Ⓔ	64 Ⓐ Ⓑ Ⓒ Ⓓ Ⓔ
5 Ⓐ Ⓑ Ⓒ Ⓓ Ⓔ	35 Ⓐ Ⓑ Ⓒ Ⓓ Ⓔ	65 Ⓐ Ⓑ Ⓒ Ⓓ Ⓔ
6 Ⓐ Ⓑ Ⓒ Ⓓ Ⓔ	36 Ⓐ Ⓑ Ⓒ Ⓓ Ⓔ	66 Ⓐ Ⓑ Ⓒ Ⓓ Ⓔ
7 Ⓐ Ⓑ Ⓒ Ⓓ Ⓔ	37 Ⓐ Ⓑ Ⓒ Ⓓ Ⓔ	67 Ⓐ Ⓑ Ⓒ Ⓓ Ⓔ
8 Ⓐ Ⓑ Ⓒ Ⓓ Ⓔ	38 Ⓐ Ⓑ Ⓒ Ⓓ Ⓔ	68 Ⓐ Ⓑ Ⓒ Ⓓ Ⓔ
9 Ⓐ Ⓑ Ⓒ Ⓓ Ⓔ	39 Ⓐ Ⓑ Ⓒ Ⓓ Ⓔ	69 Ⓐ Ⓑ Ⓒ Ⓓ Ⓔ
10 Ⓐ Ⓑ Ⓒ Ⓓ Ⓔ	40 Ⓐ Ⓑ Ⓒ Ⓓ Ⓔ	70 Ⓐ Ⓑ Ⓒ Ⓓ Ⓔ
11 Ⓐ Ⓑ Ⓒ Ⓓ Ⓔ	41 Ⓐ Ⓑ Ⓒ Ⓓ Ⓔ	71 Ⓐ Ⓑ Ⓒ Ⓓ Ⓔ
12 Ⓐ Ⓑ Ⓒ Ⓓ Ⓔ	42 Ⓐ Ⓑ Ⓒ Ⓓ Ⓔ	72 Ⓐ Ⓑ Ⓒ Ⓓ Ⓔ
13 Ⓐ Ⓑ Ⓒ Ⓓ Ⓔ	43 Ⓐ Ⓑ Ⓒ Ⓓ Ⓔ	73 Ⓐ Ⓑ Ⓒ Ⓓ Ⓔ
14 Ⓐ Ⓑ Ⓒ Ⓓ Ⓔ	44 Ⓐ Ⓑ Ⓒ Ⓓ Ⓔ	74 Ⓐ Ⓑ Ⓒ Ⓓ Ⓔ
15 Ⓐ Ⓑ Ⓒ Ⓓ Ⓔ	45 Ⓐ Ⓑ Ⓒ Ⓓ Ⓔ	75 Ⓐ Ⓑ Ⓒ Ⓓ Ⓔ
16 Ⓐ Ⓑ Ⓒ Ⓓ Ⓔ	46 Ⓐ Ⓑ Ⓒ Ⓓ Ⓔ	76 Ⓐ Ⓑ Ⓒ Ⓓ Ⓔ
17 Ⓐ Ⓑ Ⓒ Ⓓ Ⓔ	47 Ⓐ Ⓑ Ⓒ Ⓓ Ⓔ	77 Ⓐ Ⓑ Ⓒ Ⓓ Ⓔ
18 Ⓐ Ⓑ Ⓒ Ⓓ Ⓔ	48 Ⓐ Ⓑ Ⓒ Ⓓ Ⓔ	78 Ⓐ Ⓑ Ⓒ Ⓓ Ⓔ
19 Ⓐ Ⓑ Ⓒ Ⓓ Ⓔ	49 Ⓐ Ⓑ Ⓒ Ⓓ Ⓔ	79 Ⓐ Ⓑ Ⓒ Ⓓ Ⓔ
20 Ⓐ Ⓑ Ⓒ Ⓓ Ⓔ	50 Ⓐ Ⓑ Ⓒ Ⓓ Ⓔ	80 Ⓐ Ⓑ Ⓒ Ⓓ Ⓔ
21 Ⓐ Ⓑ Ⓒ Ⓓ Ⓔ	51 Ⓐ Ⓑ Ⓒ Ⓓ Ⓔ	81 Ⓐ Ⓑ Ⓒ Ⓓ Ⓔ
22 Ⓐ Ⓑ Ⓒ Ⓓ Ⓔ	52 Ⓐ Ⓑ Ⓒ Ⓓ Ⓔ	82 Ⓐ Ⓑ Ⓒ Ⓓ Ⓔ
23 Ⓐ Ⓑ Ⓒ Ⓓ Ⓔ	53 Ⓐ Ⓑ Ⓒ Ⓓ Ⓔ	83 Ⓐ Ⓑ Ⓒ Ⓓ Ⓔ
24 Ⓐ Ⓑ Ⓒ Ⓓ Ⓔ	54 Ⓐ Ⓑ Ⓒ Ⓓ Ⓔ	84 Ⓐ Ⓑ Ⓒ Ⓓ Ⓔ
25 Ⓐ Ⓑ Ⓒ Ⓓ Ⓔ	55 Ⓐ Ⓑ Ⓒ Ⓓ Ⓔ	85 Ⓐ Ⓑ Ⓒ Ⓓ Ⓔ
26 Ⓐ Ⓑ Ⓒ Ⓓ Ⓔ	56 Ⓐ Ⓑ Ⓒ Ⓓ Ⓔ	86 Ⓐ Ⓑ Ⓒ Ⓓ Ⓔ
27 Ⓐ Ⓑ Ⓒ Ⓓ Ⓔ	57 Ⓐ Ⓑ Ⓒ Ⓓ Ⓔ	87 Ⓐ Ⓑ Ⓒ Ⓓ Ⓔ
28 Ⓐ Ⓑ Ⓒ Ⓓ Ⓔ	58 Ⓐ Ⓑ Ⓒ Ⓓ Ⓔ	88 Ⓐ Ⓑ Ⓒ Ⓓ Ⓔ
29 Ⓐ Ⓑ Ⓒ Ⓓ Ⓔ	59 Ⓐ Ⓑ Ⓒ Ⓓ Ⓔ	
30 Ⓐ Ⓑ Ⓒ Ⓓ Ⓔ	60 Ⓐ Ⓑ Ⓒ Ⓓ Ⓔ	

IMPORTANT NOTES REGARDING THE EXAMINATION FOR MAIL HANDLER:

You will find an examination announcement for this job on page KB-120

The examination is in three parts:

Address Checking: This is the same as that subject in the Clerk-Carrier
    examination so you will find additional practice on pages KB-36 to KB-42
    and KB-64 and 65.

Meaning of Words: You will find added practice for this on pages KB 95
    through KB-106.

Following Oral Directions: The added practice for this is at the end of
    the book to facilitate more easy removal of the pages that whould be
    held and read by another person -- pages KB-133 through Kb-146.

Position Title	Level	Position No.	Occ Code	Craft
Time & Attendance Clerk	5	SP 1–29	0590–01xx	C,M,&MV
Tire Repairman	5	SP 5–53	4504–01xx	MV
Tool & Die Maker	9	SP 7–47	3416–01xx	
Tool & Parts Clerk	5	SP 1–31	6904–01xx	M&MV
Tractor Trailer Operator	6	SP 5–22	5756–01xx	MV
Training Technician (PEDC)	6	SP 2–621	1712–34xx	C
Transfer Clerk	6	KP–15	2330–01xx	C
Transfer Clerk, AMF	6	SP 2–217	2330–04xx	C
Translator-Correspondence	7	SP 2–620	1045–02xx	C
Typist	4	KP–7	0322–01xx	C
Typist—Label Printing	4	SP 2–580	0322–04xx	MH
Vehicle Dispatcher	6	SP 5–11	2151–01xx	MV
Vehicle Dispatcher	7	SP 5–12	2151–01xx	MV
Vehicle Maintenance Analyst	7	SP 5–56	1601–08xx	MV
Vehicle Operations Assistant	6	SP 5–1	2150–08xx	MV
Vehicle Operations Assistant— Bulk Mails	6	SP 5–66	2150–03xx	MV
Vehicle Operations Maintenance Assistant	6	SP 2–195	0341–06xx	C,SD,MV &CA
Vending Machines Mechanic	6	SP 6–68	4801–04xx	M
Warehouseman	4	SP 7–28	6907–01xx	
Warehouse Tractor Operator	4	SP 7–63	3502–13xx	
Watchman (Mail Handling Areas)	4	SP 2–216	0085–06xx	MH
Window Cleaner	4	SP 6–9	3540–01xx	M
Window Clerk	5	KP–13	2320–01xx	C
Window Services Technician	6	SP 2–388	2320–29xx	C
WLRS Control Clerk	5	SP 2–565	0301–94xx	C

UNITED STATES POSTAL SERVICE

STUDY CAREFULLY BEFORE YOU GO TO THE EXAMINATION ROOM

SAMPLE QUESTIONS

The following samples show the types of questions you will see in the written tests. They also show how the questions are to be answered. Read the directions. Then answer the sample questions. Mark your answers on the Sample Answer Sheet. Then compare your answers with those given in the Correct Answers to Sample Questions.

In the *Address Checking* test, you will have to decide whether two addresses are alike or different. If the two addresses are exactly *Alike* in every way, darken space A for the question. If the two addresses are *Different* in any way, darken space D for the question. Questions 1 to 5 are samples of this test.

Mark your answers to these sample questions on the Sample Answer Sheet on this page.

1.	Acme La	Acme La
	Since the two addresses are exactly alike, mark A for question 1 on the Sample Answer Sheet.	
2.	Orleans Mass	Orleans Mich
3.	Saxe Va	Saxis Va
4.	Chappaqua NY 10514	Chappaqua NY 10514
5.	Los Angeles Calif 90013	Los Angeles Calif 90018

The *Meaning of Words* test asks you what a word or phrase means. In each question a word or phrase is in italics. Five other words or phrases—lettered A, B, C, D, and E--are given as possible meanings. Only one is *right*. You are to pick out the one that is right. Then on the answer sheet, find the answer space numbered the same as the question, and darken the space with the letter of the right answer. Questions 6 and 7 are samples of this test.

Mark your answers to questions 6 and 7 on the Sample Answer Sheet on this page.

6. The letter was *short*. *Short* means most nearly
   A) tall
   B) wide
   C) brief
   D) heavy
   E) dark

For this question, you should darken space C because *brief* is the suggested answer that means most nearly the same as *short*, the word in italics.

7. A small crane was used to *raise* the heavy part. *Raise* means most nearly
   A) lift
   B) drag
   C) drop
   D) deliver
   E) guide

Sample Answer Sheet	
1 Ⓐ Ⓓ	5 Ⓐ Ⓓ
2 Ⓐ Ⓓ	6 Ⓐ Ⓑ Ⓒ Ⓓ Ⓔ
3 Ⓐ Ⓓ	7 Ⓐ Ⓑ Ⓒ Ⓓ Ⓔ
4 Ⓐ Ⓓ	

Correct Answers	
1 ● Ⓓ	5 Ⓐ ●
2 Ⓐ ●	6 Ⓐ Ⓑ ● Ⓓ Ⓔ
3 Ⓐ ●	7 ● Ⓑ Ⓒ Ⓓ Ⓔ
4 ● Ⓓ	

In the test of *Following Oral Directions*, you will be told to follow directions by writing in a test booklet and then on an answer sheet. The test booklet will have lines of material like the following five samples:

SAMPLE 8.   5 _____

SAMPLE 9.   1   6   4   3   7

SAMPLE 10.   D   B   A   E   C

SAMPLE 11.   (8__) (5__) (2__) (9__) (10__)

SAMPLE 12.   (7__) [6__] (1__) [12__]

To practice this test, tear off page 3.
Then have somebody read the instructions to you and you follow the instructions.
When he tells you to darken the space on the Sample Answer Sheet, use the one on this page.

EDITOR'S NOTE: You might prefer not to tear out the coming page but use the more extensive practice on this subject at the end of the book on pages KB-133 through KB-146.

Sample Answer Sheet

1 Ⓐ Ⓑ Ⓒ Ⓓ Ⓔ   7 Ⓐ Ⓑ Ⓒ Ⓓ Ⓔ

2 Ⓐ Ⓑ Ⓒ Ⓓ Ⓔ   8 Ⓐ Ⓑ Ⓒ Ⓓ Ⓔ

3 Ⓐ Ⓑ Ⓒ Ⓓ Ⓔ   9 Ⓐ Ⓑ Ⓒ Ⓓ Ⓔ

4 Ⓐ Ⓑ Ⓒ Ⓓ Ⓔ   10 Ⓐ Ⓑ Ⓒ Ⓓ Ⓔ

5 Ⓐ Ⓑ Ⓒ Ⓓ Ⓔ   11 Ⓐ Ⓑ Ⓒ Ⓓ Ⓔ

6 Ⓐ Ⓑ Ⓒ Ⓓ Ⓔ   12 Ⓐ Ⓑ Ⓒ Ⓓ Ⓔ

Instructions to be read (the words in parentheses should not be read aloud)

You are to follow the instructions that I shall read to you. I cannot repeat them.

Look at the samples. Sample 8 has a number and a line beside it. On the line write an A. (Pause 2 seconds.) Now on the Sample Answer Sheet, find number 5 (pause 2 seconds) and darken the sapce for the letter you just wrote on the line. (Pause 2 seconds.)

Look at Sample 9. (Pause slightly.) Draw a line under the third number. (Pause 2 seconds.) Now look on the Sample Answer Sheet, find the number under which you just drew a line and darken space B as in baker for that number. (Pause 5 seconds.)

Look at the letters in Sample 10. (Pause slightly.) Draw a line under the third letter in the line. (Pause 2 seconds.) Now on your answer sheet, find number 9 (pause 2 seconds) and darken the space for the letter under which you drew a line. (Pause 5 seconds.)

Look at the five circles in Sample 11. (Pause slightly.) Each circle has a number and a line in it. Write D as in dog on the blank in the last circle. (Pause 2 seconds.) Now on the Sample Answer Sheet, darken the space for the number-letter combination that is in the circle you just wrote in (Pause 5 seconds.)

Look at Sample 12. (Pause slightly.) There are two circles and two boxes of different sizes with numbers in them. (Pause slightly.) If 4 is more than 2 and if 5 is less than 3, write A in the smaller circle. (Pause slightly.) Otherwise write C in the larger box. (Pause 2 seconds.) Now on the Sample Answer Sheet, darken the space for the number-letter combination in the box or circle in which you just wrote. (Pause 5 seconds.)

Now look at the Sample Answer Sheet. (Pause slightly.) You should have darkened spaces 4B, 5A, 9A, 10D, and 12C on the Sample Answer Sheet. (If the person preparing to take the examination made any mistakes, try to help him see why he made wrong marks.)

IMPORTANT NOTES REGARDING THIS EXAMINATION:

̇You will find an announcement sheet fot his job on page KB-121.

The examination is in four parts:

Number Series: You will find added practice on number series on
   pages KB-108 through ̇KB-11̇4.

Address Coding: This is the same as the Address Coding in the Clerk-
   Carrier examination, so you will find added practice on pages
   KB-45 through KB-54 and KB-66 through KB-70. (Address Code
   Memory is a continuation of the same test to be worked without
   looking at the key boxes.)

Address Checking: This is the same as that subject in the Clerk-Carrier
   examination so you will find added material on pages KB-36 to KB-42
   and KB-64 and 65.

EXAMINATION FOR DISTRIBUTION CLERK, MACHINE

SQ-400
rev.

U.S. POSTAL SERVICE
SAMPLE QUESTIONS
EXAMINATION 400

The following sample questions show the types of questions that will be used in the test. They also show the method of answering the questions.

PART A

NUMBER SERIES

For each Number Series question there is at the left a series of numbers which follow some definite order and at the right five sets of two numbers each. You are to look at the numbers in the series at the left and find out what order they follow. Then decide what the next two numbers in that series would be if the same order were continued. Mark your answers on the Sample Answer Sheet.

1. 1 2 3 4 5 6 7 . . A) 1 2 B) 5 6 C) 8 9 D) 4 5 E) 7 8

The numbers in this series are increasing by 1. If the series were continued for two more numbers, it would read: 1 2 3 4 5 6 7 8 9. Therefore the correct answer is 8 and 9, and you should have darkened C for question 1.

2. 15 14 13 12 11 10 9 . . . A) 2 1 B) 17 16 C) 8 9 D) 8 7 E) 9 8

The numbers in this series are decreasing by 1. If the series were continued for two more numbers, it would read: 15 14 13 12 11 10 9 8 7 Therefore the correct answer is 8 and 7 and you should have darkened D for question 2.

3. 20 20 21 21 22 22 23 . . . A) 23 23 B) 23 24 C) 19 19 D) 22 23 E) 21 22

Each number in this series is repeated and then increased by 1. If the series were continued for two more numbers it would read: 20 20 21 21 22 22 23 23 24. Therefore the correct answer is 23 and 24, and you should have darkened B for question 3.

4. 17 3 17 4 17 5 17 . . . A) 6 17 B) 6 7 C) 17 6 D) 5 6 E) 17 7

This series is the number 17 separated by numbers increasing by 1, beginning with the number 3. If the series were continued for two more numbers, it would read: 17 3 17 4 17 5 17 6 17. Therefore the correct answer is 6 and 17, and you should have darkened A for question 4.

5. 1 2 4 5 7 8 10 . . . .A) 11 12 B) 12 14 C) 10 13 D) 12 13 E) 11 13

The numbers in this series are increasing first by 1 (plus 1) and then by 2 (plus 2). If the series were continued for two more numbers, it would read: 1 2 4 5 7 8 10 (plus 1) 11 (plus 2) 13. Therefore the correct answer is 11 and 13, and you should have darkened E for question 5.

Now read and work sample questions 6 through 10 and mark your answers on the Sample Answer Sheet.

6. 21 21 20 20 19 19 18 . . . . . .A) 18 18   B) 18 17   C) 17 18   D) 17 17   E) 18 19

7. 1 22 1 23 1 24 1 . . . . . . .A) 26 1   B) 25 26   C) 25 1   D) 1 26   E) 1 25

8. 1 20 3 19 5 18 7 . . . . . .A) 8 9   B) 8 17   C) 17 10   D) 17 9   E) 9 18

9. 4 7 10 13 16 19 22 . . . . . .A) 23 26   B) 25 27   C) 25 26   D) 25 28   E) 24 27

10. 30 2 28 4 26 6 24 . . . . . . .A) 23 9   B) 26 8   C) 8 9   D) 26 22   E) 8 22

```
                    Sample Answer Sheet

            1 Ⓐ Ⓑ Ⓒ Ⓓ Ⓔ       6 Ⓐ Ⓑ Ⓒ Ⓓ Ⓔ

            2 Ⓐ Ⓑ Ⓒ Ⓓ Ⓔ       7 Ⓐ Ⓑ Ⓒ Ⓓ Ⓔ

            3 Ⓐ Ⓑ Ⓒ Ⓓ Ⓔ       8 Ⓐ Ⓑ Ⓒ Ⓓ Ⓔ

            4 Ⓐ Ⓑ Ⓒ Ⓓ Ⓔ       9 Ⓐ Ⓑ Ⓒ Ⓓ Ⓔ

            5 Ⓐ Ⓑ Ⓒ Ⓓ Ⓔ      10 Ⓐ Ⓑ Ⓒ Ⓓ Ⓔ
```

The correct answers to sample questions 6 to 10 are: 6B, 7C, 8D, 9D, and 10E.

PART B

ADDRESS CODING

    In this test, you will find five boxes labeled A, B, C, D, and E. Each box
contains five addresses. For each of the addresses in the list, you are to
decide in which lettered box (A, B, C, D, or E) it belongs and then mark that
letter on the answer sheet.

A	B	C
4700-5599 Table Lismore 4800-5199 West Hesper 5500-6399 Blake	6800-6999 Table Kelford 5200-5799 West Musella 4800-5499 Blake	5600-6499 Table Joel 3200-3499 West Sardis 6400-7299 Blake

D	E
6500-6799 Table Tatum 3500-4299 West Porter 4300-4799 Blake	4400-4699 Table Ruskin 4300-4799 West Somers 7300-7499 Blake

For Part B of the test, the boxes will be shown on the same page with the addresses, but for Part C, you will not have the boxes to look at. Therefore, it is important that you memorize each of the addresses in a box, and the letter for that box. You will have 5 minutes to memorize the locations of the addresses.

Now complete the questions for Part B. Mark your answers for each question by darkening the space as was done for questions 1 and 2.

1. Musella	5. 5500-6399 Blake	9. 6400-7299 Blake	13. Porter
2. 4300-4799 Blake	6. Hesper	10. Joel	14. 7300-7499 Blake
3. 4700-5599 Table	7. Kelford	11. 5500-6399 Blake	
4. Tatum	8. Somers	12. 5200-5799 West	

SAMPLE ANSWER SHEET

1 Ⓐ ● Ⓒ Ⓓ Ⓔ   8 Ⓐ Ⓑ Ⓒ Ⓓ Ⓔ

2 Ⓐ Ⓑ Ⓒ ● Ⓔ   9 Ⓐ Ⓑ Ⓒ Ⓓ Ⓔ

3 Ⓐ Ⓑ Ⓒ Ⓓ Ⓔ   10 Ⓐ Ⓑ Ⓒ Ⓓ Ⓔ

4 Ⓐ Ⓑ Ⓒ Ⓓ Ⓔ   11 Ⓐ Ⓑ Ⓒ Ⓓ Ⓔ

5 Ⓐ Ⓑ Ⓒ Ⓓ Ⓔ   12 Ⓐ Ⓑ Ⓒ Ⓓ Ⓔ

6 Ⓐ Ⓑ Ⓒ Ⓓ Ⓔ   13 Ⓐ Ⓑ Ⓒ Ⓓ Ⓔ

7 Ⓐ Ⓑ Ⓒ Ⓓ Ⓔ   14 Ⓐ Ⓑ Ⓒ Ⓓ Ⓔ

The correct answers for questions 3 to 14 are: 3A, 4D, 5A, 6A, 7B, 8E, 9C, 10C, 11A, 12B, 13D, and 14E.

PART C

ADDRESS CODE MEMORY

In this test you will be performing the same task as in the test of ADDRESS CODING; however, you will not be allowed to refer to the address boxes. You must identify an address and recall the correct code from memory. Select the appropriate code for each of the addresses on the next page. DO NOT REFER TO THE ADDRESS BOXES ON THE PREVIOUS PAGE. Mark your answers for each question by darkening the space as you did for the previous question.

1. 4800-5199 West
2. Ruskin
3. 6800-6999 Table
4. 4800-5499 Blake
5. Tatum

6. 3200-3499 West
7. Lismore
8. Musella
9. Sardis
10. Joel

11. 7300-7499 Blake
12. 3500-4299 West
13. Hesper
14. Kelford

SAMPLE ANSWER SHEET

1 Ⓐ Ⓑ Ⓒ Ⓓ Ⓔ   8 Ⓐ Ⓑ Ⓒ Ⓓ Ⓔ

2 Ⓐ Ⓑ Ⓒ Ⓓ Ⓔ   9 Ⓐ Ⓑ Ⓒ Ⓓ Ⓔ

3 Ⓐ Ⓑ Ⓒ Ⓓ Ⓔ   10 Ⓐ Ⓑ Ⓒ Ⓓ Ⓔ

4 Ⓐ Ⓑ Ⓒ Ⓓ Ⓔ   11 Ⓐ Ⓑ Ⓒ Ⓓ Ⓔ

5 Ⓐ Ⓑ Ⓒ Ⓓ Ⓔ   12 Ⓐ Ⓑ Ⓒ Ⓓ Ⓔ

6 Ⓐ Ⓑ Ⓒ Ⓓ Ⓔ   13 Ⓐ Ⓑ Ⓒ Ⓓ Ⓔ

7 Ⓐ Ⓑ Ⓒ Ⓓ Ⓔ   14 Ⓐ Ⓑ Ⓒ Ⓓ Ⓔ

The correct answers for questions 1 to 14 are: 1A, 2E, 3B, 4B, 5D, 6C, 7A, 8B, 9C, 10C, 11E, 12D, 13A, 14B.

PART D

ADDRESS CHECKING TEST

In this test you will have to decide whether two addresses are alike or different. If the two addresses are exactly Alike in every way, darken space A for the question. If the two addresses are Different in any way, darken space D for the question.

Mark your answers to these sample questions on the Sample Answer Sheet on right.

1. . 213 S 20th St   213 S 20th St
    Since the two addresses are exactly alike, mark A for question 1 on the
Sample Answer Sheet!
2. . 4608 N Warnock St   4806 N Warnock St   **Sample Answer Sheet**
3. . 1202 W Girard Dr   1202 W Girard Rd
4. . Chappaqua NY 10514   Chappaqua NY 10514   1 Ⓐ Ⓓ
5. . 2207 Markland Ave   2207 Markham Ave
                                                          2 Ⓐ Ⓓ
    The answers to samples 2 to 5 are: 2D, 3D, 4A, and 5D
                                                          3 Ⓐ Ⓓ

                                                          4 Ⓐ Ⓓ

                                                          5 Ⓐ Ⓓ

DESCRIPTION OF THE TEST AND SAMPLE QUESTIONS

In this kind of question you have to say what a word or phrase means. (A phrase is a group of words.) This word or phrase is in *italics* in a sentence. You are also given for each question five other words or groups of words—lettered A, B, C, D, and E—as possible answers. One of these words or groups of words means the same as the word or group of words in italics. Only one is right. You are to pick out the one that is right and darken the box that has the letter of your answer.

Hints for Answering Word-Meaning Questions

- Read each question carefully.
- Choose the best answer of the five choices even though it is not the word you might use yourself
- Answer first those that you know. Then do the others.
- If you know that some of the suggested answers are not right, pay no more attention to them.
- Be sure that you have marked an answer for every question, even if you have to guess.

Now study the sample questions and explanations before going on to the Practice Tests.

Word Meaning—Sample Questions

Now try a few.

The letter was *short*. *Short* means most nearly

A) tall
B) wide
C) brief
D) heavy
E) dark

Short is a word you have used to describe something that is small, or not long, or little, etc. Therefore you would not have to spend much time figuring out the right answer. You would choose c) brief

Try another.

The young man is *vigorous*. *Vigorous* means most nearly

A) serious
B) reliable
C) courageous
D) strong
E) talented

Vigorous is a word that you have probably used yourself or read somewhere. It carries with it the idea of being active, full of pep, etc. Which one of the five choices comes closest to meaning that? Certainly not A) serious, B) reliable or E) talented; c) courageous—maybe, D) strong—maybe. But between courageous or strong, you would have to agree that strong is the better choice. Therefore you would choose D.

Now that you know what to do, try these. These words are like those in the Mail Handler examination.

For each question, darken the box for the correct answer. Mark your answers on the answer sheet on the next page.

Answer first those questions for which you know the answers. Then work on the other questions. If you can't figure out the answer, guess.

Do not spend more than *30 minutes* on this practice test.

1. *Simple* clothing should be worn to work. *Simple* means most nearly
   A) plain   D) comfortable
   B) inexpensive   E) old
   C) nice

2. Take your *finished* work to that area of the work floor. *Finished* means most nearly
   A) inspected   D) completed
   B) assigned   E) rejected
   C) outgoing

3. If we are not careful, the problem will *develop* further. *Develop* means most nearly
   A) continue   D) grow
   B) appear   E) be concerned
   C) be used

4. The mail handler was a *rapid* worker. *Rapid* means most nearly
   A) trained   D) regular
   B) rash   E) strong
   C) fast

5. The supply of envelopes is *abundant* for our use. *Abundant* means most nearly
   A) accessible   D) divided
   B) plentiful   E) scattered
   C) concentrated

6. The department is working on *experiments* in that area. *Experiments* means most nearly
   A) tests   D) plans
   B) refinements   E) patents
   C) statements

7. The members were concerned about two *fundamental* points. *Fundamental* means most nearly
   A) difficult   D) essential
   B) serious   E) final
   C) emphasized

8. The leader *asserted* that it was time to start. *Asserted* means most nearly
   A) believed   D) agreed
   B) decided   E) contradicted
   C) declared

9. All requests for supplies should be stated *exactly*. *Exactly* means most nearly
   A) briefly   D) emphatically
   B) clearly   E) accurately
   C) promptly

10. We had not meant to *alarm* them. *Alarm* means most nearly
    A) endanger   D) frighten
    B) insult   E) confuse
    C) accuse

11. The kind of car he bought was *costly*. *Costly* means most nearly
    A) custom made   D) cheap
    B) expensive   E) scarce
    C) desirable

12. The cause of the action was *revealed* before the meeting. *Revealed* means most nearly
    A) made known
    B) fully described
    C) carefully hidden
    D) guessed at
    E) seriously questioned

13. The material used to make mail sacks is *durable*. *Durable* means most nearly
    A) thick   D) elastic
    B) waterproof   E) light
    C) lasting

14. The *valiant* men and women were rewarded. *Valiant* means most nearly
    A) brave   D) loyal
    B) popular   E) famous
    C) victorious

15. The worker was affected by his *fatigue*. *Fatigue* means most nearly
    A) problem   D) sickness
    B) weariness   E) worry
    C) relaxation

16. The meeting was interrupted by an *urgent* call. *Urgent* means most nearly
    A) trivial   D) surprising
    B) annoying   E) casual
    C) pressing

17. The captain of the team will *participate in* the ceremony. *Participate in* means most nearly
A) depend upon
B) be recognized at
c) be invited to
D) supervise
E) share in

18. Each office was asked to *restrict* the number of forms it used. *Restrict* means most nearly
A) watch
B) record
c) limit
D) replace
E) provide

19. The pole was *rigid*. *Rigid* means most nearly
A) broken
B) pointed
c) bent
D) rough
E) stiff

20. The supervisor *demonstrated* the sorting procedure. *Demonstrated* means most nearly
A) changed
B) controlled
c) determined
D) showed
E) described

21. The effort was *futile*. *Futile* means most nearly
A) wasteful
B) useless
c) foolish
D) undesirable
E) unfortunate

22. There was a pile of *sundry* item on the table. *Sundry* means most nearly
A) miscellaneous
B) valuable
c) unusual
D) necessary
E) specific

23. The supervisor should not be *partial*. *Partial* means most nearly
A) biased
B) greedy
c) irresponsible
D) jealous
E) suspicious

24. The retired postal worker led an *inactive* life. *Inactive* means most nearly
A) restful
B) idle
c) peaceful
D) ordinary
E) weary

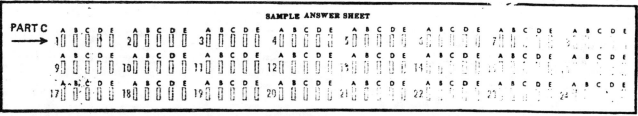

Now check your answers by comparing them with the correct answers shown below.

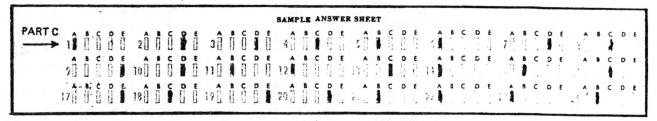

Count how many you got right, and write that number on this line
(This is your Test Score.)

Meaning of Test Score

If your Test Score is *18 or over*, you have a Good score.

If your Test Score is from *15 to 17*, you have a Fair score.

If your Test Score is *14 or less*, you are not doing too well.

This practice test is a little harder.

For each question, darken the box for the correct answer. Mark your answers on the answer sheet on the next page.

Answer first those questions for which you know the answers. Then work on the other questions. If you can't figure out the answer, guess.

Do not spend more than *30 minutes* on this practice test.

1. The officials *prevented* the action. *Prevented* means most nearly
   A) allowed
   B) urged
   C) hindered
   D) considered
   E) suggested

2. The postmaster's office expected to *report* the results next week. *Report* means most nearly
   A) decide
   B) tell
   C) approve
   D) study
   E) repeat

3. The conference room is now *vacant*. *Vacant* means most nearly
   A) empty
   B) quiet
   C) dark
   D) available
   E) lonely

4. Tapping on the desk can be an *irritating* habit. *Irritating* means most nearly
   A) nervous
   B) annoying
   C) noisy
   D) startling
   E) unsuitable

5. The package was *forwarded* by our office. *Forwarded* means most nearly
   A) returned
   B) canceled
   C) received
   D) detained
   E) sent

6. The postal service is *essential* in this country. *Essential* means most nearly
   A) inevitable
   B) needless
   C) economical
   D) indispensable
   E) established

7. The wheel turned at a *uniform* rate. *Uniform* means most nearly
   A) increasing
   B) unusual
   C) normal
   D) slow
   E) unchanging

8. Each carrier realized his *obligation*. *Obligation* means most nearly
   A) importance
   B) need
   C) duty
   D) kindness
   E) honor

9. The group was interested in the *origin* of the rumor. *Origin* means most nearly
   A) direction
   B) growth
   C) existence
   D) beginning
   E) end

10. Laws governing the *parole* of prisoners should be more flexible. *Parole* means most nearly
    A) conditional release
    B) withdrawal of privileges
    C) good behavior
    D) outside employment
    E) solitary confinement

11. That employee is *retiring* by nature. *Retiring* means most nearly
    A) complaining
    B) gruff
    C) neglected
    D) modest
    E) sluggish

12. The patron *verified* the contents of the package. *Verified* means most nearly
    A) justified
    B) explained
    C) confirmed
    D) guaranteed
    E) examined

13. The group was *repulsed* immediately. *Repulsed* means most nearly
    A) rebuffed
    B) excused
    C) mistreated
    D) loathed
    E) resented

14. The time was right for the committee to make a *decisive* statement. *Decisive* means most nearly
    A) official
    B) prompt
    C) judicial
    D) rational
    E) conclusive

15. Each person expects *compensation* for his work. *Compensation* means most nearly
    A) fulfillment
    B) remuneration
    C) appreciation
    D) approval
    E) recommendation

16. The department plans to increase the number of *novices* in the program. *Novices* means most nearly
    A) volunteers
    B) experts
    C) trainers
    D) beginners
    E) amateurs

17. The guests were overwhelmed by the *fabulous* decorations. *Fabulous* means most nearly
A) antiquated   D) immoderate
B) enormous   E) intricate
C) incredible

18. The duties of the job are mentioned *explicitly* in the handbook. *Explicitly* means most nearly
A) casually   D) exclusively
B) informally   E) specifically
C) intelligibly

19. The school is supplying opportunities for *recreation*. *Recreation* means most nearly
A) diversion   D) learning
B) eating   E) recess
C) resting

20. It was necessary to *recapitulate* the regulation. *Recapitulate* means most nearly
A) emphasize   D) interpret
B) withdraw   E) summarize
C) reinstate

21. The villagers *succumbed to* the enemy forces. *Succumbed to* means most nearly
A) aided   D) were checked by
B) opposed   E) discouraged
C) yielded to

22. The shipments have been *accelerated*. *Accelerated* means most nearly
A) anxiously awaited
B) caused to move faster
C) delayed by traffic congestion
D) given careful handling
E) routed over shorter lines

23. He was not a good employee, because he was *indolent*. *Indolent* means most nearly
A) stupid   D) lazy
B) indifferent   E) incompetent
C) selfish

24. He had been cautioned not to be *vindictive*. *Vindictive* means most nearly
A) boastful   D) revengeful
B) impolite   E) aggressive
C) impulsive

SAMPLE ANSWER SHEET

Now check your answers by comparing them with the correct answers shown below.

CORRECT ANSWERS

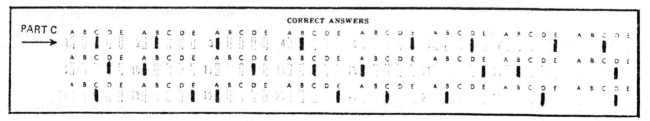

Count how many you got right, and write that number on this line ⟶ _____

(This is your Test Score. The meaning of your Test Score will be found on page KB-97

Here is another practice test.

For each question, darken the box for the correct answer. Mark your answers on the answer sheet on the next page.

Answer first those questions for which you know the answers. Then work on the other questions. If you can't figure out the answer, guess.

Do not spend more than *30 minutes* on this practice test.

1. The *power* of that organization cannot be ignored any longer. *Power* means most nearly
   A) size
   B) courage
   C) success
   D) force
   E) ambition

2. The employees reached the *shore* several days later. *Shore* means most nearly
   A) ocean
   B) reef
   C) island
   D) water
   E) coast

3. The *instructor* was enthusiastic. *Instructor* means most nearly
   A) expert
   B) foreman
   C) teacher
   D) beginner
   E) assistant

4. A *responsible* employee is an asset to any business. *Responsible* means most nearly
   A) considerate
   B) trustworthy
   C) smart
   D) experienced
   E) resourceful

5. He was a good clerk because he was *alert*. *Alert* means most nearly
   A) watchful
   B) busy
   C) honest
   D) helpful
   E) faithful

6. The machine was *revolving* rapidly. *Revolving* means most nearly
   A) working
   B) inclining
   C) vibrating
   D) turning
   E) producing

7. The canceling machine did not *function* yesterday. *Function* means most nearly
   A) finish
   B) stop
   C) overheat
   D) vibrate
   E) operate

8. The supervisor did not *comprehend* the clerk's excuse. *Comprehend* means most nearly
   A) hear
   B) understand
   C) suspect
   D) consider
   E) accept

9. His conduct was *becoming*. *Becoming* means most nearly
   A) improved
   B) heroic
   C) deliberate
   D) suitable
   E) patient

10. The men were not aware of the *hazard*. *Hazard* means most nearly
    A) peril
    B) choice
    C) decision
    D) contest
    E) damage

11. A *flexible* policy was developed to handle the situation. *Flexible* means most nearly
    A) pliable
    B) weak
    C) rigid
    D) uniform
    E) active

12. The clerk suggested an *innovation*. *Innovation* means most nearly
    A) conventional practice
    B) improvement
    C) inadequate change
    D) new method
    E) preliminary trial

13. Many parents *indulge* their children too much. *Indulge* means most nearly
    A) admire
    B) humor
    C) flatter
    D) coax
    E) discipline

14. The men were *commended* for their actions during the emergency. *Commended* means most nearly
    A) blamed
    B) reprimanded
    C) promoted
    D) encouraged
    E) praised

5. Two men were *designated* by the postmaster. *Designated* means most nearly
A) dismissed
D) named
B) assisted
E) rebuked
C) instructed

16. The package will be *conveyed* by the employees. *Conveyed* means most nearly
A) carried
D) refused
B) wrapped
E) guarded
C) exchanged

17. It seems *feasible* to start the physical fitness training now. *Feasible* means most nearly
A) praiseworthy
D) beneficial
B) justifiable
E) profitable
C) practicable

18. He was a *notorious* rebel. *Notorious* means most nearly
A) condemned
D) pretentious
B) unpleasant
E) well-known
C) vexatious

19. The main speaker appeared to be a *pompous* person. *Pompous* means most nearly
A) narrow-minded
D) self-important
B) insincere
E) rude
C) talkative

20. The office was surprised that he had *disregarded* his duty. *Disregarded* means most nearly
A) contemplated
D) resisted
B) discerned
E) renounced
C) neglected

21. The collector described the *blemish* on the new stamp. *Blemish* means most nearly
A) color
D) imprint
B) flaw
E) figure
C) design

22. The *ardor* of the patriot was contagious. *Ardor* means most nearly
A) anger
D) happiness
B) desire
E) daring
C) zeal

23. All the employees *vied* for that award. *Vied* means most nearly
A) contended
D) persevered
B) cooperated
E) prepared
C) petitioned

24. Immediately after hearing the bad news, the group was in a state of *ferment*. *Ferment* means most nearly
A) lawlessness
D) reorganization
B) indecision
E) agitation
C) disintegration

SAMPLE ANSWER SHEET

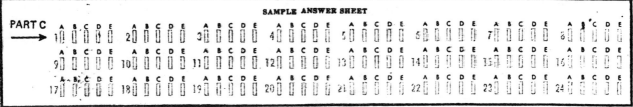

Now check your answers by comparing them with the correct answers shown below.

SAMPLE ANSWER SHEET

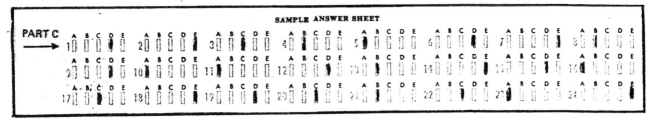

Count how many you got right, and write that number on this line———→ _____
(This is your Test Score. The meaning of your Test Score will be found on page KB-97

HINTS FOR IMPROVING YOUR VOCABULARY

Vocabulary tests are really just tests of your knowledge of the meaning of words.

Would you like to increase your vocabulary so that you will do better on this kind of test?

Here are some things that you can do:

1. Some newspapers and magazines print quizzes, or little tests, on the meaning of words. Try these quizzes when you see them. Write down the words that you miss and try to learn what they mean.

2. Read newspapers and magazines and write down all the words that you don't know. Then look them up in a dictionary. The library has dictionaries.

3. Anytime you look up a word, write a sentence using it or try to use it when you talk.

4. Borrow a book to help build up your vocabulary from your library. Then do what the book tells you to do.

To increase your knowledge of words, remember to—

1. Read more.

2. Look up words you aren't sure of.

3. Use new words often so that they will become a part of your vocabulary.

Editor's Note: You might also look up "An Easy Guide to Grammar and Vocabulary" in this Ken-Book Series.

In each question in Part C you are asked what a word or phrase means. In each question a word or phrase is in italics. Five other words or phrases—lettered A, B, C, D, and E—are given as possible meanings of the word or phrase in italics. Only one is *right*. You are to pick out the one that is right. Then on the answer sheet, find the answer space numbered the same as the question, and darken the box under the letter of the right answer.

Here are some sample questions for you to do. Mark your answers to them on the Sample Answer Sheet on this page. Do not spend more than *3 minutes* on reading and studying this page.

1. The letter was *short*. *Short* means most nearly
   A) tall
   B) wide
   C) brief
   D) heavy
   E) dark

In this question the word *short* is in italics. So you are to decide which one of the suggested answers means most nearly the same as *short*. "Brief" means most nearly the same as *short*; so you should have darkened box C for question 1.

2. A crane was used to *raise* the heavy part. *Raise* means most nearly
   A) lift
   B) drag
   C) drop
   D) deliver
   E) guide

Darken the box for your answer. Then compare the answers you have marked with those given in the Correct Answers to Sample Questions.

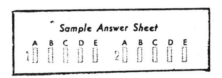

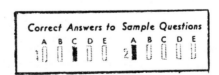

Try to answer every question in this part. Answer first the questions that are easiest for you. Then do the others. If you are not sure of an answer, guess.

You will have *25 minutes* to answer the 32 questions in this part. If you finish before the time is up, go back and check your answers for Part C.

You are to mark your answers to these questions in Part C of your answer sheet.

DO NOT TURN THIS PAGE UNTIL YOU ARE READY TO BEGIN PART C.

PART C

In each question in this part, choose the one of the five suggested answers that means most nearly the same as the word in italics.

Be sure to mark your answers for this part in Part C of the answer sheet.

1. He was asked to *speak* at the meeting. *Speak* means most nearly
   - A) vote
   - B) explain
   - c) talk
   - D) shout
   - E) decide

2. They *discovered* the missing boxes in the morning. *Discovered* means most nearly
   - A) sought
   - B) found
   - c) opened
   - D) noticed
   - E) inspected

3. The number of letters mailed by this office is *double* what it was last year. *Double* means most nearly
   - A) twice
   - B) different from
   - c) more than
   - D) almost
   - E) the same as

4. The post office had to *purchase* the new equipment. *Purchase* means most nearly
   - A) charge
   - B) construct
   - c) supply
   - D) buy
   - E) order

5. The shell was *hollow*. *Hollow* means most nearly
   - A) smooth
   - B) hard
   - c) soft
   - D) rough
   - E) empty

6. The packages were kept in a *secure* place. *Secure* means most nearly
   - A) distant
   - B) safe
   - c) convenient
   - D) secret
   - E) bad

7. It was *customary* for him to be at work on time. *Customary* means most nearly
   - A) curious
   - B) necessary
   - c) difficult
   - D) common
   - E) important

8. An attempt was made to *unite* the groups. *Unite* means most nearly
   - A) improve
   - B) serve
   - c) uphold
   - D) advise
   - E) combine

9. The leader *defended* his followers. *Defended* means most nearly
   - A) praised
   - B) liked
   - c) informed
   - D) protected
   - E) delayed

10. The *aim* of the employees is to do their work well. *Aim* means most nearly
    - A) hope
    - B) purpose
    - c) duty
    - D) promise
    - E) idea

11. The workers will *assemble* the sacks of mail before loading them on the truck. *Assemble* means most nearly
    - A) bring together
    - B) examine carefully
    - c) locate
    - D) fill
    - E) mark

12. The mayor of the city sent a letter to each of the *merchants*. *Merchants* means most nearly
    - A) producers
    - B) advertisers
    - c) bankers
    - D) executives
    - E) storekeepers

USE ANSWER SHEET ON PAGE KB-107

13. The clerk was *compelled* to concentrate on his job. *Compelled* means most nearly
   A) tempted
   B) persuaded
   c) forced
   D) unable
   E) content

14. The clerk *extended* his vacation. *Extended* means most nearly
   A) limited
   B) deserved
   c) enjoyed
   D) lengthened
   E) started

15. The *territory* is too large to see in one day. *Territory* means most nearly
   A) swamp
   B) region
   c) city
   D) beach
   E) terminal

16. The technicians *created* a new machine. *Created* means most nearly
   A) planned
   B) copied
   c) invented
   D) tried
   E) replaced

17. The *mended* mail sacks will be delivered. *Mended* means most nearly
   A) repaired
   B) torn
   c) clean
   D) labelled
   E) tied

18. The new post office building is *huge*. *Huge* means most nearly
   A) ugly
   B) tall
   c) sturdy
   D) immense
   E) narrow

19. He was asked to *mingle* with the other guests. *Mingle* means most nearly
   A) consult
   B) visit
   c) sing
   D) mix
   E) dance

20. The director of the program is *likewise* chairman of the committee. *Likewise* means most nearly
   A) also
   B) often
   c) thus
   D) however
   E) meanwhile

21. Doctors are determined to *conquer* the disease. *Conquer* means most nearly
   A) study
   B) fight
   c) overcome
   D) eliminate
   E) trace

22. The machine was *designed* for stamping envelopes. *Designed* means most nearly
   A) fine
   B) used
   c) essential
   D) approved
   E) intended

23. He *mourned* the loss of his friend. *Mourned* means most nearly
   A) resented
   B) grieved
   c) remembered
   D) avenged
   E) faced

24. The meeting will take place at the *usual* time. *Usual* means most nearly
   A) proper
   B) old
   c) customary
   D) best
   E) earliest

25. The employee was given *distinct* instructions. *Distinct* means most nearly
   A) clear
   B) short
   c) new
   D) regular
   E) loud

26. The worker will *bind* the pages together. *Bind* means most nearly
   A) press
   B) receive
   c) make
   D) return
   E) fasten

27. He *startled* the person standing next to him. *Startled* means most nearly
    A) alarmed
    B) touched
    C) scolded
    D) reassured
    E) avoided

28. He *deceived* them by claiming to be rich. *Deceived* means most nearly
    A) favored
    B) tricked
    C) impressed
    D) imitated
    E) angered

29. The flood brought *distress* to many families. *Distress* means most nearly
    A) shock
    B) illness
    C) suffering
    D) risk
    E) hunger

30. Some of the statements made at the meeting were *absurd*. *Absurd* means most nearly
    A) clever
    B) original
    C) careless
    D) foolish
    E) serious

31. The supervisor *implied* that the schedule would be changed. *Implied* means most nearly
    A) acknowledged
    B) imagined
    C) suggested
    D) predicted
    E) insisted

32. Each person works to earn his own *livelihood*. *Livelihood* means most nearly
    A) salary
    B) employment
    C) fortune
    D) education
    E) maintenance

If you finish before the time is up, check your answers to this part. Do not go to any other part.

ANSWER SHEET FOR PAGES KB 104-106

SAMPLE ANSWER SHEET

	A B C D E		A B C D E		A B C D E		A B C D E		A B C D E		A B C D E		A B C D E		A B C D E
1	⫿ ⫿ ⫿ ⫿ ⫿	2	⫿ ⫿ ⫿ ⫿ ⫿	3	⫿ ⫿ ⫿ ⫿ ⫿	4	⫿ ⫿ ⫿ ⫿ ⫿	5	⫿ ⫿ ⫿ ⫿ ⫿	6	⫿ ⫿ ⫿ ⫿ ⫿	7	⫿ ⫿ ⫿ ⫿ ⫿	8	⫿ ⫿ ⫿ ⫿ ⫿
9	⫿ ⫿ ⫿ ⫿ ⫿	10	⫿ ⫿ ⫿ ⫿ ⫿	11	⫿ ⫿ ⫿ ⫿ ⫿	12	⫿ ⫿ ⫿ ⫿ ⫿	13	⫿ ⫿ ⫿ ⫿ ⫿	14	⫿ ⫿ ⫿ ⫿ ⫿	15	⫿ ⫿ ⫿ ⫿ ⫿	16	⫿ ⫿ ⫿ ⫿ ⫿
17	⫿ ⫿ ⫿ ⫿ ⫿	18	⫿ ⫿ ⫿ ⫿ ⫿	19	⫿ ⫿ ⫿ ⫿ ⫿	20	⫿ ⫿ ⫿ ⫿ ⫿	21	⫿ ⫿ ⫿ ⫿ ⫿	22	⫿ ⫿ ⫿ ⫿ ⫿	23	⫿ ⫿ ⫿ ⫿ ⫿	24	⫿ ⫿ ⫿ ⫿ ⫿
25	⫿ ⫿ ⫿ ⫿ ⫿	26	⫿ ⫿ ⫿ ⫿ ⫿	27	⫿ ⫿ ⫿ ⫿ ⫿	28	⫿ ⫿ ⫿ ⫿ ⫿	29	⫿ ⫿ ⫿ ⫿ ⫿	30	⫿ ⫿ ⫿ ⫿ ⫿	31	⫿ ⫿ ⫿ ⫿ ⫿	32	⫿ ⫿ ⫿ ⫿ ⫿

ANSWERS TO QUESTIONS ON PAGES KB 104-106

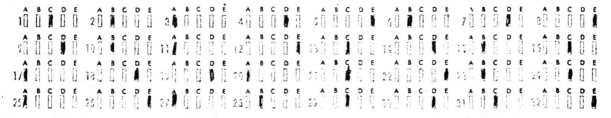

DESCRIPTION OF THE TEST AND SAMPLE QUESTIONS

The Number Series test is used only in the Clerk-Carrier examination. If you do not plan to take this examination, you need not study this section.

This test measures your ability to think with numbers instead of words.

In each problem, you are given a series of numbers that are changing according to a rule—followed by five sets of 2 numbers each. Your problem is to figure out a rule that would make one of the five sets the next two numbers in the series.

The problems do not use hard arithmetic. The task is merely to see how the numbers are related to each other. The sample questions will explain several types in detail so that you may become familiar with what you have to do.

Hints for Answering Number Series Questions

- Do the ones that are easiest for you first. Then go back and work on the others.
  Enough time is allowed for you to do all the questions, providing you don't stay too long on the ones you have trouble answering.
- Sound out the series to yourself. You may hear the rule: 2 4 6 8 10 12 14 . . . What are the next two numbers?
- Look at the series carefully. You may see the rule: 9 2 9 4 9 6 9 . . . What are the next two numbers?
- If you can't hear it or see it, you may have to figure it out by writing down how the numbers are changing: 6 8 16 18 26 28 36 . . . What are the next two numbers?
  $6^{+2}\ 8^{+8}\ 16^{+2}\ 18^{+8}\ 26^{+2}\ 28^{+8}\ 36$ . . . What are the next two numbers if this is $+2\ +8$?
  $36+2=38+8=46$ or 38 46. You would mark the letter of the answer that goes with 38 46.
- If none of the answers given fit the rule you have figured out, try again. Try to figure out a rule that makes one of the five answers a correct one.

DON'T SPEND TOO MUCH TIME ON ANY ONE QUESTION. SKIP IT AND COME BACK. A FRESH LOOK SOMETIMES HELPS.

Let's try a few—

Mark your answers for these samples on the Sample Answer Sheet on this page.

1. 1 2 3 4 5 6 7.........A) 1 2   B) 5 6   C) 8 9   D) 4 5   E) 7 8
How are these numbers changing? The numbers in this series are increasing by 1 or the rule is "add 1." If you apply this rule to the series, what would the next two numbers be? $7+1=8+1=9$. Therefore, the correct answer is 8 and 9, and you would select c) 8 9 as your answer.

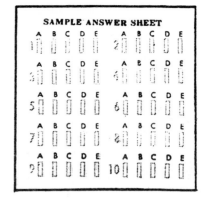

2. 15 14 13 12 11 10 9....A) 2 1   B) 17 16   C) 8 9   D) 8 7   E) 9 8
The numbers in this series are decreasing by 1 or the rule is "subtract 1." If you apply that rule, what would the next two numbers be? $9-1=8-1=7$. The correct answer is 8 and 7, and you would select D) 8 7 as your answer.

3. 20 20 21 21 22 22 23.......A) 23 23   B) 23 24   c) 19 19   D) 22 23   E) 21 22
In this series each number is repeated and then increased by 1. The rule is "repeat, add 1, repeat, add 1, etc." The series would be $20^{+0}\ 20^{+1}\ 21^{+0}\ 21^{+1}\ 22^{+0}\ 22^{+1}\ 23^{+0}\ 23^{+1}\ 24$. The correct answer is 23 and 24, and you should have darkened B on the Sample Answer Sheet for question 3.

4. 17 3 17 4 17 5 17.........A) 6 17   B) 6 7   c) 17 6   D) 5 6   E) 17 7
If you can't find a single rule for all the numbers in a series, see if there are really two series in the problem. This series is the number 17 separated by numbers increasing by 1, starting with 3. If the series were continued for two more numbers, it would read 17 3 17 4 17 5 17 6 17. The correct answer is 6 and 17, and you should have darkened A on the Sample Answer Sheet for question 4.

5. 1 2 4 5 7 8 10.............A) 11 12   B) 12 14   c) 10 13   D) 12 13   E) 11 13
The rule in this series is not easy to see until you actually set down how the numbers are changing: $1^{+1}\ 2^{+2}\ 4^{+1}\ 5^{+2}\ 7^{+1}\ 8^{+2}\ 10$. The numbers in this series are increasing first by 1 (that is plus 1) and then by 2 (that is plus 2). If the series were continued for two more numbers, it would read: 1 2 4 5 7 8 10 (plus 1) which is *11* (plus 2) which is *13*. Therefore the correct answer is 11 and 13, and you should have darkened E on the Sample Answer Sheet for question 5.

Now read and work sample questions 6 through 10 and mark your answers on the Sample Answer Sheet on this page.

6. 21 21 20 20 19 19 18....... A) 18 18   B) 18 17   c) 17 18   D) 17 17   E) 18 19
7. 1 22 1 23 1 24 1........... A) 2 61   B) 25 26   c) 25 1   D) 1 26   E) 1 25
8. 1 20 3 19 5 18 7........... A) 8 9   B) 8 17   c) 17 10   D) 17 9   E) 9 18
9. 4 7 10 13 16 19 22........ A) 23 26   B) 25 27   c) 25 26   D) 25 28   E) 24 27
10. 30 2 28 4 26 6 24......... A) 23 9   B) 26 8   c) 8 9   D) 26 22   E) 8 22

The correct answers to sample questions 6 to 10 are: 6B, 7C, 8D, 9D, and 10E.

Explanations for questions 6 through 10.

6. Each number in the series repeats itself and then decreases by 1 or minus 1; *21* (repeat) *21* (minus 1) which makes *20* (repeat) *20* (minus 1) which makes *19* (repeat) *19* (minus 1) which makes *18* (repeat) ? (minus 1) ?

7. The number *1* is separated by numbers which begin with *22* and increase by 1; *1 22 1* (increase 22 by 1) which makes *23 1* (increase 23 by 1) which makes *24 1* (increase 24 by 1) which makes ?

8. This is best explained by two alternating series—one series starts with *1* and increases by 2 or plus 2; the other series starts with *20* and decreases by 1 or minus 1.

$$1 \uparrow 3 \uparrow 5 \uparrow 7 \uparrow ?$$
$$20 \quad 19 \quad 18 \quad ?$$

9. This series of numbers increases by 3 (plus 3) beginning with the first number —4 (plus 3) 7 (plus 3) 10 (plus 3) 13 (plus 3) 16 (plus 3) 19 (plus 3) 22 (plus 3) ? (plus 3) ?

10. Look for two alternating series—one series starts with 30 and decreases by 2 (minus 2); the other series starts with 2 and increases by 2 (plus 2).

$$30 \uparrow 28 \uparrow 26 \uparrow 24 \uparrow \ ?$$
$$2 \quad 4 \quad 6 \quad ?$$

Now try questions 11 to 18. Mark your answers on the Sample Answer Sheet on this page.

	A)	B)	C)	D)	E)
11. 5 6 20 7 8 19 9	10 18	18 17	10 17	18 19	10 11
12. 9 10 1 11 12 2 13	2 14	3 14	14 3	14 15	14 1
13. 4 6 9 11 14 16 19	21 24	22 25	20 22	21 23	22 24
14. 8 8 1 10 10 3 12	13 13	12 5	12 4	13 5	4 12
15. 14 1 2 15 3 4 16	5 16	6 7	5 17	5 6	17 5
16. 10 12 50 15 17 50 20	50 21	21 50	50 22	22 50	22 24
17. 1 2 3 50 4 5 6 51 7 8	9 10	9 52	51 10	10 52	10 50
18. 20 21 23 24 27 28 32 33 38 39 .	45 46	45 52	44 45	44 49	40 46

Hints for questions 11 through 18.

11. Alternating series: 5 6 ↑ 7 8 ↑ 9 ? ↑
    20   19   ?

12. Alternating series: 9 10 ↑ 11 12 ↑ 13 ? ↑
    1   2   ?

13. Increases alternately by 2 (plus 2) then 3 (plus 3) —4 (plus 2) 6 (plus 3) 9 (plus 2) 11 (plus 3) 14 (plus 2) 16 (plus 3) 19 (plus 2) ? (plus 3) ?

14. Alternating series: 8 8 ↑ 10 10 ↑ 12 ? ↑
    1   3   ?

15. Alternating series: 14 ↑ ↑15 ↑ ↑ 16 ↑ ↑
    1 2   3 4   ? ?

16. Alternating series: 10 12 ↑ 15 17 ↑ 20 ? ↑
    50   50   ?

17. Alternating series: 1 2 3 ↑ 4 5 6 ↑ 7 8 ? ↑
    50   51   ?

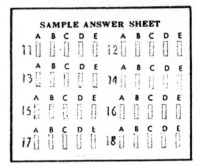

18. Increases alternately by (plus 1), (plus 2), (plus 1), (plus 3), (plus 1), (plus 4), etc. —20 (plus 1) 21 (plus 2) 23 (plus 1) 24 (plus 3) 27 (plus 1) 28 (plus 4) 32 (plus 1) 33 (plus 5) 38 (plus 1) 39 (plus 6) ? (plus 1) ?

The correct answers to the sample questions above are: 11A, 12C, 13A, 14B, 15D, 16D, 17B, and 18A.

These number series questions are like the ones in the Clerk-Carrier examination.

Do first those questions that you can do easily. Then go back and do the ones that you skipped.

Work *20 minutes* on this test. No more. No less. If you finish before the 20 minutes are up, go over your answers again. Mark your answers on the Answer Sheet .

1. 10 11 12 10 11 12 10......	A) 10 11	B) 12 10	C) 11 10	D) 11 12	E) 10 12
2. 4 6 7 4 6 7 4.............	A) 6 7	B) 4 7	C) 7 6	D) 7 4	E) 6 8
3. 7 7 3 7 7 4 7.............	A) 4 5	B) 4 7	C) 5 7	D) 7 5	E) 7 7
4. 3 4 10 5 6 10 7...........	A) 10 8	B) 9 8	C) 8 14	D) 8 9	E) 8 10
5. 6 6 7 7 8 8 9......•.....	A) 10 11	B) 10 10	C) 9 10	D) 9 9	E) 10 9
6. 3 8 9 4 9 10 5............	A) 6 10	B) 10 11	C) 9 10	D) 11 6	E) 10 6
7. 2 4 3 6 4 8 5.............	A) 6 10	B) 10 7	C) 10 6	D) 9 6	E) 6 7
8. 11 5 9 7 7 9 5.............	A) 11 3	B) 7 9	C) 7 11	D) 9 7	E) 3 7
9. 12 10 8 8 6 7 4...........	A) 2 2	B) 6 4	C) 6 2	D) 4 6	E) 2 6
10. 20 22 22 19 21 21 18......	A) 22 22	B) 19 19	C) 20 20	D) 20 17	E) 19 17
11. 5 7 6 10 7 13 8...........	A) 16 9	B) 16 10	C) 9 15	D) 10 15	E) 15 9
12. 13 10 11 15 12 13 17......	A) 18 14	B) 18 15	C) 15 16	D) 14 15	E) 15 18
13. 30 27 24 21 18 15 12......	A) 9 3	B) 9 6	C) 6 3	D) 12 9	E) 8 5
14. 3 7 10 5 8 10 7...........	A) 10 11	B) 10 5	C) 10 9	D) 10 10	E) 9 10
15. 12 4 13 6 14 8 15.........	A) 10 17	B) 17 10	C) 10 12	D) 16 10	E) 10 16
16. 21 8 18 20 7 17 19........	A) 16 18	B) 18 6	C) 6 16	D) 5 15	E) 6 18
17. 14 16 16 18 20 20 22......	A) 22 24	B) 26 28	C) 24 26	D) 24 24	E) 24 28
18. 5 6 8 9 12 13 17..........	A) 18 23	B) 13 18	C) 18 22	D) 23 24	E) 18 19
19. 1 3 5 5 2 4 6 6 3.........	A) 7 4	B) 5 5	C) 1 3	D) 5 7	E) 7 7
20. 12 24 15 25 18 26 21......	A) 27 22	B) 24 22	C) 29 24	D) 27 27	E) 27 24
21. 17 15 21 18 10 16 19......	A) 20 5	B) 5 11	C) 11 11	D) 11 20	E) 15 14
22. 12 16 10 14 8 12 6........	A) 10 14	B) 10 8	C) 10 4	D) 4 10	E) 4 2
23. 13 4 5 13 6 7 13..........	A) 13 8	B) 8 13	C) 8 9	D) 8 8	E) 7 8
24. 10 10 9 11 11 10 12.......	A) 13 14	B) 12 11	C) 13 13	D) 12 12	E) 12 13

SAMPLE ANSWER SHEET

Now check your answers by comparing them with the correct answers shown below.

CORRECT ANSWERS

Count how many you got right, and write that number on this line————→ _____
(This is your Test Score.)

Meaning of Test Score

If your Test Score is *17 or more*, you have a Good score.
If your Test Score is *from 12 to 16*, you have a Fair score.
If your Test Score is *11 or less*, you are not doing too well.

These number series questions are like the ones in the Clerk-Carrier examination.

Do first those questions that you can do easily. Then go back and do the ones that you skipped.

Work *20 minutes* on this test. No more. No less. If you finish before the 20 minutes are up, go over your answers again. Mark your answers on the Answer Sheet .

	A)	B)	C)	D)	E)
1. 8 9 9 8 10 10 8............	11 8	8 13	8 11	11 11	8 8
2. 10 10 11 11 12 12 13......	15 15	13 13	14 14	13 14	14 15
3. 6 6 10 6 6 12 6............	6 14	13 6	14 6	6 13	6 6
4. 17 11 5 16 10 4 15........	13 9	13 11	8 5	9 5	9 3
5. 1 3 2 4 3 5 4.............	6 8	5 6	6 5	3 4	3 5
6. 11 11 10 12 12 11 13......	12 14	14 12	14 14	13 14	13 12
7. 18 5 6 18 7 8 18..........	9 9	9 10	18 9	8 9	18 7
8. 7 8 9 13 10 11 12 14 13 14 .	15 16	13 15	14 15	15 15	13 14
9. 5 7 30 9 11 30 13.........	15 16	15 17	14 17	15 30	30 17
10. 5 7 11 13 17 19 23........	27 29	25 29	25 27	27 31	29 31
11. 9 15 10 17 12 19 15 21 19..	23 24	25 23	17 23	23 31	21 24
12. 34 37 30 33 26 29 22......	17 8	18 11	25 28	25 20	25 18
13. 10 16 12 14 14 12 16......	14 12	10 18	10 14	14 18	14 16
14. 11 12 18 11 13 19 11 14....	18 11	16 11	20 11	11 21	17 11
15. 20 9 8 19 10 9 18 11 10....	19 11	17 10	19 12	17 12	19 10
16. 28 27 26 31 30 29 34......	36 32	32 31	33 32	33 36	35 36
17. 10 16 14 20 18 24 22......	28 32	27 26	28 26	26 28	27 28
18. 9 9 7 8 7 7 9 10 5:.......	5 11	11 12	5 9	9 11	5 5
19. 5 7 11 17 10 12 16 22 15 17...	27 26	19 23	19 27	21 23	21 27
20. 12 19 13 20 14 21 15......	16 17	22 16	16 22	15 22	15 16
21. 6 6 8 10 10 12 14.........	14 14	14 16	16 16	12 14	10 10
22. 8 1 9 3 10 5 11...........	7 12	6 12	12 6	7 8	6 7
23. 30 11 24 12 19 14 15 17 12 21 10....................	23 8	25 8	26 9	24 9	25 9
24. 24 30 29 22 28 27 19 26 25 15 24...................	14 23	19 18	23 22	25 11	23 10

Now check your answers by comparing them with the correct answers shown below.

(This is your Test Score.)

Meaning of Test Score

    If your Test Score is *17 or more,* you have a Good score.

    If your Test Score is *from 12 to 16,* you have a Fair score.

    If your Test Score is *11 or less,* you are not doing too well.

These number series questions are like the ones in the Clerk-Carrier examination.

Do first those questions that you can do easily. Then go back and do the ones that you skipped.

Work *20 minutes* on this test. No more. No less. If you finish before the 20 minutes are up, go over your answers again. Mark your answers on the Sample Answer Sheet

		A)	B)	C)	D)	E)
1.	13 12 8 11 10 8 9	8 7	6 8	8 6	8 8	7 8
2.	13 18 13 17 13 16 13	15 13	13 14	13 15	14 15	15 14
3.	13 13 10 12 12 10 11	10 10	10 9	11 9	9 11	11 10
4.	6 5 4 6 5 4 6	4 6	6 4	5 4	5 6	4 5
5.	10 10 9 8 8 7 6	5 5	5 4	6 5	6 4	5 3
6.	20 16 18 14 16 12 14	16 12	10 12	16 18	12 12	12 10
7.	7 12 8 11 9 10 10	11 9	9 8	9 11	10 11	9 10
8.	13 13 12 15 15 14 17	17 16	14 17	16 19	19 19	16 16
9.	19 18 12 17 16 13 15	16 12	14 14	12 14	14 12	12 16
10.	7 15 12 8 16 13 9	17 14	17 10	14 10	14 17	10 14
11.	18 15 6 16 14 6 14	12 6	14 13	6 12	13 12	13 6
12.	6 6 5 8 8 7 10 10	8 12	9 12	12 12	12 9	9 9
13.	17 20 23 26 29 32 35	37 40	41 44	38 41	38 42	36 39
14.	15 5 7 16 9 11 17	18 13	15 17	12 19	13 15	12 13
15.	19 17 16 16 13 15 10	14 7	12 9	14 9	7 12	10 14
16.	11 1 16 10 6 21 9	12 26	26 8	11 26	11 8	8 11
17.	21 21 19 17 17 15 13	11 11	13 11	11 9	9 7	13 13
18.	23 22 20 19 16 15 11	6 5	10 9	6 1	10 6	10 5
19.	17 10 16 9 14 8 11	7 11	7 7	10 4	4 10	7 4
20.	11 9 14 12 17 15 20 18 23 ..	21 24	26 21	21 26	24 27	26 29
21.	7 5 9 7 11 9 13	11 14	10 15	11 15	12 14	10 14
22.	9 10 11 7 8 9 5	6 7	7 8	5 6	6 4	7 5
23.	8 9 10 10 9 10 11 11 10 11 12 ..	11 12	12 10	11 11	12 11	11 13
24.	5 6 8 9 12 13 17 18 23 24	30 31	25 31	29 30	25 30	30 37

SAMPLE ANSWER SHEET

PART D →

Now check your answers by comparing them with the correct answers shown below.

SAMPLE ANSWER SHEET

PART D →

WHAT DO THE POSTAL SERVICE EMPLOYEES DO who occupy the positions for which these examinations are given?   To answer that, we have on the coming pages:

Excerpts from the Occupational Outlook Handbook, 1980-1981. This book is published every second year by the Bureau of Statistics of the United States Department of Labor. Here are its notes on Postal Service employment. Although it says on the chart on page KB-118 that "little growth is likely" note that there is some growth and the number of Postal Service employees is nearly 700,000 and that, as the article says, "Many of thousands of job openings will result annually as workers retire, die, or transfer to other fields.

And the pay is good.

Announcements for recent examinations for the three jobs discussed herein are to be found on pages KB-119, 120, and 121.

Mail Carriers

(D.O.T. 230.363-010 and .367-010)

Nature of the Work

Most mail carriers travel planned routes delivering and collecting mail. Carriers start work at the post office early in the morning, where they spend a few hours arranging their mail for delivery and taking care of other details.

A carrier may cover the route on foot, by vehicle, or by a combination of both. On foot, carriers tote a heavy load of mail in a satchel or push it in a cart. In outlying suburban or rural areas, a car or small truck is used to deliver mail. Residential carriers cover their routes only once a day, but carriers assigned to a business district may make two trips a day. Deliveries are made house-to-house, to roadside mailboxes, and to large buildings, such as apartments, which have all the mailboxes on the first floor.

Besides making deliveries, carriers collect postage-due and c.o.d. cash on delivery fees and obtain signed receipts for registered, certified, and, sometimes, insured mail. If a customer is not home the carrier leaves a notice that tells where special mail is being held.

After completing their routes, carriers return to the post office with mail gathered from street collection boxes and homes. They turn in the mail receipts and money collected during the day and may separate letters and parcels so that they can be canceled easily.

Many carriers have more specialized duties. Some deliver only parcel post while others collect mail from street boxes and office mail chutes. In contrast, rural carriers provide a wide variety of postal services. In addition to delivering and picking up mail, they sell stamps and money orders and accept parcels and letters to be registered or insured.

All carriers answer customers' questions about postal regulations and service and provide change-of-address cards and other postal forms when requested.

Working Conditions

Most carriers begin work early in the morning, in some cases as early as 4 a.m. if they have routes in the business district. Carriers spend most of their time outdoors in all kinds of weather delivering mail. Even those who drive often must walk when making deliveries and must lift heavy sacks of parcel post when loading their vehicles.

Mail carriers often tote mail in a heavy satchel when making deliveries on foot.

The job, however, has its advantages. Carriers who begin work early in the morning are through by early afternoon. They are also free to work at their own pace as long as they cover their routes within a certain period of time.

Places of Employment

The U.S. Postal Service employed 245,000 mail carriers in 1978, three-quarters of them full time. Although about 50,000 were rural carriers, most worked in cities and suburban communities throughout the Nation.

Training, Other Qualifications, and Advancement

Mail carriers must be U.S. citizens and at least 18 years old. They must qualify on a written examination that tests their clerical accuracy and abilities to memorize mail distribution systems, read, and do simple arithmetic.

If the carrier job involves driving, applicants must have a driver's license, a good driving record, and pass a road test. Before appointment, mail carriers must pass a physical examination and may be asked to show that they can lift and handle mail sacks weighing up to 70 pounds.

Applicants for mail carrier jobs should apply at a post office in the general area where they wish to work. Applicants' names are listed in order of their examination scores. Five points are added to the score of an honorably discharged veteran, and te points to the score of a veteran wounded i combat or disabled. When a vacancy occur: the appointing officer chooses one of the x three applicants; the rest of the names rema. on the list to be considered for future ope: ings.

Mail carriers are classified as casua. part-time flexible, part-time regular, or fu: time. Casual workers are not career em ployees, but are hired to help deliver mai during peak mailing periods of the year Part-time flexible carriers are career em ployees who do not have a regular work schedule, but replace absent workers anc help with extra work as the need arises Part-time flexible carriers sometimes wor! as many as 40 hours per week. Part-time regulars have a set work schedule—for example, 4 hours a day. Full-time carrier; usually work a 40-hour week.

New carriers are trained on the job They may begin as part-time flexible city carriers and become regular or full-time carriers in order of seniority as vacancie occur. Advancement possibilities are lim ited, but carriers can look forward to ob taining preferred routes or higher level job: such as carrier technician as their seniority increases.

Employment Outlook

Employment of mail carriers is expecte to increase more slowly than the average for all occupations through the 1980's. Although the number of homes and business establishments is expected to increase along with growth in population and business activity, anticipated cutbacks in the frequency of mail delivery should limit the need for additional carriers. Nevertheless, thousands of job openings will result from the need to replace experienced carriers who retire, die, or transfer to other occupations. Openings will be concentrated in metropolitan areas.

Earnings

In 1978, experienced full-time mail carriers earned an average salary of $17,168 a year, about one and one-half times as much as average earnings for all nonsupervisory workers in private industry, except farming. Full-time carriers started at a rate of $14,603 a year and could rise to a maximum of $17,-188 after 8 years. They also received 10 percent additional pay for work between 6 p.m. and 6 a.m. Part-time flexible carriers began at $7.27 an hour in 1978, with provision for periodic increases up to $8.56 an hour after 8 years of satisfactory service.

The earnings of rural carriers are determined through an evaluation of the amount of work required to service their particular routes. Carriers with longer, more populated routes generally earned more than those with shorter routes that served fewer homes. Rural carriers also received an equipment maintenance allowance for the use of their automobiles. They work either a 5-or a 6-day week. For information on fringe benefits, see the statement on postal service occupations elsewhere in the *Handbook*.

Related Occupations

Although mail carriers play an important role in moving the Nation's mail, postal clerks and mailhandlers also provide necessary services, and their work and qualifications are closely related to those of mail carriers. Other related delivery occupations include messengers, merchandise delivers, delivery-route truck drivers, newspaper delivery drivers, and newspaper carriers.

Sources of Additional Information

Local post offices and State employment service offices can supply details about entrance examinations and employment opportunities for mail carriers.

Telephone Operators

Nature of the Work

Although millions of telephone numbers are dialed directly each day, making a call sometimes requires the assistance of a telephone operator. Often an operator is needed because a caller wants to reverse long-dis-

In many telephone company central offices, manual switchboards have been replaced with sophisticated computerized equipment.

tance charges, find out a telephone number in another city, or know the cost of a call. Operators also may be needed to contact the police or fire departments in an emergency or arrange a conference call for business executives.

Providing these services are two groups of telephone operators. The operators who work in telephone company central offices probably are the most familiar. But many business and large organizations receive so many calls that they employ operators to run their private branch exchange (PBX) switchboards. Sometimes operators place calls by inserting and removing plugs that make switchboard connections and by listening and speaking into their headsets. However, many switchboards, especially those in telephone company central offices, are now operated by pushbuttons or dials.

Telephone company operators may be assigned either to handle long-distance calls or to give directory assistance. *Long-distance operators* (D.O.T. 235.462-010) obtain the information needed to complete the call, make the necessary connections, and record the details for billing. *Directory assistance operators* (D.O.T. 235.662-018) look up and provide telephone numbers. Service assistants train and help new operators to complete difficult calls.

PBX operators (D.O.T. 235.662-022) run switchboards for business offices and other establishments. They connect interoffice or house calls, answer and relay outside calls, assist company employees in making outgoing calls, supply information to callers, and record charges. In many small establishments, PBX operators work at switchboards that serve only a limited number of telephones. These operators may do other

office work such as typing or sorting mail and many also act as receptionists or information clerks. (The work of receptionists is described elsewhere in the *Handbook*.)

Working Conditions

Most telephone company and PBX operators work between 35 and 40 hours a week. Often, their scheduled hours are the same as those of other office clerical workers. In telephone companies, however, and in hotels, hospitals, and other places where telephone service is needed on a 24-hour basis, operators work on shifts and on holidays and weekends. Some operators work split shifts—that is, they are on duty during the peak calling periods in the late morning and early evening and have time off in between.

Operators usually work in pleasant, well-lighted, air-conditioned surroundings. The job of a telephone operator requires little physical exertion; however, during the peak calling periods, the pace at the switchboard may be very hectic. Often operators are unable to leave their seats during these periods.

Places of Employment

About 310,000 telephone operators were employed in 1978. More than one-half worked as PBX operators in manufacturing plants, hospitals, department stores, or businesses. The remainder worked in telephone companies. About one-fourth of all operators work only part time.

Both telephone company and PBX operators are concentrated in heavily populated areas. Nearly one-fifth work in the New York City, Chicago, and Los Angeles metropolitan areas.

Occupations in the Postal Service

The U.S. Postal Service is the most highly visible Federal Government agency—daily accepting millions of letters and packages and delivering them to our homes, places of employment, and throughout the world. An army of workers is needed to provide this vital public service, and although many postal employees—mail carriers, for example —may be seen at work in our communities, many others work in jobs that the public seldom sees.

A national postal system was recognized as essential before the United States was founded. In one of its first official acts, the Continental Congress created the U.S. postal system in 1775 and named Benjamin Franklin to head it as the first Postmaster General. The system later became the Post Office Department and grew as the Nation's needs for postal services increased. In 1970, the Post Office Department was reorganized and became the U.S. Postal Service, which is now operated independently of all other agencies of the Federal Government.

The Nation's first postal system had fewer than 50 post offices. In 1978, the more than 40,000 post offices, stations, branches, and community post offices operated by the Postal Service handled over 96 billion pieces of mail, more than 400 pieces for every individual in the country.

Postal workers are employed at postal facilities located throughout the Nation. Facilities range in size from large metropolitan post offices and mail processing centers that employ hundreds of workers to small stations that employ only a few. Most are post offices, but some are facilities that serve special purposes, such as handling packages and other bulk mail, maintaining vehicles, or processing payroll records.

Although every community receives mail service, employment is concentrated in large metropolitan areas. Post offices in cities such as New York, Chicago, and Los Angeles employ a great number of workers not only because they process huge amounts of mail for their own populations but also because they serve as mail processing centers for the smaller communities that surround them.

Occupations in the Industry

The U.S. Postal Service employed nearly 660,000 workers in mid-1978; 1 out of 5 worked part time or on a casual or substitute basis. Although 5 out of 6 postal employees worked in mail processing occupations, the U.S. Postal Service also employed more than 30,000 workers in maintenance and repair jobs, and about 80,000 professional, administrative, and clerical workers. The more than 500,000 mail carriers and postal clerks employed in mid-1978 constituted the vast majority of mail processing workers, as well as of all postal workers. Mail carriers and postal clerks are discussed in more detail elsewhere in the *Handbook*.

Mail Processing Occupations. Most people are familiar with the duties of the mail carrier, yet few are aware of the many different tasks required in processing mail. At all hours of the day and night, a steady stream of letters, packages, magazines, and papers moves through the postal system. *Mail carriers* (D.O.T. 230.363-010 and .367-010) collect mail from neighborhood mailboxes and bring it to post offices that truck it to the nearest mail processing center for sorting by *postal clerks* (D.O.T. 243.367-014). There are more than 300 large mail processing centers, each responsible for sorting the outgoing and incoming mail for an area of the United States. Outgoing mail is sorted and sent by truck or airplane to the appropriate mail processing center in another area of the country. Incoming mail is sorted for the various local post offices in the area, trucked to the post offices, and then sorted again for delivery by mail carriers to homes and business establishments.

Mailhandlers (D.O.T. 209.687-014) load, unload, and move mail sacks and bulk mail, such as parcels and packages. They separate and distribute mail sacks to postal clerks for processing. Some also rewrap parcels and packages or operate canceling machines, forklift trucks, or addressograph and mimeograph machines.

Maintenance and Repair Occupations. The U.S. Postal Service employs large numbers of workers to maintain the buildings, equipment, and vehicles used in processing mail. Custodians, maintenance technicians, carpenters, painters, and other maintenance workers keep buildings and facilities clean and in good repair. Electronics technicians and *mail processing equipment mechanics* (D.O.T. 633.261-014) maintain, test, repair, and overhaul electronic equipment and other machinery used to sort and process mail. Automobile and truck mechanics service and repair the Postal Service's nearly 200,000 vehicles.

Professional, Administrative, and Clerical Occupations. The U.S. Postal Service employs workers in a variety of supervisory, administrative, and clerical jobs. It employs administrators, lawyers, secretaries, and typists at its regional as well as national headquarters.

Postmasters (D.O.T. 188.167-066) and *mail supervisors* (D.O.T. 230.137-01 nd 243.137-010) are responsible for the day-to-day operation of the post offices. They supervise mailhandlers, clerks, and technicians; hire and train employees; and set up work schedules.

Postal inspectors (D.O.T. 168.267-062) audit post offices' operations to see that they are run efficiently, that funds are spent prop-

Mailhandlers unload mail sacks and bulk mail and distribute them to postal clerks for processing.

erly, and that postal laws and regulations are observed. They also investigate crimes such as theft, forgery, and fraud involving use of the mail.

Working Conditions

Except for mail carriers, most postal employees work indoors. Mail carriers spend much of their time outdoors or driving vehicles, regardless of weather conditions.

Training, Other Qualifications, and Advancement

An applicant for a Postal Service job must pass a written examination, meet minimum age requirements, and be a U.S. citizen. Generally, the mimimum age is 18, but a high school graduate may begin work at 16 if the job is not hazardous and does not require use of a motor vehicle. Many Postal Service jobs do not require formal education or special training. Applicants for these jobs are hired on the basis of their examination scores.

Applicants should apply at the post office where they wish to work and take the entrance examination for the job they want. Examinations for most jobs include a written test that checks an applicant's vocabulary and reading ability, as well as any special abilities required, such as aptitude for remembering addresses. A physical examination is required, as well. Applicants for jobs that require strength and stamina are sometimes given a special test. For example, mailhandlers must be able to lift and carry mail sacks weighing up to 70 pounds. The names of applicants who pass the examinations are placed on a list in the order of their scores. Five points are added to the score of an honorably discharged veteran, and ten extra points to the score of a veteran wounded in combat or disabled. When a job opens, the appointing officer chooses one of the top three applicants. Others are left on the list so that they can be considered for future openings.

New employees are trained either on the job by supervisors and other experienced employees or in local training centers. Training ranges from a few days to several months, depending on the job. For example, mailhandlers and custodians can learn their jobs in a relatively short time while postal inspectors need months of training.

Postal workers are classified as casual, part-time flexible, part-time regular, or full time. Casual workers are not career employees, but are hired to help handle the large amounts of mail during the Christmas season and for other short-term assignments. Part-time flexible employees, although they have career status, do not have a regular work schedule but replace absent workers or help with extra workloads as the need arises. Part-time regulars have a set work schedule—for example, 4 hours a day. Carriers, clerks, and mailhandlers may start as part-time flexible workers and move into full-time jobs according to their seniority as vacancies occur.

Postal workers can advance to better paying positions by learning new skills. Training programs are available for low-skilled workers who wish to become technicians or mechanics. Also, employees can get preferred assignments, such as the day shift or a more desirable delivery route, as their seniority increases. When an opening occurs, eligible employees may submit written requests, called "bids," for assignment to the vacancy. The bidder who meets the qualifications for the assignment and has the most seniority gets the job.

For supervisory jobs, requirements for promotion may include training or education, a satisfactory work record, and appropriate personal characteristics such as leadership ability. Although opportunities for promotion to supervisory positions in smaller post offices are limited, workers may apply for vacancies in a larger post office and thus increase their chances.

Employment Outlook

Little change is expected in Postal Service employment through the 1980's as mail processing systems become more automated and as mail volume increases very slowly because of rising postal rates and increasing reliance on the telephone for personal communication. Possible cutbacks in the frequency of home deliveries may temper any employment growth stemming from increases in the number of homes and business establishments. Employment in maintenance and repair occupations is expected to increase as mail processing machines grow in numbers and complexity. Many thousands of job openings will result annually as workers retire, die, or transfer to other fields.

Earnings

In late 1978, most full-time employees of the U.S. Postal Service earned annual salaries of at least $14,000. The average annual salary of all full-time postal workers was about $17,350, about one and one-half times the average earnings for all non-supervisory workers in private industry, except farming.

Postal Service employees are paid under three principal pay schedules depending upon the duties of the job. There is one schedule for production workers, such as clerks, city mail carriers, and mailhandlers; one for rural carriers; and one for supervisory, administrative, technical, and clerical workers. (Earnings of postal clerks and mail carriers are discussed elsewhere in the *Handbook*.) Most production employees receive periodic "step" increases up to a specified maximum if their job performance is satisfactory. In addition, salaries of most postal workers are automatically adjusted for changes in the cost of living. Full-time employees work an 8-hour day 5 days a week. They receive extra pay for night and Sunday work.

In 1978, postal employees earned 13 days of annual leave (vacation) during each of their first 3 years of service, including prior Federal civilian and military service; 20 days each year for 3 to 15 years of service; and 26 days after 15 years. In addition, they earned 13 days of paid sick leave a year regardless of length of service.

Other benefits included retirement and survivorship annuities, low-cost health insurance programs paid for in part by the Postal Service, and fully paid life insurance.

Most postal workers are members of unions and are covered by one of several negotiated bargaining agreements between the Postal Service and the unions.

Sources of Additional Information

Local post offices and State employment service offices can supply details about entrance examinations and employment opportunities in the Postal Service.

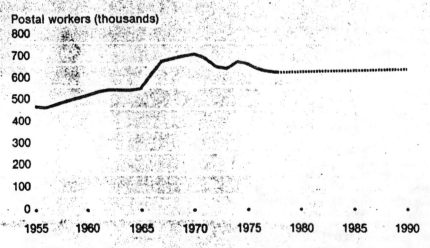

As a result of automation, little growth is likely in postal service employment

Postal workers (thousands)

Source: Bureau of Labor Statistics

THE UNITED STATES POSTAL SERVICE ANNOUNCES AN EXAMINATION FOR

CLERK & CARRIER

POSITIONS IN THE POST OFFICES AT

OAKLAND, CA 94615

(NAME OF POST OFFICE(S) AND STATE)

It is estimated that the resultant register of eligibles will be used to fill approximately 240 career positions during the next two years.

THE OPPORTUNITY

Applications are now being accepted, and examinations will be given to establish a register of eligibles or to expand the current register of eligibles from which future clerk and carrier vacancies in this Post Office will be filled. All interested persons who meet the requirements described in this announcement are urged to apply.

QUALIFICATION REQUIREMENTS

No experience is required. All applicants will be required to take a written examination designed to test aptitude for learning and performing the duties of the position. The test will consist of 4 parts: (1) Address Checking, (2) Memory for Addresses, (3) General Abilities (word meaning and reading), and (4) Number Series. The test and completion of the forms will require approximately 3 hours. Competitors will be rated on a scale of 100. They must score at least 70 on the examination as a whole.

DUTIES

Clerks work indoors. Clerks have to handle sacks of mail weighing as much as 70 pounds. They sort mail and distribute it by using a complicated scheme which must be memorized. Some clerks work at a public counter or window doing such jobs as selling stamps and weighing parcels and are personally responsible for all money and stamps. A clerk may be on his feet all day. He also has to stretch, reach, and throw mail. Assignments to preferred positions, such as window clerks, typist and stenographic positions, etc., are filled by open bid and reassignment of the senior qualified clerk.

Carriers have to collect and deliver mail. Some carriers walk, other carriers drive. Carriers must be out in all kinds of weather. Almost all carriers have to carry mail bags on their shoulders; loads weigh as much as 35 pounds. Carriers sometimes have to load and unload sacks of mail weighing as much as 70 pounds.

The duties of newly appointed Clerks and Carriers are at times interchangeable. As representatives of the Postal Service, they must maintain pleasant and effective public relations with patrons and others, requiring a general familiarity with postal laws, regulations, and procedures commonly used.

Employees may be assigned to work in places exposed to public view. Their appearance influences the general public's confidence and attitude toward the entire Postal Service.

Employees appointed under this standard are therefore expected to maintain neat and proper personal attire and grooming appropriate to conducting public business, including the wearing of a uniform when required.

> ALL QUALIFIED APPLICANTS WILL RECEIVE CONSIDERATION FOR EMPLOYMENT WITHOUT REGARD TO RACE, RELIGION, COLOR, NATIONAL ORIGIN, SEX, POLITICAL AFFILIATIONS, OR ANY OTHER NON-MERIT FACTOR.

CARRIER POSITIONS REQUIRING DRIVING

Before eligibles may be appointed to carrier positions which require driving, they must demonstrate a Safe Driving record and must pass the Road Test to show they can safely drive a vehicle of the type used on the job.

Eligibles who fail to qualify in the Road Test will not be given the test again in the same group of hires. Those who fail the test a second time will not again be considered as a result of the same examination for appointment to a position that requires driving.

A valid driver's license from the state in which this post office is located must be presented at the time of appointment. Persons who do not have the license will not be appointed but their names will be restored to the register. They may not again be considered for carrier positions until they have obtained the required driver's license. After hire, individuals must also be able to obtain the required type of Government operator's permit.

PHYSICAL REQUIREMENTS

Applicants must be physically able to perform the duties described elsewhere in this announcement. Any physical condition which would cause the applicant to be a hazard to himself or to others will be disqualifying for appointment.

The distant vision for Clerk and Carrier positions not involving driving duties must test at least 20/30 (Snellen) in one eye, glasses permitted, and applicants generally must be able to hear ordinary conversation with or without a hearing aid, but some clerk positions may be filled by the deaf.

THE UNITED STATES POSTAL SERVICE ANNOUNCES AN EXAMINATION FOR
MAIL HANDLER
POSITIONS IN THE POST OFFICES AT

OAKLAND, CA 94615
(NAME OF POST OFFICE(S) AND STATE)

It is estimated that the resultant register of eligibles will be used to fill approximately 130 career positions during the next two years.

THE OPPORTUNITY

Applications are now being accepted, and examinations will be given to establish a register of eligibles from which future mail handler vacancies in the above Post Office(s) will be filled. All interested persons who meet the requirements described in this announcement are urged to apply.

It is estimated that the resultant register of eligibles will be used to fill approximately .... career positions in the post office(s) listed on this announcement during the next two years.

QUALIFICATION REQUIREMENTS

No experience is required. All applicants will be required to take a written examination designed to test (1) Address Checking, (2) Following Oral Directions, and (3) Understanding of Meaning of Words. The test and completion of the forms will require approximately 2 hours. Competitors will be rated on a scale of 100. They must score at least 70 on the examination as a whole.

DUTIES

Loads, unloads, and moves bulk mail, and performs duties incidental to the movement and processing of mail. Duties may include separation of mail sacks, facing letter mail, canceling stamps on parcel post; operating canceling machines, addressograph, mimeograph; operating fork-lift truck; rewrapping parcels, etc.

PHYSICAL REQUIREMENTS

Persons with amputation of arm, leg or foot should not apply.

A physical examination will be required before appointment.

STRENGTH AND STAMINA TEST

When eligibles are within reach for appointment they will be required to pass a test of strength and stamina. In this test they will be required to lift, shoulder, and carry two 70-pound sacks—one at a time—15 feet and load them on a hand truck. They will be required to push that truck to where there are some 40-, 50-, and 60-pound sacks. They will be required to load those sacks onto the truck. They will then have to unload the truck and return the truck to its original location. Eligibles will be notified when and where to report for the test of strength and stamina.

Persons with certain physical conditions will not be permitted to take the test of strength and stamina without prior approval of a physician. These physical conditions are (a) hernia or rupture, (b) back trouble, (c) heart trouble, (d) pregnancy, (e) or any other condition which makes it dangerous to the eligible to lift and carry 70-pound weights. Persons with these physical conditions will be given special instruction at the time they are notified to report for the strength and stamina test.

Eligibles being considered for an appointment who fail to qualify on the test will not be tested again in the same group of hires. If an eligible fails the test a second time, his/her eligibility for the position of mail handler will be cancelled.

ALL QUALIFIED APPLICANTS WILL RECEIVE CONSIDERATION FOR EMPLOYMENT WITHOUT REGARD TO RACE, RELIGION, COLOR, NATIONAL ORIGIN, SEX, POLITICAL AFFILIATIONS, OR ANY OTHER NON-MERIT FACTOR.

ELIGIBILITY

A passing score of 70 points on the examination places the applicant's name on a register of eligibles for two years. Applicants may extend this eligibility for a third year, after the 18th month, by making a written request to the postmaster of the installation where the register is maintained. An individual's score is important in the selection process, since names are placed on the register according to the score received on the examination. Scores of Veteran Preference eligibles are increased by 5 or 10 points, depending on the preference. Those with a 10-percent or greater compensable service-connected disability are placed at the top of the register in the order of their scores. Other eligibles are listed below this group in rank order. The Veterans Preference Act applies to the Postal Service as it does to other Federal agencies.

Applicants for postal employment who entered on active duty with the military after OCTOBER 14, 1976, are not entitled to veteran preference for employment purposes. There are only two exceptions to this requirement.

1. Applicants with active duty service during a war, a campaign, or expedition for which a campaign badge has been authorized are PREFERENCE ELIGIBLES and are entitled to a 5 point veteran preference.

2. Applicants with service-connected disabilities are PREFERENCE ELIGIBLES and are entitled to a 10 point veteran preference.

QUALIFICATION REQUIREMENTS

No experience is required. All applicants will be required to take a written examination designed to test the abilities required to perform the duties of the position. The test will consist of 4 parts: (1) Number Series, (2) Address Coding, (3) Address Code Memory, and (4) Address Checking. Competitors will be rated on a scale of 100. They must score at least 70 on the examination.

DUTIES

Individuals in this position are required to operate a machine which sorts and distributes letters. Individuals must read address ZIP Codes and key codes using a special purpose keyboard. Operators of this machine are required to key address codes at a maximum rate of sixty (60) addresses per minute and maintain an average keying accuracy of ninety-eight per cent (98%). Operators must also perform allied duties such as loading/stacking letters on letter sorting machine consoles and checking/verifying that the letters are correctly sorted.

Candidates must have a willingness to maintain close visual attention for sustained periods and must be able to meet performance standards. Upon successful completion of a training program, employees will be assigned to work as a member of a team under the direction of an immediate supervisor.

PHYSICAL REQUIREMENTS

Applicants must be physically able to perform the duties previously described. Any physical condition which would cause the applicant to be a hazard to himself or to others will be cause for disqualification.

Applicants must pass a vision test and possess the manual dexterity required to operate a two-handed keyboard. The following are vision requirements: (Glasses permitted)

> Near Acuity Both Eyes...7 or higher
> Near Acuity Left Eye....7 or higher
> Near Acuity Right Eye...3 or higher
> Near Lateral Phoria
>   (Titmus).............3 or higher
> Near Lateral Phoria
>   (Bausch & Lomb).......2 or higher

2

FIRST -- WATCH FOR ANNOUNCEMENTS OF JOBS THAT INTEREST YOU.

As we have said, announcements of Federal examinations are posted in Federal Buildings, post offices, and court houses throughout the United States. State and local announcements are to be found in city halls, state buildings, court houses, libraries, etc. They are often published in newspapers. If you are really interested in a civil service job, you should get into the habit of stopping by, about every two weeks, at the nearest offices of your state and local civil service offices, and the nearest place where Federal announcements are posted. Also, many civil service boards will, if you leave your name, send you a post card when an examination that you are interested in is announced. You are under no obligation if you ask them to do this; they are looking for qualified personnel, too.

WHAT ARE THE BASIC REQUIREMENTS? In most cases, you must be a citizen

of the United States. You must be at least 18 or 21 depending on the job (there might be occasional jobs where 17 will qualify) and healthy enough to hold down the job and belong to the retirement system. Local authorities sometimes but not always require a period of local residence. Sometimes there are maximum age limits; sometimes not. Don't take any of these things for granted; read the announcement sheet of the examination.

GET THE ANNOUNCEMENT SHEET OF THE EXAMINATION AND READ IT!

The announcement sheet or "scope sheet" gives the title of the job, the pay, the requirements (education, experience, age, physical, etc.), the duties of the position, and in most cases, some idea of the subjects upon which the questions will be based. The Federal Government often gives a sheet of sample questions.

THE ANNOUNCEMENT SHEET MEANS WHAT IT SAYS! If it gives a list of

subjects upon which you will be examined, you should prepare yourself as well as you can on each of those subjects. Here is a current one:

SCOPE OF EXAMINATION: Points

Subjects

Written test on ability to perform clerical duties of a routine nature, tests on general knowledge and intelligence, and may include tests on alphabetical filing, spelling, grammar, punctuation, word knowledge, arithmetic and tests on ability to deal intelligently with the general public - - -   1000

These, then, are the subjects in one general clerical examination. This book will give you a lot of help with each of them, but you need not stop there; keep asking yourself questions on these subjects -- and make it your business to find out the answers.

THE FACT THAT YOU HAVE DONE THE WORK IS NOT ENOUGH. Remember

that modern examinations seek to test your knowledge of the materials, processes, procedures, laws, and terminology in the field. If the scope sheet says "knowledge of bookkeeping procedures" it is not enough that you once helped keep books for the Smith Company; it is now your business to refresh your knowledge of the entire field of bookkeeping.

MAKING OUT THE APPLICATION. The civil service office will give you, along with the announcement sheet, an application to take the examination. In some Federal examinations, it is now the practice to have you submit this when you take the examination, rather than before; the first step is to turn in a card. Read the application carefully and be sure that you meet all the requirements : sex, age, residence, education, experience, etc. Make it out neatly, legibly, and truthfully. False statements might catch up with you years later. If you file for something for which you know you do not have the requirements, you are looking for trouble; misrepresentation might do you harm when you are filing for another job for which you do have the necessary background. But remember that this procedure is like making out your income tax return: tell the truth but take advantage of anything that is in your favor. Perhaps you have forgotten some experience that might qualify you. It is the work that counts, not what it is called, so if the application requires a year of clerical experience, perhaps they will accept the year you spent doing some of the paper work in helping your uncle run his store, even though you never thought of yourself as a "clerk." Perhaps that experience would even qualify you for a bookkeeping job. Think! Also, be sure that your application is neat; very often it is weighed as part of your examination. Unless handwriting is required, print or type it. Make it easy to read. The examiners have many to go through; a clear, bright one will be given more attention than one that has to be deciphered with a microscope!

VETERANS' PREFERENCE. The United States Government gives 5 extra points to honorably discharged war veterans. Ten points preference are given to disabled veterans or their wives, the widows of veterans, and the widowed or divorced mothers of veterans who lost their lives while in the armed forces or who were totally disabled while on active duty. State and local agencies usually have similar provisions in their regulations. Years in the service often count, too, towards experience requirements. If special forms must be filled out to get these extra credits, be sure you take care of these details.

BE SURE THAT YOUR APPLICATION IS PROPERLY SIGNED AND IN ON TIME!
Be sure that every question is answered and every box filled in. Filling out a Federal "Standard Form 57", for instance, is a long job. Go over it to be sure you haven't missed anything. Keep a copy, so the next time you have to fill one out, you won't have to look up the same facts all over again. Be sure your application is signed in the proper place, and turned in by the "closing date." If applications must be in by October 3, the best application in the world isn't worth the traditional plugged nickel on October 4. (The Federal Government has an exception to this; there are special provisions for people in the military service or are working out of the United States for a Government agency or for the United Nations.)

ONCE YOUR APPLICATION IS FILED -- STUDY! Make a list of the things about the job that you do not know -- and dig out the answers. If you want the job so much that you are willing to make this preparation the principal interest in your life in the month or two between the filing and the examination -- then nothing can stop you!

THE WRITTEN EXAMINATION: COME PREPARED! If your application is accepted, you will be sent a card telling you when to appear for the written test. Guard this credential! Its loss might bar you from taking the examination! Also, be on time! Some examination authorities, if the cards say "8:30" will bolt the door at that exact time, and if you knock at 8:31, you might as well be a week late for all the good it will do. So allow yourself plenty of time to catch the bus or find a place to park; even allow for a bus break-down or a flat tire. If you are told to bring pencil or ink or paper, be sure to do so, and bring enough; be prepared for a broken pencil or an empty pen.

BE CALM! There is nothing to get excited about. The room is quiet and nobody will bother you. The public agency wants everybody to have an equal chance. If you go in there in a state of internal unrest, you spoil that effort and your own chances. Nothing can beat thorough preparation and a calm attitude. (Some people, these days, if they are excitable, take pills to calm down. It is suggested that this only be done under a doctor's direction.)

GO THROUGH THE PRELIMINARIES ACCORDING TO THE DIRECTIONS. The proctor in charge will tell you to write your name somewhere and seal it, or copy your identifying number someplace, or fill in application forms. There can be no argument about these things; listen carefully and do just what you are told. Don't be the one to stop the proceedings to ask a question that was just answered, if you had only listened. Answer truthfully the written forms about whether you will accept a smaller salary or temporary or out-of-town appointments. Many examinations are graded by number; the envelope in which you seal your name and address is not opened until the rating for the corresponding number has been established.

DO NOT ASK THE PROCTOR A LOT OF UNNECESSARY QUESTIONS! The directions that the proctor reads are usually prepared in advance, and nothing is left out. Most proctors will run an examination for clerk on Monday and for Assistant Oyster Inspector on Tuesday, and Personnel Assistant on Wednesday -- so they don't know anything about your questions, and wouldn't tell you if they did. If the question seems to be ambiguous, answer it as well as you can; maybe you can protest it when the examination is over. The only occasions when you would have to consult the proctor would be if the examination were illegible or a page missing, or your chair is breaking down, etc. The proctor will tell you what the rules are about leaving the room. The best policy is to prepare for this, too, in advance. In many examinations, you just don't.

BE SMART ABOUT THE TIMING! There are usually gong or bell signals. Sometimes you must complete a part of the examination within a given time, and cannot go back over your questions after that time, or forward to the next section before that time. Do an intelligent job of dividing the time; if you have an hour for 100 questions, try to average 25 to the quarter hour.

WHEN DOING SPEED TESTS -- KEEP WORKING! Some tests contain more material than anybody can complete in the required time; the idea is to see how far you get. In these, just keep working; don't lose time looking back to see if you were right. You probably were, so use the "second look" time go get others done.

ANSWER THE EASY ONES FIRST! This is the primary rule for taking examinations. Too many people worry about Question number 6 for ten minutes, instead of going ahead and getting another 20 done. The idea is to get as many correct answers down as you can; usually they all count for an equal number of points. But be sure you mark somewhere which ones you skipped so can easily find them later; if you are allowed to mark the question book put a small x next to the ones you have not answered. When using electrical grading sheets, special precaution must be taken; there is further discussion on this type of examination a few paragraphs below.

IT IS A GOOD IDEA TO STAY THE FULL TIME. If you finish ahead of time, stay there and re-check your answers. Perhaps you marked something that you didn't mean to mark at all. (There is a divided opinion about changing answers; some people contend that the first choice is usually the best. We feel that this is quite possible, but it is still a good idea to go over answers if there is time; you might find something that, on second look, you are sure you marked wrong the first time. If you are still in doubt -- it might be better to leave the first answer "be.")

WHY NOT GUESS? It was once a custom to deduct "wrongs" from "rights". Thus, if you got 70 right out of a hundred, the 30 wrong were deducted from the 70, giving you a score of 40. This system was used in True-False tests where by pure chance a person might get half of the answers right. The idea was that it was safer not to guess -- not to mark it at all if you weren't sure, for if the question were not answered at all, there would be no wrong answer to deduct. Unless you know that this system is being used, however, why not guess at everything? Every right answer counts -- and there is no penalty for a wrong one. Many examination takers, when they run behind and find that they have two minutes left to answer 50 questions, will quickly put some answer down for all of the 50; a certain percentage are bound to be right!

BE CAREFUL OF QUESTIONS THAT SAY ALWAYS, IN ALL CASES, NEVER. Particularly in True-False type tests, some questions will say that something is always so, or never so; one exception will make the answer necessarily false. It is not true that a question mark is never used in the middle of a sentence because sometimes it is. It is not true that all states have a two-house legislature, because Nebraska does not. Of course, there are exceptions: some things are always or never true. But be on your guard.

HOW TO TAKE CIVIL SERVICE EXAMINATIONS

ELECTRICALLY GRADED EXAMINATIONS. In most modern examinations for which there are a large number of applicants, a machine grades the answers. A sheet, separate from the booklet in which the questions are given, has perhaps 150 to 300 spaces on a side, like those shown in the illustration. If the question has five possible answers, you answer it by filling in between the numbered answer lines as shown. You must use the special pencil given to you in the examination room, and no other ! Only this pencil has lead that the electrical grading impulse will pick up. If you erase, erase thoroughly; a bit of lead on the wrong pair of lines might throw out the answer. Be sure that you put your answer by the right question number in each case; often the numbers go half way down the sheet and then start at the top again. If you omit a question, be sure to check that number in the question book and be sure to skip it on the answer sheet! Other- wise you might throw all of your answers out of place. Some people say to themselves "Answer B to Question 18, " as they answer each question, just to be sure that they never get off the track.

TYPES OF EXAMINATION QUESTIONS. "Essay" types of questions are rarely given today; it is too difficult to try to grade long writings. The "True-False" type : "Thomas Jefferson was the second President. True False, " is, as we have said, not used so much as it once was, as by pure chance the applicant should get about half of the answers right. The modern trend is to the "multiple choice" question with four or five possible answers. Usually, out of the four or five, there are two that are very plausible, and the choice between them is difficult. A good examination must be "valid" in that it tests what it is is intended to test; and "reliable" in that it always gives the same results, no matter how or where it is given.

TYPES OF EXAMINATIONS. Test questions divide themselves into three main types. All three types are illustrated in this book:

Achievement tests: These demonstrate what you know or can do. They might be written, to measure your knowledge of spelling or arithmetic or statistics, for instance; or they might be "performance" tests in which you actually operate a typewriter, an automobile, a key-punch machine, or a drill-press.

Aptitude tests: These determine in what direction your talents lie: do you have the type of mind for clerical, mechanical, law enforcement work, or what? Many modern examinations for policemen and fireman, for instance, are more directed to measuring the aptitude for the work than knowledge of the work itself; the job can always be taught later.

Intelligence tests. These procedures, to be discussed more fully later in this book, are used to determine your basic brain power. If you are quick at seeing a relation- ship between parts, or the missing number in a series, this is to your credit, whether you know much about the work or not; if you have it, you can learn the rest.

PHYSICAL EXAMINATIONS. Usually there are medical examinations some time before actual employment. The public authorities want to know if you are well enough to do the work, and also whether you are a good risk for their health and retirement plans. If you want to go into civil service, and suspect there is anything wrong, it might be a good idea to see your doctor as soon as possible; perhaps it can be cleared up before you go before an official doctor or board.

FOR SOME JOBS, THERE ARE TESTS OF STRENGTH AND AGILITY. These vary with the job, the time and the place. In these days when most work is open to both sexes, the requirements are usually such that either sex can qualify. We suggest that you check carefully the required height, weight, etc., and the types of physical tests that are generally given for the job that you want. It might be possible to practice and prepare yourself for the running, jumping, weight lifting, sack dragging, or whatever will be expected of you. Perhaps even go to a gymnasium for a while.

ORAL INTERVIEWS. The scope sheet will tell you whether these are part of the examination. Be at your best, of course; the best hair-do, or the pants pressed, as the case may be. The talk will probably range from your personal background to the subject matter of the job. Take it easy, say what must be said, and don't prolong the session after it has been indicated that your time is up. People have talked themselves into jobs and then out of them. Do not go in with the idea that the interview is fixed for a favorite; usually the interviewers do not know anything about the hiring but are outside experts in the subject matter field, paid to do a job, and rating you by an impartial scale. A new wrinkle, sometimes used, is the "stress interview." The aim is to badger or insult you, to see if you will "blow your top." Be prepared for these!

FINALLY, PROTESTS. Most examining boards allow you to see a "key" to the examination you have taken, and allow you to file complaints if you feel that the answers given are wrong. Do not fail to do this if you are so allowed. Your protest will be fairly considered, and if the question is wrongly answered, the answer will be changed or the question eliminated. One or two of these can make the difference between your success or failure in an examination.

INTRODUCTION: The following, which is taken from a pamphlet issued by the Personnel Board of a large state, should be helpful to those who are to take oral examinations. While the procedures in giving such interviews vary according to the state or locality concerned, we believe that many of the suggestions as to how to prepare yourself for and conduct yourself during such questionings should be of use everywhere.

INFORMATION ABOUT YOUR INTERVIEW

"This leaflet is sent to you to help you understand and prepare for the oral part of your state examination. It was written primarily for candidates who are going before a qualifications board for the first time, but it may also be useful to more experienced candidates.

"The main purpose of the interview is to rate two factors: (1) how well your experience, education, and personal qualifications fit you to perform the duties of the position; and (2) how your qualifications compare with the qualifications of other candidates. The interview board must also determine whether your qualifications meet the established minimums. (At the time of reviewing applications reasonable doubts as to possession of the required education and experience are resolved in favor of the candidate, and are subject to review by the interview board.

"The board which conducts your interview will probably be composed of three members. Generally, the chairman is from the staff of the State Personnel Board. The second member is usually a person from within the state service who is familiar with the job requirements. The third member comes from outside the state service and often gives his time as a contribution to good government. You will be told who your board members are shortly before you meet them.

WHAT HAPPENS IN THE INTERVIEW

"First, the chairman will introduce the other board members and help you to feel at ease. The board realizes that appearing for an interview is not something that happens every day and that you may be a bit nervous and uncertain.

"Board members will have your original application before them and will probably ask you a variety of questions about your present work and your previous positions. (In a promotional examination they may wish to know what you have done to prepare yourself for promotion.) They may also be interested in your plans for the future and in any leisure time activities which could have a bearing on your qualifications. They may also ask you to describe your qualifications as you see them. In describing your qualifications try to present an accurate picture without either undue modesty or boasting. State the facts honestly as you see them. The board's opinion of your qualifications will probably not be determined by your answer to any single question, but will be based on the over-all picture you give them of your training, experience, and personal fitness for the position you seek.

"It may be that one or more of the board members will express some doubts about your qualifications. You should welcome such expressions for two reasons. First, when a board member expresses his reservations, you have an opportunity to correct a possible misunderstanding and to supply additional information. Second, these frank expressions show you where, in the opinion of the board members, your qualifications could be stronger. They give clues as to the areas you may wish to strengthen for a possible future examination and for your success in general.

'For some positions, it may be necessary for the board to ask pointed and provocative questions. These are not asked to put you "on the spot" but to help you demonstrate your qualifications.

"Just before the end of the interview, the chairman will ask if you have any further information you would like to add. Keep in mind that this question does not mean that you have omitted anything or that you have made an inadequate presentation of your qualifications. The chairman just wants to make sure that you have the opportunity to present everything you wish.

"The length of the interview will depend upon the class for which you are being interviewed. Most interviews run about 15 minutes.

HOW QUALIFICATIONS ARE RATED

"Your qualifications will be rated by the board after they have discussed your qualifications and the qualifications of other candidates. If the board members feel that you are qualified, they will give you a rating between 70% and 99%. (In some examinations only a "qualified" and "not qualified" rating is given instead of a percentage figure.) If the board members do not believe you are qualified at this time or if it appears that you qualifications are below the level of acceptable competitors, they will give you a rating of 65%. (Editor's Note: Remember, again, that these customs and percentages vary with the locality; this is merely the rating procedure of one state system.)

IN CASE OF DISQUALIFICATION

'If you should receive a rating below 70%, remember that there are usually more candidates than there are vacant positions and that the purpose of the interview is to pick out the best qualified of the candidates who compete. Thus, a disqualifying score does not necessarily mean that you could not do the job successfully. It may merely mean that in competition with other candidates, your qualifications were not such as to support a passing score. A disqualification in one examination does not lessen your chances in the future. In fact, the experience you have gained in the examination may be very useful in long range planning for your career.

SUGGESTIONS ABOUT YOUR INTERVIEW

"You will wish to present your qualifications as effectively as possible. We offer these suggestions:

"1. You should review the examination announcement to obtain a clear picture of the requirements and duties of the position. (This information is sometimes omitted from announcements for promotional examinations where the duties are well-known to the competitors.)

"2. You should be prepared to tell the interview board why you are interested in the position and why you believe that your education, experience, and personal qualifications would make you a success in the position. You do not have to prepare a speech, but you should be able to present a clear, concise statement of your qualifications for the position. Throughout the interview, the board members will give you whatever help they can, but you have the basic responsibility for the presentation of your qualifications.

"3. Listen carefully to the questions asked by the board members and answer them as frankly and directly as you can, keeping in mind the requirements of the position."

(Editor's Note: We might add to this that there is no excuse for not being prepared for questions that will probably arise, such as, 'Why do you want the position?" or 'Why do you think you are qualified for the position." You should also be prepared to give some defense to questions that might arise concerning weak points in your case, such as, 'Why did you leave that position?" when the truth is that you were discharged.

"4. Do not be concerned about the microphone you will probably notice on the table in front of you or suspended over the table. Interviews are recorded so that a transcript can be made if needed.

"5. It is not necessary for you to furnish letters of recommendation or other documents relating to your proficiency or character. In the interest of fairness and uniformity, board members usually prefer to judge a candidate's qualifications on the basis of his application and his oral presentation.

"6. Be yourself ; people usually make their most favorable impression when they act naturally."

THE PAMPHLET JUST QUOTED also contains information about appeals from interviews.   This procedure is not universal so we have not included it here.

THE FOLLOWING IS FROM A SIMILAR PUBLICATION, issued by a large city:

THE CITIZEN'S TEST

"Almost every examination for the City has an interview. (Ed. Note: This is not universally true, however.) This is because the ability to work well with other employees and to serve the citizens of this community requires a high order of personal qualifications.   The interviewers are there to rate these personality tests.   They may ask you many questions which seem to have nothing to do with the job for which you are applying.   Their job is to inquire into your outside interests and hobbies, what kind of citizen you are, how well you have demonstrated your ability to be a good employee in the past, and whether you are ready to meet the high requirements which the public service demands."

FINALLY A NOTE ON ORAL INTERVIEWS FOR SUPERVISORY POSITIONS:

"What are the basic attitudes and interests that should be given greatest weight in interviews for supervisory positions? First would seem to be attitudes towards other persons.   Does he seem to have a friendly attitude toward other persons or is he hostile, shy, or aloof? Next is poise and self-confidence. Is he sure of himself (but not to an obnoxious degree)? Is he anxious, tense, or suspicious of others? Would he get rattled easily? Is he likely to be unduly critical or sarcastic, and blame others for his mistakes? Third is the willingness to teach and supervise others.   Would he prefer to do the work rather than to lead and teach others? Does he take the role of leader or follower? Would he prefer bearing the responsibility for only his own work or for the work of others? Next is his attitude towards learning and keeping up with new developments. Is he satisfied with his present knowledge? Is he primarily interested in activities away from his work?

"The evaluation of the technical competence of the applicant, when such competence is highly important for job success, can also be included in the interview."

from "Selecting Supervisors," U.S. Government Printing Office, 1956.

IT MIGHT BE NOTED that many of the factors mentioned in the last quotation could also be in the interviewers' minds in questioning applicants for positions that are not supervisory.

This is a test that at present is used only for the Mail Handler examination, apparently on the theory that they must follow a lot of orders that are given to them by work of mouth. Thus, the test is different from the others discussed herein in that it is essential that the directions be read to you by another person -- as that is the way the examination will be given. Please insist that that other person read carefully the manner in which he or she is to give the directions as explained on page KB-143 et seq.

Following Oral Directions

DESCRIPTION OF THE TEST AND SAMPLE QUESTIONS

This test is included only in the Mail Handler Examination. If you do not plan to take the Mail Handler Examination, you may skip this section.

A large part of the Mail Handler's job is listening to the supervisor and following his instructions. Since it is important that each employee does exactly as he is instructed, this test is used to make sure that each applicant can and will listen carefully and follow through without extra supervision.

The directions in the test are not hard to follow, but you must listen carefully and do exactly what you are told to do.

In order to do this practice section, you must have a friend who will read the directions to you.

Hints for Doing the Test of Following Oral Directions

- Listen carefully to the directions.
- Do exactly what the examiner tells you to do.
- Do not try to get ahead of the examiner.
- If you missed an instruction, wait for the next one.
- Make sure that you darken only one box for each number on the answer sheet.

For your convenience, the Instructions for this test that someone else is to read to you are placed at the end of the book so that you can cut them out for him or her to hold.

The material which you will use for practice on the Following Oral Directions Test is on pages KB136-140

Do not read the material on KB-143-6 yourself; because, if you do, you will lose the value of this practice.

Following Oral Directions—Sample Questions

The directions are to be read at the rate of 80 words per minute. Since not everybody speaks at this speed, your friend should practice reading the 1-minute practice on page 31 until he can read it in exactly 1 minute whenever he wants to. He will also need a watch with a second hand.

To do the sample questions tear out KB143 which has the 1-minute practice and the directions for the sample questions. Give it to your friend to use. (Each friend who is helping you will have to use it to practice, so don't throw it away.)

When your friend reads the directions to you, listen carefully and do what he says. If you fall behind and miss a direction, don't get excited. Let that one go and listen for the next one. Since B and D sound very much alike, he will say "B as in baker" when he means B and "D as in dog" when he means D.

He will tell you some things to do with the 5 sample questions below. Then, when he tells you to darken a box on the Sample Answer Sheet, use the one on this page.

QUESTION 1. 5_____

QUESTION 2. 1 6 4 3 7

QUESTION 3. D B A E C

QUESTION 4. (8__) (5__) (2__) (9__) (10__)

QUESTION 5. (7__) [6__] (1__) [12__]

SAMPLE ANSWER SHEET

	A	B	C	D	E			A	B	C	D	E			A	B	C	D	E			A	B	C	D	E			A	B	C	D	E			A	B	C	D	E			A	B	C	D	E			A	B	C	D	E
1							2							3							4							5														7							8					

	A	B	C	D	E			A	B	C	D	E			A	B	C	D	E			A	B	C	D	E			A	B	C	D	E			A	B	C	D	E			A	B	C	D	E			A	B	C	D	E
9							10							11							12							13							14							15							16					

WORKSHEET FOR PRACTICE TEST 1

1.   45_____   43_____   83_____

2. |__A| |__E| |__C| |__B| |__D|

3.   69   87   50   54   25   47   20   80   27

4.   (71__)   (36__)   (49__)   (11__)

5.   [42__]   (44__)   (14__)   [56__]

6.   (88__)   (68__)   (61__)   (70__)   (34__)

7.   28   67   29   77   26

8.

A	B	C
CHESTNUT STREET	HYDE PARK	PRUDENTIAL PLAZA
_____	_____	_____

9. |85__| |86__| |63__| |39__|

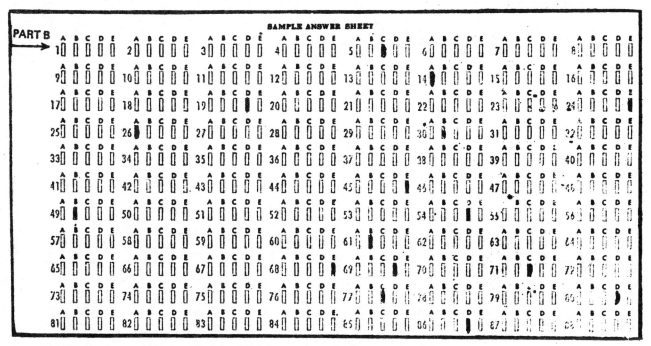

Now check your answers by comparing your answers with the correct answers shown below.

Your Test Score on this Practice Test is the number you got right.

Count how many you got right, and write that number on this line——————→

Meaning of Test Score

If your Test Score is *15 or 16*, you have a Good score.

If your Test Score is *13 or 14*, you have a Fair score.

If your Test Score is *12 or less*, you are not doing too well.

You may be working too slowly or you may not be doing exactly what you are told to do. You need more practice.

WORKSHEET FOR PRACTICE TEST 2

1.   40   85   17   87   52   55   56   45   75

2. | 65___ | | 37___ | | 12___ | | 4___ |

3.   X O O O X O O X X O X O X

4. | 78___ | (25__) | 27___ | (73__)

5.   88   2   69   84   34

6.   (63__)   (38__)   (76__)   (53__)   (57__)

7. | 435 ___B | | 466 ___C | | 474 ___E | | 467 ___A | | 489 ___D |

8.   79_____   39_____

9. | ___C | | ___E | | ___A | | ___D | | ___B |

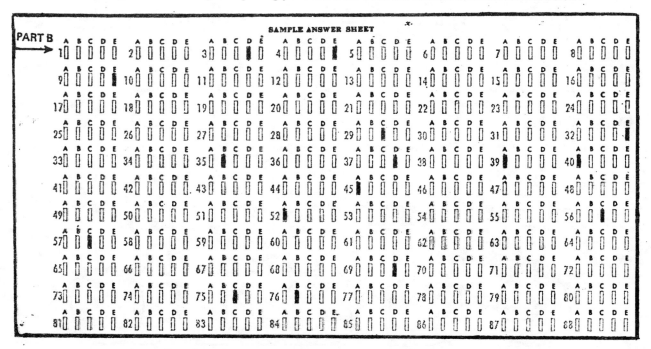

Now check your answers by comparing your answers with the correct answers shown below.

Your Test Score on this Practice Test is the number you got right.

Count how many you got right, and write that number on this line — — — — — — — — > _____

Meaning of Test Score

If your Test Score is *15 or 16*, you have a Good score.

If your Test Score is *13 or 14*, you have a Fair score.

If your Test Score is *12 or less*, you are not doing too well.

You may be working too slowly or you may not be doing exactly what you are told to do. You need more practice.

WORKSHEET FOR PRACTICE TEST 3

1.   59   35   62   58   8

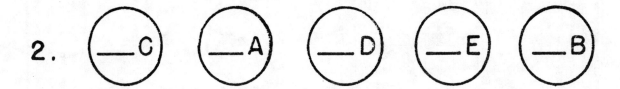

2.   (__C)   (__A)   (__D)   (__E)   (__B)

3.   15 _____   20 _____

4. | 3__ | | 37__ | | 36__ | CURE   DAMP   BEAR

5.   A   C   B   A   B   D   C   E   D

6. | 48__ | | 28__ | | 22__ | | 43__ |

7.   51 _____   69 _____   50 _____

8.   (65__)   (13__)   (87__)   (31__)   (17__)

9 | 55__ | | 44__ | | 74__ | | 25__ |

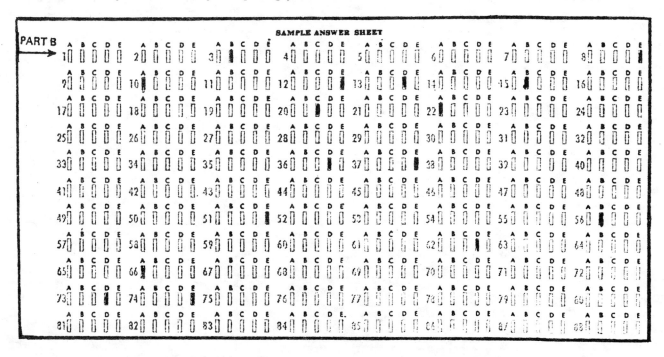

Now check your answers by comparing your answers with the correct answers shown below.

Your Test Score on this Practice Test is the number you got right.

Count how many you got right, and write that number on this line ⟶ _____

Meaning of Test Score

If your Test Score is *15 or 16*, you have a Good score.

If your Test Score is *13 or 14*, you have a Fair score.

If your Test Score is *12 or less*, you are not doing too well.

You may be working too slowly or you may not be doing exactly what you are told to do.

You need more practice.

The following four pages are for the person who is to read to you the Instructions

for this test. They can be cut out of the book for this purpose. We suggest

that the reader familiarize himself or herself with the method and timing to

be used, as explained on the bottom of page KB 113 and elsewhere in the set.

The directions should be read at about 80 words per minute. Practice reading aloud the material in the box below until you can do it in exactly 1 minute. This will give you a feel for the way you should read the test material.

1-MINUTE PRACTICE

(This is for practice in reading aloud. It is not the sample test.)

> Look at line 20 in your work booklet. There are two circles and two boxes of different sizes with numbers in them. If 7 is less than 3 and if 2 is smaller than 4, write a G in the larger circle. Otherwise write B as in baker in the smaller box. Now on your Code Sheet darken the space for the number-letter combination in the box or circle.

DIRECTIONS to be read. (The words in parentheses should *not* be read aloud. They tell you how long you should pause at the various spots. You should time the pauses with a watch with a second hand. The instruction "Pause slightly" means that you should stop long enough to take a breath.) You should not repeat any directions.

THIS IS THE SAMPLE.

> You are to follow the instructions that I read to you. I cannot repeat them.
>
> Look at the Sample Questions. Question 1 has a number and a line beside it. On the line write an A. (Pause 2 seconds.) Now on the Sample Answer Sheet, find number 5 (pause 2 seconds) and darken the box for the letter you just wrote on the line. (Pause 5 seconds.)
>
> Look at Question 2. (Pause slightly.) Draw a line under the third number. (Pause 2 seconds.) Now on the Sample Answer Sheet, find the number under which you just drew a line and darken box B as in baker for that number. (Pause 5 seconds.)
>
> Look at the letters in Question 3. (Pause slightly.) Draw a line under the third letter in the line. (Pause 2 seconds.) Now on your answer sheet, find number 9 (pause 2 seconds) and darken the box for the letter under which you drew a line. (Pause 5 seconds.)
>
> Look at the five circles in Question 4. (Pause slightly.) Each circle has a number and a line in it. Write D as in dog on the blank in the last circle. (Pause 2 seconds.) Now on the Sample Answer Sheet, darken the space for the number-letter combination that is in the circle you just wrote in. (Pause 5 seconds.)
>
> Look at Question 5. (Pause slightly.) There are two circles and two boxes of different sizes with numbers in them. (Pause slightly.) If 4 is more than 2 and if 5 is less than 3, write A in the smaller circle. (Pause slightly.) Otherwise write C in the larger box. (Pause 2 seconds.) Now on the Sample Answer Sheet, darken the space for the number-letter combination in the box or circle in which you just wrote. (Pause 5 seconds.)
>
> Now look at the Sample Answer Sheet. (Pause slightly.) You should have darkened spaces 4B, 5A, 9A, 10D, and 12C on the Sample Answer Sheet.

FOLLOWING ORAL DIRECTIONS—PRACTICE TEST 1

When you are ready to try Practice Test 1, tear this sheet out and give it to your friend who is helping you practice the Following Oral Directions Test.

To the Person Who Is to Read the Directions—Directions are to be read at the rate of 80 words per minute. Do not read aloud the material which is in parentheses. Do not repeat any directions.

Read the following directions aloud.

For this practice test you are to use the worksheet that is on KB136 and the answer sheet which is on KB137. (Pause until the person studying has turned to page KB-136

Look at line 1 on your worksheet. (Pause slightly.) Next to the left-hand number write the letter E. (Pause 2 seconds.) Now on your answer sheet, find the space for the number beside which you wrote and darken box E. (Pause 5 seconds.)

Now look at line 2 on your worksheet. (Pause slightly.) There are 5 boxes. Each box has a letter. (Pause slightly.) In the fifth box write the answer to this question: Which of the following numbers is largest: 18, 9, 15, 19, 13? (Pause 5 seconds.) Now on your answer sheet, darken the space for the number-letter combination that is in the box you just wrote in. (Pause 5 seconds.) In the fourth box on the same line do nothing. In the third box write 5. (Pause 2 seconds.) Now on your answer sheet, darken the space for the number-letter combination that is in the box you just wrote in. (Pause 5 seconds.) In the second box, write the answer to this question: How many hours are there in a day? (Pause 2 seconds.) Now on your answer sheet, darken the space for the number-letter combination that is in the box you just wrote in. (Pause 5 seconds.)

Look at line 3 on your worksheet. (Pause slightly.) Draw a line under every number that is more than 50 but less than 85. (Pause 12 seconds.) Now on your answer sheet, for each number that you drew a line under, darken box D as in dog. (Pause 25 seconds.)

Look at line 4 on your worksheet. (Pause slightly.) Write a B as in baker in the third circle. (Pause 2 seconds.) Now on your answer sheet, find the number in that circle and darken box B for that number. (Pause 5 seconds.)

Look at line 4 again. (Pause slightly.) Write C in the first circle. (Pause 2 seconds.) Now on your answer sheet, find the number in that circle and darken box C for that number. (Pause 5 seconds.)

Look at line 5 on your worksheet. (Pause slightly.) There are two circles and two boxes of different sizes with numbers in them. (Pause slightly.) If 4 is more than 6 and if 9 is less than 7, write D as in dog in the smaller box. (Pause slightly.) Otherwise write A in the larger circle. (Pause 2 seconds.) Now on your answer sheet, darken the space for the number-letter combination for the box or circle you just wrote in. (Pause 5 seconds.)

Now look at line 6 on your worksheet. (Pause slightly.) Write an E in the second circle. (Pause 2 seconds.) Now on your answer sheet, find the number in that circle and darken box E for that number. (Pause 5 seconds.)

Now look at line 6 again. (Pause slightly.) Write a B as in baker in the middle circle. (Pause 2 seconds.) Now on your answer sheet, find the number in that circle and darken box B as in baker for that number. (Pause 5 seconds.)

Look at the numbers on line 7 on your worksheet. (Pause slightly.) Draw a line under the largest number in the line. (Pause 2 seconds.) Now on your answer sheet, find the space for that number and darken box C for that number. (Pause 5 seconds.)

Now look at line 7 again. (Pause slightly.) Draw a circle around the smallest number in the line. (Pause 2 seconds.) Now on your answer sheet, find the space for the number which you just drew a circle around and darken box A for that number. (Pause 5 seconds.)

Now look at line 8 on your worksheet. There are 3 boxes with words and letters in them. (Pause slightly.) Each box represents a station in a large city. Station A delivers mail in the Chestnut Street area, Station B delivers mail in Hyde Park, and Station C delivers mail in the Prudential Plaza. Mr. Adams lives in Hyde Park. Write the number 30 on the line inside the box which represents the station that delivers Mr. Adams' mail. (Pause 2 seconds.) Now on your answer sheet, find the space for number 30 and darken the box for the letter that is in the box you just wrote in. (Pause 5 seconds.)

Now look at line 9 on your worksheet. (Pause slightly.) Write a D as in dog in the second box. (Pause 2 seconds.) Now on your answer sheet, find the number that is in the box you just wrote in and darken box D as in dog for that number. (Pause 5 seconds.)

Now check your answers by comparing them with the correct answers on page KB-137

When you are ready to try Practice Test 2, tear this sheet out and give it to your friend who is helping you practice the Following Oral Directions Test.

*To the Person Who Is to Read the Directions—*The Directions are to be read at the rate of 80 words per minute. Do not read aloud the material which is in parentheses. Do not repeat any directions.

Read the following directions aloud.

For this practice test you are to use the worksheet that is on KB138 and the answer sheet which is on KB138. (Pause until the person studying has turned to KB138.)

Look at line 1 on your worksheet. (Pause slightly.) Draw a line under every number that is more than 35 but less than 55. (Pause 12 seconds.) Now on your answer sheet, for each number that you drew a line under darken box A. (Pause 25 seconds.)

Now look at line 1 on your worksheet again. (Pause slightly.) Draw two lines under every number that is more than 55 and less than 80. (Pause 12 seconds.) Now on your answer sheet for each number that you drew two lines under darken box C. (Pause 25 seconds.)

Look at line 2 on your worksheet. (Pause slightly.) Write an E in the last box. (Pause 2 seconds.) Now on your answer sheet, find the number in that box and darken box E for that number. (Pause 5 seconds.)

Now look at line 2 on your worksheet again. (Pause slightly.) Write a D as in dog in the second box. (Pause 2 seconds.) Now on your answer sheet, find the number in that box and darken box D as in dog for that number. (Pause 5 seconds.)

Look at line 3 on your worksheet. (Pause slightly.) Draw a line under every "X" in the line. (Pause 5 seconds.) Count the number of lines that you have drawn, add 3, and write that number at the end of the line. (Pause 5 seconds.) Now on your answer sheet, find that number and darken space E for that number. (Pause 5 seconds.)

Look at line 4 on your worksheet. (Pause slightly.) If the number in the right-hand box is larger than the number in the left-hand circle, add 4 to the number in the left-hand circle, and change the number in the circle to this number. (Pause 8 seconds.) Then write C next to the new number. (Pause slightly.) Otherwise, write A next to the number in the smaller box. (Pause 3 seconds.) Now on your answer sheet, darken the space for the number-letter combination that is in the box or circle you just wrote in. (Pause 5 seconds.)

Now look at line 5 on your worksheet. (Pause slightly.) Draw a line under the middle number in the line. (Pause 2 seconds.) Now on your answer sheet, find the number under which you just drew the line and darken box D as in dog for that number. (Pause 5 seconds.)

Now look at line 6 on your worksheet. (Pause slightly.) Write a B as in baker in the third circle. (Pause 2 seconds.) Now on your answer sheet, find the number in that circle and darken box B as in baker for that number. (Pause 5 seconds.)

Now look at line 6 again. (Pause slightly.) Write a C in the last circle. (Pause 2 seconds.) Now on your answer sheet, find the number in that circle and darken box C for that number. (Pause 5 seconds.)

Look at the drawings on line 7 on your worksheet. The number in each box is the number of employees in a post office. (Pause slightly.) In the box for the post office with the smallest number of employees, write on the line the last two figures of the number of employees. (Pause 5 seconds.) Now on your answer sheet, darken the space for the number-letter combination that is in the box you just wrote in. (Pause 5 seconds.)

Now look at line 8 on your worksheet. (Pause slightly.) Write an A on the line next to the right-hand number. (Pause 2 seconds.) Now on your answer sheet find the space for the number next to which you just wrote and darken box A. (Pause 5 seconds.)

Look at line 9 on your worksheet. (Pause slightly.) In the fourth box, write the answer to this question: How many feet are in a yard? (Pause 2 seconds.) Now on your answer sheet darken the space for the number-letter combination that is in the box you just wrote in. (Pause 5 seconds.)

Look at line 9 again. (Pause slightly.) In the second box, write the number 32. (Pause 2 seconds.) Now on your answer sheet, find the number-letter combination that is in the box you just wrote in. (Pause 5 seconds.)

Now check your answers by comparing them with the Correct Answers on KB-139.

When you are ready to try Practice Test 3, tear this sheet out and give it to your friend who is helping you practice the Following Oral Directions Test.

To the Person Who Is to Read the Directions—The Directions are to be read at the rate of 80 words per minute. Do not read the material which is in parentheses aloud. Do not repeat any directions.

Read the following directions aloud.

For this practice test you are to use the worksheet that is on KB140 and the answer sheet that is on KB141 (Pause until the person preparing for the examination has turned to KB140.)

Look at line 1 on your worksheet. (Pause slightly.) Draw a line under the largest number in the line. (Pause 2 seconds.) Now on your answer sheet, find the number under which you just drew a line and darken box D as in dog for that number. (Pause 5 seconds.)

Look at line 1 on your worksheet again. (Pause slightly.) Draw two lines under the smallest number in the line. (Pause 2 seconds.) Now on your answer sheet, find the number under which you just drew two lines and darken box E. (Pause 5 seconds.)

Look at the circles in line 2 on your worksheet. (Pause slightly.) In the second circle, write the answer to this question: How much is 6 plus 4? (Pause 8 seconds.) In the third circle, write the answer to this question: Which of the following numbers is largest: 67, 48, 15, 73, 61? (Pause 5 seconds.) In the fourth circle, write the answer to this question: How many months are there in a year? (Pause 2 seconds.) Now, on your answer sheet, darken the number-letter combinations that are in the circles you wrote in. (Pause 10 seconds.)

Now look at line 3 on your worksheet. (Pause slightly.) Write the letter C on the blank next to the right-hand number. (Pause 2 seconds.) Now on your answer sheet, find the space for the number beside which you wrote and darken box C. (Pause 5 seconds.)

Now look at line 3 on your worksheet again. (Pause slightly.) Write the letter B as in baker on the blank next to the left-hand number. (Pause 2 seconds.) Now on your answer sheet, find the space for the number beside which you just wrote and darken box B as in baker. (Pause 5 seconds.)

Look at the boxes and words in line 4 on your worksheet. (Pause slightly.) Write the first letter of the second word in the third box. (Pause 2 seconds.) Write the last letter of the first word in the second box. (Pause 2 seconds.) Write the first letter of the third word in the first box. (Pause 2 seconds.) Now on your answer sheet, darken the spaces for the number-letter combinations that are in the three boxes you just wrote in. (Pause 10 seconds.)

Look at the letters on line 5 on your worksheet. (Pause slightly.) Draw a line under the fifth letter in the line. (Pause 2 seconds.) Now on your answer sheet, find the number 56 (pause 2 seconds) and darken the space for the letter under which you drew a line. (Pause 5 seconds.)

Look at the letters on line 5 on your worksheet again. (Pause slightly.) Draw two lines under the fourth letter in the line. (Pause 2 seconds.) Now on your answer sheet, find the number 66 (pause 2 seconds) and darken the space for the letter under which you drew two lines. (Pause 5 seconds.)

Look at the drawings on line 6 on your worksheet. (Pause slightly.) The four boxes indicate the number of buildings in four different carrier routes. In the box for the route with the fewest number of buildings, write an A. (Pause 2 seconds.) Now on your answer sheet, darken the space for the number-letter combination that is in the box you just wrote in. (Pause 5 seconds.)

Now look at line 7 on your worksheet. (Pause slightly.) If fall comes before summer, write the letter B as in baker on the line next to the middle number. (Pause slightly.) Otherwise, write an E on the blank next to the left-hand number. (Pause 5 seconds.) Now on your answer sheet, darken the space for the number-letter combination that you have just written. (Pause 5 seconds.)

Now look at line 8 on your worksheet. (Pause slightly.) Write a D as in dog in the circle with the lowest number. (Pause 2 seconds.) Now on your answer sheet, darken the space for the number-letter combination that is in the circle you just wrote in. (Pause 5 seconds.)

Look at the drawings in line 9 on your worksheet. The four boxes are planes for carrying mail. (Pause slightly.) The plane with the highest number is to be loaded first. Write an E in the box with the highest number. (Pause 2 seconds.) Now on your answer sheet, darken the space for the number-letter combination that is in the box you just wrote in. (Pause 5 seconds.)

Now check your answers by comparing them with the Correct Answers on page KB-141

1 Ⓐ Ⓑ Ⓒ Ⓓ Ⓔ	31 Ⓐ Ⓑ Ⓒ Ⓓ Ⓔ	61 Ⓐ Ⓑ Ⓒ Ⓓ Ⓔ
2 Ⓐ Ⓑ Ⓒ Ⓓ Ⓔ	32 Ⓐ Ⓑ Ⓒ Ⓓ Ⓔ	62 Ⓐ Ⓑ Ⓒ Ⓓ Ⓔ
3 Ⓐ Ⓑ Ⓒ Ⓓ Ⓔ	33 Ⓐ Ⓑ Ⓒ Ⓓ Ⓔ	63 Ⓐ Ⓑ Ⓒ Ⓓ Ⓔ
4 Ⓐ Ⓑ Ⓒ Ⓓ Ⓔ	34 Ⓐ Ⓑ Ⓒ Ⓓ Ⓔ	64 Ⓐ Ⓑ Ⓒ Ⓓ Ⓔ
5 Ⓐ Ⓑ Ⓒ Ⓓ Ⓔ	35 Ⓐ Ⓑ Ⓒ Ⓓ Ⓔ	65 Ⓐ Ⓑ Ⓒ Ⓓ Ⓔ
6 Ⓐ Ⓑ Ⓒ Ⓓ Ⓔ	36 Ⓐ Ⓑ Ⓒ Ⓓ Ⓔ	66 Ⓐ Ⓑ Ⓒ Ⓓ Ⓔ
7 Ⓐ Ⓑ Ⓒ Ⓓ Ⓔ	37 Ⓐ Ⓑ Ⓒ Ⓓ Ⓔ	67 Ⓐ Ⓑ Ⓒ Ⓓ Ⓔ
8 Ⓐ Ⓑ Ⓒ Ⓓ Ⓔ	38 Ⓐ Ⓑ Ⓒ Ⓓ Ⓔ	68 Ⓐ Ⓑ Ⓒ Ⓓ Ⓔ
9 Ⓐ Ⓑ Ⓒ Ⓓ Ⓔ	39 Ⓐ Ⓑ Ⓒ Ⓓ Ⓔ	69 Ⓐ Ⓑ Ⓒ Ⓓ Ⓔ
10 Ⓐ Ⓑ Ⓒ Ⓓ Ⓔ	40 Ⓐ Ⓑ Ⓒ Ⓓ Ⓔ	70 Ⓐ Ⓑ Ⓒ Ⓓ Ⓔ
11 Ⓐ Ⓑ Ⓒ Ⓓ Ⓔ	41 Ⓐ Ⓑ Ⓒ Ⓓ Ⓔ	71 Ⓐ Ⓑ Ⓒ Ⓓ Ⓔ
12 Ⓐ Ⓑ Ⓒ Ⓓ Ⓔ	42 Ⓐ Ⓑ Ⓒ Ⓓ Ⓔ	72 Ⓐ Ⓑ Ⓒ Ⓓ Ⓔ
13 Ⓐ Ⓑ Ⓒ Ⓓ Ⓔ	43 Ⓐ Ⓑ Ⓒ Ⓓ Ⓔ	73 Ⓐ Ⓑ Ⓒ Ⓓ Ⓔ
14 Ⓐ Ⓑ Ⓒ Ⓓ Ⓔ	44 Ⓐ Ⓑ Ⓒ Ⓓ Ⓔ	74 Ⓐ Ⓑ Ⓒ Ⓓ Ⓔ
15 Ⓐ Ⓑ Ⓒ Ⓓ Ⓔ	45 Ⓐ Ⓑ Ⓒ Ⓓ Ⓔ	75 Ⓐ Ⓑ Ⓒ Ⓓ Ⓔ
16 Ⓐ Ⓑ Ⓒ Ⓓ Ⓔ	46 Ⓐ Ⓑ Ⓒ Ⓓ Ⓔ	76 Ⓐ Ⓑ Ⓒ Ⓓ Ⓔ
17 Ⓐ Ⓑ Ⓒ Ⓓ Ⓔ	47 Ⓐ Ⓑ Ⓒ Ⓓ Ⓔ	77 Ⓐ Ⓑ Ⓒ Ⓓ Ⓔ
18 Ⓐ Ⓑ Ⓒ Ⓓ Ⓔ	48 Ⓐ Ⓑ Ⓒ Ⓓ Ⓔ	78 Ⓐ Ⓑ Ⓒ Ⓓ Ⓔ
19 Ⓐ Ⓑ Ⓒ Ⓓ Ⓔ	49 Ⓐ Ⓑ Ⓒ Ⓓ Ⓔ	79 Ⓐ Ⓑ Ⓒ Ⓓ Ⓔ
20 Ⓐ Ⓑ Ⓒ Ⓓ Ⓔ	50 Ⓐ Ⓑ Ⓒ Ⓓ Ⓔ	80 Ⓐ Ⓑ Ⓒ Ⓓ Ⓔ
21 Ⓐ Ⓑ Ⓒ Ⓓ Ⓔ	51 Ⓐ Ⓑ Ⓒ Ⓓ Ⓔ	81 Ⓐ Ⓑ Ⓒ Ⓓ Ⓔ
22 Ⓐ Ⓑ Ⓒ Ⓓ Ⓔ	52 Ⓐ Ⓑ Ⓒ Ⓓ Ⓔ	82 Ⓐ Ⓑ Ⓒ Ⓓ Ⓔ
23 Ⓐ Ⓑ Ⓒ Ⓓ Ⓔ	53 Ⓐ Ⓑ Ⓒ Ⓓ Ⓔ	83 Ⓐ Ⓑ Ⓒ Ⓓ Ⓔ
24 Ⓐ Ⓑ Ⓒ Ⓓ Ⓔ	54 Ⓐ Ⓑ Ⓒ Ⓓ Ⓔ	84 Ⓐ Ⓑ Ⓒ Ⓓ Ⓔ
25 Ⓐ Ⓑ Ⓒ Ⓓ Ⓔ	55 Ⓐ Ⓑ Ⓒ Ⓓ Ⓔ	85 Ⓐ Ⓑ Ⓒ Ⓓ Ⓔ
26 Ⓐ Ⓑ Ⓒ Ⓓ Ⓔ	56 Ⓐ Ⓑ Ⓒ Ⓓ Ⓔ	86 Ⓐ Ⓑ Ⓒ Ⓓ Ⓔ
27 Ⓐ Ⓑ Ⓒ Ⓓ Ⓔ	57 Ⓐ Ⓑ Ⓒ Ⓓ Ⓔ	87 Ⓐ Ⓑ Ⓒ Ⓓ Ⓔ
28 Ⓐ Ⓑ Ⓒ Ⓓ Ⓔ	58 Ⓐ Ⓑ Ⓒ Ⓓ Ⓔ	88 Ⓐ Ⓑ Ⓒ Ⓓ Ⓔ
29 Ⓐ Ⓑ Ⓒ Ⓓ Ⓔ	59 Ⓐ Ⓑ Ⓒ Ⓓ Ⓔ	
30 Ⓐ Ⓑ Ⓒ Ⓓ Ⓔ	60 Ⓐ Ⓑ Ⓒ Ⓓ Ⓔ	

KB-148

1 Ⓐ Ⓑ Ⓒ Ⓓ Ⓔ   31 Ⓐ Ⓑ Ⓒ Ⓓ Ⓔ   61 Ⓐ Ⓑ Ⓒ Ⓓ Ⓔ
2 Ⓐ Ⓑ Ⓒ Ⓓ Ⓔ   32 Ⓐ Ⓑ Ⓒ Ⓓ Ⓔ   62 Ⓐ Ⓑ Ⓒ Ⓓ Ⓔ
3 Ⓐ Ⓑ Ⓒ Ⓓ Ⓔ   33 Ⓐ Ⓑ Ⓒ Ⓓ Ⓔ   63 Ⓐ Ⓑ Ⓒ Ⓓ Ⓔ
4 Ⓐ Ⓑ Ⓒ Ⓓ Ⓔ   34 Ⓐ Ⓑ Ⓒ Ⓓ Ⓔ   64 Ⓐ Ⓑ Ⓒ Ⓓ Ⓔ
5 Ⓐ Ⓑ Ⓒ Ⓓ Ⓔ   35 Ⓐ Ⓑ Ⓒ Ⓓ Ⓔ   65 Ⓐ Ⓑ Ⓒ Ⓓ Ⓔ
6 Ⓐ Ⓑ Ⓒ Ⓓ Ⓔ   36 Ⓐ Ⓑ Ⓒ Ⓓ Ⓔ   66 Ⓐ Ⓑ Ⓒ Ⓓ Ⓔ
7 Ⓐ Ⓑ Ⓒ Ⓓ Ⓔ   37 Ⓐ Ⓑ Ⓒ Ⓓ Ⓔ   67 Ⓐ Ⓑ Ⓒ Ⓓ Ⓔ
8 Ⓐ Ⓑ Ⓒ Ⓓ Ⓔ   38 Ⓐ Ⓑ Ⓒ Ⓓ Ⓔ   68 Ⓐ Ⓑ Ⓒ Ⓓ Ⓔ
9 Ⓐ Ⓑ Ⓒ Ⓓ Ⓔ   39 Ⓐ Ⓑ Ⓒ Ⓓ Ⓔ   69 Ⓐ Ⓑ Ⓒ Ⓓ Ⓔ
10 Ⓐ Ⓑ Ⓒ Ⓓ Ⓔ   40 Ⓐ Ⓑ Ⓒ Ⓓ Ⓔ   70 Ⓐ Ⓑ Ⓒ Ⓓ Ⓔ
11 Ⓐ Ⓑ Ⓒ Ⓓ Ⓔ   41 Ⓐ Ⓑ Ⓒ Ⓓ Ⓔ   71 Ⓐ Ⓑ Ⓒ Ⓓ Ⓔ
12 Ⓐ Ⓑ Ⓒ Ⓓ Ⓔ   42 Ⓐ Ⓑ Ⓒ Ⓓ Ⓔ   72 Ⓐ Ⓑ Ⓒ Ⓓ Ⓔ
13 Ⓐ Ⓑ Ⓒ Ⓓ Ⓔ   43 Ⓐ Ⓑ Ⓒ Ⓓ Ⓔ   73 Ⓐ Ⓑ Ⓒ Ⓓ Ⓔ
14 Ⓐ Ⓑ Ⓒ Ⓓ Ⓔ   44 Ⓐ Ⓑ Ⓒ Ⓓ Ⓔ   74 Ⓐ Ⓑ Ⓒ Ⓓ Ⓔ
15 Ⓐ Ⓑ Ⓒ Ⓓ Ⓔ   45 Ⓐ Ⓑ Ⓒ Ⓓ Ⓔ   75 Ⓐ Ⓑ Ⓒ Ⓓ Ⓔ
16 Ⓐ Ⓑ Ⓒ Ⓓ Ⓔ   46 Ⓐ Ⓑ Ⓒ Ⓓ Ⓔ   76 Ⓐ Ⓑ Ⓒ Ⓓ Ⓔ
17 Ⓐ Ⓑ Ⓒ Ⓓ Ⓔ   47 Ⓐ Ⓑ Ⓒ Ⓓ Ⓔ   77 Ⓐ Ⓑ Ⓒ Ⓓ Ⓔ
18 Ⓐ Ⓑ Ⓒ Ⓓ Ⓔ   48 Ⓐ Ⓑ Ⓒ Ⓓ Ⓔ   78 Ⓐ Ⓑ Ⓒ Ⓓ Ⓔ
19 Ⓐ Ⓑ Ⓒ Ⓓ Ⓔ   49 Ⓐ Ⓑ Ⓒ Ⓓ Ⓔ   79 Ⓐ Ⓑ Ⓒ Ⓓ Ⓔ
20 Ⓐ Ⓑ Ⓒ Ⓓ Ⓔ   50 Ⓐ Ⓑ Ⓒ Ⓓ Ⓔ   80 Ⓐ Ⓑ Ⓒ Ⓓ Ⓔ
21 Ⓐ Ⓑ Ⓒ Ⓓ Ⓔ   51 Ⓐ Ⓑ Ⓒ Ⓓ Ⓔ   81 Ⓐ Ⓑ Ⓒ Ⓓ Ⓔ
22 Ⓐ Ⓑ Ⓒ Ⓓ Ⓔ   52 Ⓐ Ⓑ Ⓒ Ⓓ Ⓔ   82 Ⓐ Ⓑ Ⓒ Ⓓ Ⓔ
23 Ⓐ Ⓑ Ⓒ Ⓓ Ⓔ   53 Ⓐ Ⓑ Ⓒ Ⓓ Ⓔ   83 Ⓐ Ⓑ Ⓒ Ⓓ Ⓔ
24 Ⓐ Ⓑ Ⓒ Ⓓ Ⓔ   54 Ⓐ Ⓑ Ⓒ Ⓓ Ⓔ   84 Ⓐ Ⓑ Ⓒ Ⓓ Ⓔ
25 Ⓐ Ⓑ Ⓒ Ⓓ Ⓔ   55 Ⓐ Ⓑ Ⓒ Ⓓ Ⓔ   85 Ⓐ Ⓑ Ⓒ Ⓓ Ⓔ
26 Ⓐ Ⓑ Ⓒ Ⓓ Ⓔ   56 Ⓐ Ⓑ Ⓒ Ⓓ Ⓔ   86 Ⓐ Ⓑ Ⓒ Ⓓ Ⓔ
27 Ⓐ Ⓑ Ⓒ Ⓓ Ⓔ   57 Ⓐ Ⓑ Ⓒ Ⓓ Ⓔ   87 Ⓐ Ⓑ Ⓒ Ⓓ Ⓔ
28 Ⓐ Ⓑ Ⓒ Ⓓ Ⓔ   58 Ⓐ Ⓑ Ⓒ Ⓓ Ⓔ   88 Ⓐ Ⓑ Ⓒ Ⓓ Ⓔ
29 Ⓐ Ⓑ Ⓒ Ⓓ Ⓔ   59 Ⓐ Ⓑ Ⓒ Ⓓ Ⓔ
30 Ⓐ Ⓑ Ⓒ Ⓓ Ⓔ   60 Ⓐ Ⓑ Ⓒ Ⓓ Ⓔ

1 Ⓐ Ⓑ Ⓒ Ⓓ Ⓔ	31 Ⓐ Ⓑ Ⓒ Ⓓ Ⓔ	61 Ⓐ Ⓑ Ⓒ Ⓓ Ⓔ
2 Ⓐ Ⓑ Ⓒ Ⓓ Ⓔ	32 Ⓐ Ⓑ Ⓒ Ⓓ Ⓔ	62 Ⓐ Ⓑ Ⓒ Ⓓ Ⓔ
3 Ⓐ Ⓑ Ⓒ Ⓓ Ⓔ	33 Ⓐ Ⓑ Ⓒ Ⓓ Ⓔ	63 Ⓐ Ⓑ Ⓒ Ⓓ Ⓔ
4 Ⓐ Ⓑ Ⓒ Ⓓ Ⓔ	34 Ⓐ Ⓑ Ⓒ Ⓓ Ⓔ	64 Ⓐ Ⓑ Ⓒ Ⓓ Ⓔ
5 Ⓐ Ⓑ Ⓒ Ⓓ Ⓔ	35 Ⓐ Ⓑ Ⓒ Ⓓ Ⓔ	65 Ⓐ Ⓑ Ⓒ Ⓓ Ⓔ
6 Ⓐ Ⓑ Ⓒ Ⓓ Ⓔ	36 Ⓐ Ⓑ Ⓒ Ⓓ Ⓔ	66 Ⓐ Ⓑ Ⓒ Ⓓ Ⓔ
7 Ⓐ Ⓑ Ⓒ Ⓓ Ⓔ	37 Ⓐ Ⓑ Ⓒ Ⓓ Ⓔ	67 Ⓐ Ⓑ Ⓒ Ⓓ Ⓔ
8 Ⓐ Ⓑ Ⓒ Ⓓ Ⓔ	38 Ⓐ Ⓑ Ⓒ Ⓓ Ⓔ	68 Ⓐ Ⓑ Ⓒ Ⓓ Ⓔ
9 Ⓐ Ⓑ Ⓒ Ⓓ Ⓔ	39 Ⓐ Ⓑ Ⓒ Ⓓ Ⓔ	69 Ⓐ Ⓑ Ⓒ Ⓓ Ⓔ
10 Ⓐ Ⓑ Ⓒ Ⓓ Ⓔ	40 Ⓐ Ⓑ Ⓒ Ⓓ Ⓔ	70 Ⓐ Ⓑ Ⓒ Ⓓ Ⓔ
11 Ⓐ Ⓑ Ⓒ Ⓓ Ⓔ	41 Ⓐ Ⓑ Ⓒ Ⓓ Ⓔ	71 Ⓐ Ⓑ Ⓒ Ⓓ Ⓔ
12 Ⓐ Ⓑ Ⓒ Ⓓ Ⓔ	42 Ⓐ Ⓑ Ⓒ Ⓓ Ⓔ	72 Ⓐ Ⓑ Ⓒ Ⓓ Ⓔ
13 Ⓐ Ⓑ Ⓒ Ⓓ Ⓔ	43 Ⓐ Ⓑ Ⓒ Ⓓ Ⓔ	73 Ⓐ Ⓑ Ⓒ Ⓓ Ⓔ
14 Ⓐ Ⓑ Ⓒ Ⓓ Ⓔ	44 Ⓐ Ⓑ Ⓒ Ⓓ Ⓔ	74 Ⓐ Ⓑ Ⓒ Ⓓ Ⓔ
15 Ⓐ Ⓑ Ⓒ Ⓓ Ⓔ	45 Ⓐ Ⓑ Ⓒ Ⓓ Ⓔ	75 Ⓐ Ⓑ Ⓒ Ⓓ Ⓔ
16 Ⓐ Ⓑ Ⓒ Ⓓ Ⓔ	46 Ⓐ Ⓑ Ⓒ Ⓓ Ⓔ	76 Ⓐ Ⓑ Ⓒ Ⓓ Ⓔ
17 Ⓐ Ⓑ Ⓒ Ⓓ Ⓔ	47 Ⓐ Ⓑ Ⓒ Ⓓ Ⓔ	77 Ⓐ Ⓑ Ⓒ Ⓓ Ⓔ
18 Ⓐ Ⓑ Ⓒ Ⓓ Ⓔ	48 Ⓐ Ⓑ Ⓒ Ⓓ Ⓔ	78 Ⓐ Ⓑ Ⓒ Ⓓ Ⓔ
19 Ⓐ Ⓑ Ⓒ Ⓓ Ⓔ	49 Ⓐ Ⓑ Ⓒ Ⓓ Ⓔ	79 Ⓐ Ⓑ Ⓒ Ⓓ Ⓔ
20 Ⓐ Ⓑ Ⓒ Ⓓ Ⓔ	50 Ⓐ Ⓑ Ⓒ Ⓓ Ⓔ	80 Ⓐ Ⓑ Ⓒ Ⓓ Ⓔ
21 Ⓐ Ⓑ Ⓒ Ⓓ Ⓔ	51 Ⓐ Ⓑ Ⓒ Ⓓ Ⓔ	81 Ⓐ Ⓑ Ⓒ Ⓓ Ⓔ
22 Ⓐ Ⓑ Ⓒ Ⓓ Ⓔ	52 Ⓐ Ⓑ Ⓒ Ⓓ Ⓔ	82 Ⓐ Ⓑ Ⓒ Ⓓ Ⓔ
23 Ⓐ Ⓑ Ⓒ Ⓓ Ⓔ	53 Ⓐ Ⓑ Ⓒ Ⓓ Ⓔ	83 Ⓐ Ⓑ Ⓒ Ⓓ Ⓔ
24 Ⓐ Ⓑ Ⓒ Ⓓ Ⓔ	54 Ⓐ Ⓑ Ⓒ Ⓓ Ⓔ	84 Ⓐ Ⓑ Ⓒ Ⓓ Ⓔ
25 Ⓐ Ⓑ Ⓒ Ⓓ Ⓔ	55 Ⓐ Ⓑ Ⓒ Ⓓ Ⓔ	85 Ⓐ Ⓑ Ⓒ Ⓓ Ⓔ
26 Ⓐ Ⓑ Ⓒ Ⓓ Ⓔ	56 Ⓐ Ⓑ Ⓒ Ⓓ Ⓔ	86 Ⓐ Ⓑ Ⓒ Ⓓ Ⓔ
27 Ⓐ Ⓑ Ⓒ Ⓓ Ⓔ	57 Ⓐ Ⓑ Ⓒ Ⓓ Ⓔ	87 Ⓐ Ⓑ Ⓒ Ⓓ Ⓔ
28 Ⓐ Ⓑ Ⓒ Ⓓ Ⓔ	58 Ⓐ Ⓑ Ⓒ Ⓓ Ⓔ	88 Ⓐ Ⓑ Ⓒ Ⓓ Ⓔ
29 Ⓐ Ⓑ Ⓒ Ⓓ Ⓔ	59 Ⓐ Ⓑ Ⓒ Ⓓ Ⓔ	
30 Ⓐ Ⓑ Ⓒ Ⓓ Ⓔ	60 Ⓐ Ⓑ Ⓒ Ⓓ Ⓔ	

KB-150

1 Ⓐ Ⓑ Ⓒ Ⓓ Ⓔ	31 Ⓐ Ⓑ Ⓒ Ⓓ Ⓔ	61 Ⓐ Ⓑ Ⓒ Ⓓ Ⓔ
2 Ⓐ Ⓑ Ⓒ Ⓓ Ⓔ	32 Ⓐ Ⓑ Ⓒ Ⓓ Ⓔ	62 Ⓐ Ⓑ Ⓒ Ⓓ Ⓔ
3 Ⓐ Ⓑ Ⓒ Ⓓ Ⓔ	33 Ⓐ Ⓑ Ⓒ Ⓓ Ⓔ	63 Ⓐ Ⓑ Ⓒ Ⓓ Ⓔ
4 Ⓐ Ⓑ Ⓒ Ⓓ Ⓔ	34 Ⓐ Ⓑ Ⓒ Ⓓ Ⓔ	64 Ⓐ Ⓑ Ⓒ Ⓓ Ⓔ
5 Ⓐ Ⓑ Ⓒ Ⓓ Ⓔ	35 Ⓐ Ⓑ Ⓒ Ⓓ Ⓔ	65 Ⓐ Ⓑ Ⓒ Ⓓ Ⓔ
6 Ⓐ Ⓑ Ⓒ Ⓓ Ⓔ	36 Ⓐ Ⓑ Ⓒ Ⓓ Ⓔ	66 Ⓐ Ⓑ Ⓒ Ⓓ Ⓔ
7 Ⓐ Ⓑ Ⓒ Ⓓ Ⓔ	37 Ⓐ Ⓑ Ⓒ Ⓓ Ⓔ	67 Ⓐ Ⓑ Ⓒ Ⓓ Ⓔ
8 Ⓐ Ⓑ Ⓒ Ⓓ Ⓔ	38 Ⓐ Ⓑ Ⓒ Ⓓ Ⓔ	68 Ⓐ Ⓑ Ⓒ Ⓓ Ⓔ
9 Ⓐ Ⓑ Ⓒ Ⓓ Ⓔ	39 Ⓐ Ⓑ Ⓒ Ⓓ Ⓔ	69 Ⓐ Ⓑ Ⓒ Ⓓ Ⓔ
10 Ⓐ Ⓑ Ⓒ Ⓓ Ⓔ	40 Ⓐ Ⓑ Ⓒ Ⓓ Ⓔ	70 Ⓐ Ⓑ Ⓒ Ⓓ Ⓔ
11 Ⓐ Ⓑ Ⓒ Ⓓ Ⓔ	41 Ⓐ Ⓑ Ⓒ Ⓓ Ⓔ	71 Ⓐ Ⓑ Ⓒ Ⓓ Ⓔ
12 Ⓐ Ⓑ Ⓒ Ⓓ Ⓔ	42 Ⓐ Ⓑ Ⓒ Ⓓ Ⓔ	72 Ⓐ Ⓑ Ⓒ Ⓓ Ⓔ
13 Ⓐ Ⓑ Ⓒ Ⓓ Ⓔ	43 Ⓐ Ⓑ Ⓒ Ⓓ Ⓔ	73 Ⓐ Ⓑ Ⓒ Ⓓ Ⓔ
14 Ⓐ Ⓑ Ⓒ Ⓓ Ⓔ	44 Ⓐ Ⓑ Ⓒ Ⓓ Ⓔ	74 Ⓐ Ⓑ Ⓒ Ⓓ Ⓔ
15 Ⓐ Ⓑ Ⓒ Ⓓ Ⓔ	45 Ⓐ Ⓑ Ⓒ Ⓓ Ⓔ	75 Ⓐ Ⓑ Ⓒ Ⓓ Ⓔ
16 Ⓐ Ⓑ Ⓒ Ⓓ Ⓔ	46 Ⓐ Ⓑ Ⓒ Ⓓ Ⓔ	76 Ⓐ Ⓑ Ⓒ Ⓓ Ⓔ
17 Ⓐ Ⓑ Ⓒ Ⓓ Ⓔ	47 Ⓐ Ⓑ Ⓒ Ⓓ Ⓔ	77 Ⓐ Ⓑ Ⓒ Ⓓ Ⓔ
18 Ⓐ Ⓑ Ⓒ Ⓓ Ⓔ	48 Ⓐ Ⓑ Ⓒ Ⓓ Ⓔ	78 Ⓐ Ⓑ Ⓒ Ⓓ Ⓔ
19 Ⓐ Ⓑ Ⓒ Ⓓ Ⓔ	49 Ⓐ Ⓑ Ⓒ Ⓓ Ⓔ	79 Ⓐ Ⓑ Ⓒ Ⓓ Ⓔ
20 Ⓐ Ⓑ Ⓒ Ⓓ Ⓔ	50 Ⓐ Ⓑ Ⓒ Ⓓ Ⓔ	80 Ⓐ Ⓑ Ⓒ Ⓓ Ⓔ
21 Ⓐ Ⓑ Ⓒ Ⓓ Ⓔ	51 Ⓐ Ⓑ Ⓒ Ⓓ Ⓔ	81 Ⓐ Ⓑ Ⓒ Ⓓ Ⓔ
22 Ⓐ Ⓑ Ⓒ Ⓓ Ⓔ	52 Ⓐ Ⓑ Ⓒ Ⓓ Ⓔ	82 Ⓐ Ⓑ Ⓒ Ⓓ Ⓔ
23 Ⓐ Ⓑ Ⓒ Ⓓ Ⓔ	53 Ⓐ Ⓑ Ⓒ Ⓓ Ⓔ	83 Ⓐ Ⓑ Ⓒ Ⓓ Ⓔ
24 Ⓐ Ⓑ Ⓒ Ⓓ Ⓔ	54 Ⓐ Ⓑ Ⓒ Ⓓ Ⓔ	84 Ⓐ Ⓑ Ⓒ Ⓓ Ⓔ
25 Ⓐ Ⓑ Ⓒ Ⓓ Ⓔ	55 Ⓐ Ⓑ Ⓒ Ⓓ Ⓔ	85 Ⓐ Ⓑ Ⓒ Ⓓ Ⓔ
26 Ⓐ Ⓑ Ⓒ Ⓓ Ⓔ	56 Ⓐ Ⓑ Ⓒ Ⓓ Ⓔ	86 Ⓐ Ⓑ Ⓒ Ⓓ Ⓔ
27 Ⓐ Ⓑ Ⓒ Ⓓ Ⓔ	57 Ⓐ Ⓑ Ⓒ Ⓓ Ⓔ	87 Ⓐ Ⓑ Ⓒ Ⓓ Ⓔ
28 Ⓐ Ⓑ Ⓒ Ⓓ Ⓔ	58 Ⓐ Ⓑ Ⓒ Ⓓ Ⓔ	88 Ⓐ Ⓑ Ⓒ Ⓓ Ⓔ
29 Ⓐ Ⓑ Ⓒ Ⓓ Ⓔ	59 Ⓐ Ⓑ Ⓒ Ⓓ Ⓔ	
30 Ⓐ Ⓑ Ⓒ Ⓓ Ⓔ	60 Ⓐ Ⓑ Ⓒ Ⓓ Ⓔ	